THE MEDIA IN LATIN AMERICA

Edited by Jairo Lugo-Ocando

 Open University Press

Open University Press
McGraw-Hill Education
McGraw-Hill House
Shoppenhangers Road
Maidenhead
Berkshire
England
SL6 2QL

email: enquiries@openup.co.uk
world wide web: www.openup.co.uk

and Two Penn Plaza, New York, NY 10121—2289, USA

First published 2008

A catalogue record of this book is available from the British Library

ISBN-13: 9780335222018 (pb)   9780335222025 (Hb)
ISBN-10: 0335222013 (pb)   0335222021 (Hb)

Typeset by Kerrypress, Luton, Bedfordshire
Printed in Great Britain by Bell and Bain Ltd, Glasgow

The *McGraw-Hill* Companies

The Media in Latin America

NATIONAL MEDIAS

Series editor: Brian McNair, University of Strathclyde

National Medias is a series of textbooks designed to give readers an insight into some of the most important media systems throughout the world. Each book in the series provides a comprehensive overview of the media of a particular country or a geographical group of countries or nation states.

Titles in the series

The Media in Latin America

Ed. Jairo Lugo-Ocando

The Media in Italy: Press, Cinema and Broadcasting from Unification to Digital

Matthew Hibberd

To my mentors and friends Pablo Bassim and Antonio J. Marcano, so Latin America becomes what they always wanted it to be ... a space for justice and freedom.

CONTENTS

THE CONTRIBUTORS

Celia Aldana-Durán holds a BA from the University of Lima (Peru) and an MA in media studies from the University of Sussex (UK). She currently teaches communication and development at the University of Lima, and has worked extensively as a researcher and activist in the area with the media and communication think-tank Calandria. She is a strategic communication officer at Oxfam America and has published several works on the media, diversity and racism.

Susana Aldana-Amabile holds a BA in communication studies and an MA in communication from the Methodist University of San Pablo (Brazil). She is director of the School of Communication Science at the Universidad Católica Nuestra Señora de la Asunción in Paraguay. She is co-author of 'Las y los periodistas', *in Género y comunicación: el lado oscuro de los medios* (2003) among other publications.

Marcelo Belinche is the vice-dean of the Faculty of Communication and Journalism and a researcher at the Universidad Nacional de la Plata (Argentina). He is the editor of *Medios, Política y Poder La Conformación de Los Multimedios En La Argentina de Los 90* (2003) and co-author with Walter Miceli of *Los procesos de edición periodística en los medios gráficos: el caso Clarín.*

Jorge Iván Bonilla, V. is an associated professor in the department of politics at the Escuela de Administración, Finanzas y Tecnología in Medellin. Before this he was an associate professor of the Department of Communication at the Pontifical Javeriana University (Colombia) and director of the masters programme. He is director of the think-tank Communication, Culture and Media and co-editor of the journal *Signos.* He has published extensively on the subject of media and violence in Colombia.

Andrés Cañizález is a lecturer and researcher at the Universidad Católica Andres Bello in Caracas. He has published on political communication and speech freedom in Venezuela; among others *Libertad de expressión: El gobierno de Hugo Chávez* (2005), *Politicas de ciudadanía y sociedad civil en tiempos de globalización* (2004), *Historianínima de los medios de comunicacion en Venezuela* (2004). He was director of the Journal Communication, published by the Jesuit think-tank the *Centro Gumilla* and has just finished a project on media coverage of poverty funded by the Konrad Adenauer Foundation.

Gustavo González-Rodríguez is an associate professor at the University of Chile and director of the Media and Communication School. He holds a BA in cultural journalism and a masters in political communication at the University of Chile. He is a former IPS correspondent in Chile and Ecuador, and has been an editor in Italy and Costa Rica. He has worked for several newspapers and magazines in Spain, Uruguay, Mexico and Chile. He has published extensively on communication, ethical issues, media and journalism.

Olga Guedes-Bailey is a lecturer at Nottingham Trent University (UK). She holds a BA from the University of Ceara (Brazil), an MA from the Minas Gerais University (Brazil), and a PhD from Loughborough University (UK). She has taught at the University of Ceara (Brazil), the University of the West of England (UK) and Liverpool John Moores University (UK). Before becoming an academic she worked as a journalist in Brazil. She has published in both Portuguese and English in the areas of media, communication and journalism.

Sallie Hughes is an assistant professor of journalism at the University of Miami and author of *Newsrooms in Conflict: Journalism and the Democratization of Mexico* (2006). A working journalist before receiving her PhD, she has published extensively on Latin American journalism and mass media in academic journals such as the *Latin American Research Review*, *Political Communication*, and the *Harvard International Journal of Press/Politics*, among others.

Othon F. Jambeiro Barbosa graduated in journalism from the Universidade Federal da Bahia, has a masters in social science from the Universidade de São Paulo and a PhD from the Polytechnic of Central London (today the University of Westminster). He is currently a professor at the Universidade Federal da Bahia and has published widely on broadcasting and media technologies in Brazil and Latin America.

Jairo Lugo-Ocando is a lecturer in journalism studies in the department of Film, Media & Journalism at the University of Stirling (UK). His research interests include media and democratization in South America, and digital technologies and development policies. He has worked as a correspondent, staff writer and editor for several newspapers, magazines and radio stations in Venezuela, Colombia and the USA. His publications include *Información de Estado* (1998), *Latin America's New Cultural Industries still Play Old Games: From the Banana Republic to Donkey Kong* (2002) and *Modern Conflicts in Latin America* (2007), among others.

Ancízar Narváez Montoya is a lecturer at the Universidad Pedagógica Nacional in Colombia. He is a member of the Asociación Latinoamericana de Investigadores de la Comunicación (ALAIC). His published works include *Puentes tecnológicos, abismos sociales* (2002); *Cultura mediática y política: Esfera pública, intereses y códigos* (2003); *La sociedad de la* *información o la utopía económica y cultural del neoliberalismo* (2004); and *Comunicación mediática y educación formal: Un punto de vista comunicacional* (2004). He currently coordinates the research group on education, communication and language at ALAIC.

Juan Orlando Pérez holds a BA in journalism from the University of Havana and a masters degree and PhD from the University of Westminster (UK). He taught journalism for ten years in Cuba. He has also worked as a journalist in Cuba and most recently for the BBC World Service in the UK. He is currently a lecturer in journalism and a researcher at Roehampton University (UK). He has published in both Spanish and English in the areas of media, communication and journalism.

Carlos Sandoval-García is Professor of Communication at the Communication School and the Institute for Social Research, both at the University of Costa Rica. He obtained his PhD from the Department of Cultural Studies and Sociology at the University of Birmingham (UK). He has been researching on the media, immigration, nationhood, football and masculinities in Costa Rica. His books include *Threatening Others: Nicaraguans and the Formation of National Identities in Costa Rica* (2004) and *Fuera de Juego: Fútbol, masculinidades e identidades nacionales in Costa Rica* (2006).

Erick Torrico Villanueva is currently the president of the Latin American Association of Communication Researchers and director of the Postgraduate Programme in Journalism and Communication at the Simón Bolívar Andean University in La Paz (Bolivia). He is author of several publications and monographs, including *Conceptos y hechos de la sociedad informacional: miradas desde y sobre Bolivia* (2003) and *Abordajes y Periodos de La Teoría de La Comunicación* (2004).

Christian Tovar is a lecturer and a researcher at the Universidad Nacional de la Plata (Argentina). He is a member of the Centro de Estudio y Observación de Medios, a think-tank that focuses on media ownership, structures and technologies in Argentina, based at the Faculty of Communication and Journalism at the Universidad de la Plata (Argentina). He is co-author of *Medios, Política y Poder: La conformación de los multimedios en la Argentina: de los '90* and *Mapa de las Alianzas de las Telecomunicaciones* (2004).

Patricia Vialey is a researcher at the Universidad Nacional de la Plata (Argentina). She is a member of the Centro de Estudio y Observación de Medios, and of the Asociación Latinoamericana de Investigadores de la Comunicación (ALAIC). She is co-author of *Medios, Política y Poder: La conformación de los multimedios en la Argentina de los '90* and *Mapa de las Alianzas de las Telecomunicaciones* (2004).

Arturo Wallace-Salinas is a lecturer in media and communications at the Universidad Centroamericana in Managua, Nicaragua. He is the author of *Sangre en la pantalla, y otras tendencias del periodismo nicaragüense* (2007). A former BBC producer and correspondent, he holds a BA in social communication from the Universidad Centroamericana (Nicaragua) and an MSc in media and communications from the London School of Economics and Political Science (UK). He currently coordinates the UK Department for International Development's governance programme in Nicaragua.

ACKNOWLEDGEMENTS

This book was made possible by the initiative and interest of Professor Brian McNair, the series editor, and the patience and support of Christopher Cudmore, senior commissioning editor at Open University Press/ McGraw-Hill. I am grateful for their understanding of the potential and usefulness of a volume on the media in Latin America. I offer my sincere thanks to the contributors to this volume, which is a collective effort. Each chapter author has made considerable efforts to deliver concise yet comprehensive overviews of each country featured here. I also wish to acknowledge the work of Valerie Brown, Dianela Lugo, Celina Lavallesi and Rossana Viñas in doing the initial translation of some of the chapters. I offer special thanks to Corinne Fowler at Lancaster University, who made useful editorial suggestions for each of the chapters.

I also wish to acknowledge the Centro de Estudios y Observación de Medios (CEOM) at the University Nacional de La Plata in Argentina. Its students and graduates, F. Niggli, G. Annuasi, R. Viñas, P. Balatti, R. Brecevich, G. Verne, M. Iparraguirre, B. Villar, N. Carmona, C. Bernal, P. Leme, L. López Silva, F. Guiot, L. Retta and M. Di Francesco, provided much of the data for the chapter on that country. Equally important was the contribution of the Centro Gumilla and the Universidad Católica Andrés Bello in Venezuela, which provided data and academic space in that country.

A special thanks to Nicola Rocco from *El Universal* (Venezuela) whose photography in the cover of this book illustrates very well the contrasting and complex nature of Latin America's media systems; needless to say that one picture speaks more than a thousand words.

1 AN INTRODUCTION TO THE *MAQUILAS* OF POWER: MEDIA AND POLITICAL TRANSITION IN LATIN AMERICA

Jairo Lugo-Ocando

The term '*maquila*' is often used to describe factories in duty and tariff-free areas that assemble products already manufactured in other countries, in order to re-export them to the USA as if they were produced there. Originally established in the North of Mexico, the *maquilas* took advantage of bilateral commerce treaties that aimed to promote industrialization – in reality, however, they were nothing but assembly lines on the cheap. Increasingly, the term *maquila* has been used to denote this kind of industrial arrangement throughout Latin America. Critics charge that the *maquilas* do not add value to the local economies in which they operate, but instead perpetuate existing conditions of dependency (Wilson 1992: 137). In the past, scholars have argued that Latin America's media systems have operated in a similar way to the *maquilas*, being little more than factories in which cultural products from the USA and western Europe were assembled and then recycled 'on the cheap' across the continent (Colomina 1968; Mattelart 1972; Catalán and Sunkel 1992). However, as the contributors to this volume assert, this analysis is unequal to the task of explaining the last 20 years' growth and development of media systems in the region. Instead, a more nuanced analysis is required, one that attends to the specificities of Latin America's diverse media systems and their relation to global trends.

The construction of Latin America's media spaces was not the result of particular struggles for participation and debate. From the beginning, these spaces were derived from elite power, being conceived as (a) commodities to be exploited by the private sector and (b) mechanisms of political and societal control. While the USA and Great Britain saw the rise of the 'penny press' up until the first half of the twentieth century (McNair 2003), Latin America's media system was characterized by limited reach and heavy censorship (Rockwell and Janus 2003). With very few exceptions, the dictatorships and elitist democracies which exchanged power throughout the nineteenth and twentieth centuries were careful to craft the media systems so as to prevent general access, and guarantee their role as mechanisms of control. However, things have now moved on.

Today, the analysis of Latin America's media systems faces some key challenges. One of these is the need to question the traditional paradigm that assumes that the region's realities can be interpreted as a whole. This is not to argue that, once national specificities have been taken into account, general trends cannot be observed across the region. However, as is discussed in this book, there are very distinctive and particular realities to take into consideration. As some authors have already pointed out, to understand the media systems in Latin America we must consider both global *and* local specificities (Fox and Waisbord 2002: xxii). Indeed, despite the process of globalization, national contexts still provide by far the most crucial explanatory frameworks for national media systems throughout Latin America.

Given the multi-authored nature of this book, it is inevitable that style, structure and emphases will vary. This is one of its strengths, since it has allowed each co-author to balance the need to consider the international dimensions of each country's media systems with the need for historically informed analyses of specific local contexts and realities. In some cases, such as Brazil, this has required close attention to broadcasting. In others, such as Venezuela and Bolivia, it has meant looking more closely at the relationship between the media and the current political process taking place. In so doing, not only does this book aim to explore the role of the media in modern Latin America and to analyse its adaptation to the post-dictatorship period, but it also aspires to discussing these systems in the context of politics, economic globalization and technological innovation. As a result, we hope to offer an insight into the process of re-accommodating the various media as agents of power.

One of the elements that emerged during the writing of this book was that the media as a whole in Latin America has become an increasingly sophisticated mechanism of control, one that is less politicized and more oriented towards satisfying market needs within the ideological framework of liberal democracies in the region. Nevertheless, the different chapters' readings also suggest that many repressive elements of the dictatorship period remain in place or have mutated into more subtle means of censorship and control. On the other hand, media owners and political elites are more than keen to use the media's increasingly prominent role in politics to pursue their own agendas and interests. However, this has created uneasy, fragile and tense relationships. While, more often than not, it has resulted in an inappropriate degree of collaboration between politicians and the media, in other aspects it has translated into open confrontation. The result, in the first case, is a perverse scenario in which both the media and elites have forged alliances to protect their own markets and interests. Subject as it is to the concentration of power that results from these alliances, journalism is reduced to a decorative role. It engages with politics, but only by means of scandals. It prioritizes fashion, gossip and sports and is less willing to adopt controversial political agendas, unless they reflect dissidence among the ruling elites. Superficiality, then, becomes a journalistic strategy of survival and a modus vivendi for media owners. In the second case, the outcome is the realignment of interests and a new subversive role for the media, which has, in some cases, been proactive in conspiracies to overthrow governments. The confrontation between political leaderships and the media has also meant that these leaderships have strengthened their control by means of implementing new legal frameworks, drying up resources for opposing media and restricting access to official sources.

Democracy and the media

Liberal democracy remains, by and large, a relatively new concept in the region. Many institutions have not evolved sufficiently to strike a balance between different powers and interests. Many democracies in Latin America are increasingly coming under question for their inability to provide sustainable ways of life for their citizens and for having fallen short of meeting initial expectations. After less than two decades of democracy, some of these societies are only just beginning to realize what free speech really means: a persistent clash of elites' interests. Meanwhile, these democracies have to deal with weak institutions, political confrontation and extreme poverty. In many Latin American countries, this explosive cocktail creates too volatile a political environment to permit what would be, in other circumstances, a rational, peaceful and necessary political debate. Explicit censorship and strict media-state control are still the norm in many cases, even in those nations where democratic values such as freedom of speech are constitutionally guaranteed. In reality, the institutions entrusted to safeguard these rights are still too frail, or are unwilling to do so. Faced with this scenario, newly elected governments have opted to perpetuate the censorship mechanisms created by the former military regimes, a phenomenon that still defines the normative and legal framework of the media in many places.

Equally important to this scenario are other less explicit constraints. Educational and political limitations arise from functional illiteracy, poverty and social exclusion. These are, in many senses, Latin America's true 'axis of evil'. It has been well documented that, in order for citizens to take part in the democratic process, it is imperative that they have access both to *knowledge*, which could serve as a basis for informed participation (Wisdom 2001: 24), and also, above all, to *knowledge creation*. Despite the hyperbole of the information society, Latin American citizens are more often than not deprived of the process of knowledge creation and excluded from accessing legitimate and useful resources. Besides struggling with very high absolute illiteracy rates and functional illiteracy, people across the region must also deal with the prohibitive costs of accessing the available information. The myth that information is now freely available and accessible to all obviates 'the huge gaps in these societies' (Norris 2001: 62), gaps which determine how information is accessed and who accesses it. The internet is still a chimerical aspiration limited to the rich, indirectly subsidized by the state and exploited by corporations as a pure entertainment commodity; one could say that the poorest in the region have to pay to sit in the back of someone else's car to drive them through the information superhighway.

Furthermore, many of these nations find themselves obliged to divert resources from areas such as infrastructure, education or agricultural subsidies to acquire digital and interactive technologies developed in the first world. The drive to reduce the 'digital divide' intra-nationally and internationally (Norris 2001: 4) verges on an obsession for policy-makers. The problem is exacerbated by the fact that these are not additional resources poured into the system by the private sector (as if often presented to us), but public money diverted from other areas without proper cost-effectiveness studies according to development criteria. Because of this, the 1990s saw an increasing gap between the info-rich and the info-poor across the developing world (Norris 2001: 39), despite significant amounts of public investment in the area.[1] In many cases, the reallocation of resources to developing digital and interactive media has been little more than a futile attempt to grasp the elusive opportunities offered by the mirage of the so-called new economy.[2] The result has instead been to exacerbate the old determinants of wealth and poverty. Contrary to what the World Bank and other lending and development agencies assert, there is little if any evidence to suggest that the massive investment in information and communication technology and telecommunications during the past ten years has made a significant difference to the lives of millions. Instead, for every new computer bought by the state, there is less money for paying teachers and greater dependency on the manufacturing corporations and the lending institutions that finance these projects.

However, the situation for Latin America is by no means hopeless. In many cases the region has embraced these media technologies while embarking on some interesting initiatives. Some of these have been more successful than others, but they do not indicate any general trend. There are mixed signs, too, in terms of media consumption. The region has seen an exponential growth in telecommunications and media consumption, although it is still a minority who have access to these from home or who can make any contribution in terms of content-creation. It is a problematic dilemma. While, traditionally, media production and consumption had to deal with the fluctuating costs of items such as paper, ink and electricity, the emerging digital and interactive media now need to face the test posed by trying to acquire knowledge technology and creativity as intangible goods. Furthermore, hundreds of new satellite and cable channels bring a new dimension to competition. In some cases, they have killed any possibility of local content production, due to market saturation and fragmentation. In others, they have allowed the re-emergence of an incipient audiovisual and film industry, but only in very concentrated locations. Consumption of mobile phones with G3 technology has seen a rapid growth, but at a much slower pace than the ability to produce the content or technical support to be received by such phones. This has had the effect of increasing dependency on key technological centres to provide content and support. In Latin American countries, the telecommunication companies, which were privatized during the 1990s, have concentrated on making profits from the exploitation of specific urban markets, while neglecting the delivery of universal access to the network. In most cases, governments are still the only actors with sufficient resources to maintain or subsidize universal access to the media and telecommunications, but have stopped doing so because their role has been displaced by the private sector. Both internal arrangements with the media elites and international agreements with multi-lateral institutions such as the World Trade Organization and telecom and media giants have put governments in a straitjacket, preventing them from participating and delivering universal access to what is in principle a public service. It is not that these governments were able to do this in the past. The history of the telecommunications in Latin America shows that both private and public sectors have an equally poor record on this front. Nevertheless, in more recent times the election of a series of left-wing governments that are more inclined towards state intervention has come to challenge the status quo. This phenomenon is discussed widely in the pages of this book. The challenge has not been drawn up in terms of changing the relations of power, but more along the lines of displacing traditional actors' stake in the media and substituting them with new ones. In some countries this has meant actively inviting or at least permitting international corporations to take control of specific segments of the media and telecommunications markets. In others, it has translated into the configuration of new media groups, the integration of others, or the simple sale of media outlets to individuals close to the government. In a few cases, it has also meant re-nationalizing telecommunication companies.

Looking at Latin America

This book has managed to incorporate an integrated view of the region by providing chapters that discuss generalities *and* specificities in the context of global trends. As mentioned earlier, we have asked the authors of each chapter to provide an overview, while emphasizing the particular circumstances that characterize the media systems in each country. The contributors have been chosen for their long-standing experience of living and working in these countries. For the most part, the authors are native researchers, although in other cases – such as Sallie Hughes – their work has been so consistently informative over the years that they have become a reference even for local academics and researchers.

In Chapter 2, Patricia Vialey, Marcelo Belinche and Christian Tovar examine the process of change that has taken place in both the economy and the politics of Argentina. They use this contextual analysis to explore how these changes and processes have affected the composition of Argentina's media systems. They argue that, after emerging from years of dictatorship, Argentina was one of the first countries in the region to embrace a neo-liberal economic agenda, which had a series of consequences for its national media system. As the authors explain, the process of privatization and deregulation led to a concentration of ownership in the media industries, first in the hands of international groups and later in those of Argentinean groups. The chapter also provides statistical information about media audiences, consumption and regulation.

In Chapter 3, Erick Torrico Villanueva explains the role of the media in Bolivia's profound political transformations of recent years, together with an assessment of how the media has been affected by these changes. His critical analysis of the positions assumed by the media with regard to the re-emergence of social movements and union organizations is provocative and challenging. The chapter provides an interesting explanation for Evo Morales' rise to power, which in itself is one of the most transcendental events in that country's history. Indeed, as Torrico Villanueva explains, Bolivia is experiencing a democratic transition towards a model that pretends to recover the economic position of the state and generate concrete results in social development – a process that recognizes Bolivia's social diversity. A new tension has been established by this new paradigm since the mainstream news media is, in many cases, a traditional ally of the political and economic elites. The mainstream media is starting to behave more as a political actor that, willingly or not, has contributed to the country's increasing social polarization. In so doing, the media has been dragged into the political arena while at the same time losing legitimacy and credibility among its wider audience.

In Chapter 4, Olga Guedes-Bailey and Othon F. Jambeiro Barbosa offer several insights into one of the biggest broadcasting markets in the world, Brazil. They argue that the 2006 decision of the left-wing Brazilian government to adopt the Japanese model of digital television is both revealing and problematic. The decision was taken in the face of strong opposition from academics, grassroots movements, left-wing MPs and social scientists, who have been researching digital technologies in Brazil for many years. President Luiz Inácio Lula da Silva eventually opted for the model ostensibly favoured by Globo Network and the other Brazilian broadcasters, which have historically had great power and influence in the country. The authors ask if there is any real change in the Brazilian media political environment following the election of a self-declared left-wing government that was supposed to challenge traditional structures and privileges. They examine the continuity and changes in the media system in Brazil as an explanatory framework, referring to the US system as a predominant inspiration for the commercial model of broadcasting that has prevailed in Brazil. Their picture is one of continuity in traditional settings, but changes in modus operandi.

By contrast, in Chapter 5, Gustavo González-Rodríguez argues that Chile's democratic governments succeeded where Pinochet failed. He explains the profound irony in the increasing concentration of ownership following the fall of Pinochet's dictatorship. He explores the impoverishment of the mass media's structure, which is now completely determined by the powerful dominance of market forces. For him the media system in Chile reflects quasi-monopolistic concentration and dependency on advertisers, which accounts for the current lack of pluralism and diversity. The supposed consensus that was established in the 1980s to oust Pinochet, and that continued thereafter to preserve the fragile democracy, has since become an ideological monopoly that promotes neo-liberalism as the only possible social and economic paradigm.

In Chapter 6, Jorge Iván Bonilla, V. and Ancízar Narváez Montoya offer a salient analysis of the media system in Colombia. They investigate the media's evolution and its inextricable link to the country's history. Their description of the structure and characteristics of the media also assists an understanding of how power and politics are engineered in a country that is still dominated by violence and social exclusion. The authors, two of the most important researchers in Colombia, explain the frameworks in which media outlets operate, the characteristics of concentrated ownership and how armed conflict is managed and dealt with. They ask if it is possible for the media to develop a national cultural project given the limitations imposed by ownership structure, self-censorship and political violence. Their suggestion is that it is perhaps possible, but not necessarily in terms of democracy and self-determination.

In Chapter 7 on Costa Rica, Carlos Sandoval-García, one of Central America's leading scholars, offers an overview of the country's media institutions. He analyses the media in the context of the wider processes of urbanization, literacy and secularization. Assessing the media in terms of ownership and audiences, he underlines the existence of oligopolies in the television, advertising and printed media sectors. For him, the country's media programming is characterized by a situation in which homogeneity rules over diversity in content and cultural forms – while the distribution of audiences of printed media depends upon income and literacy. Offering an illuminating series of original data, he argues that this phenomenon does not seem to affect television viewers' habits of consumption in the same way. He also explores the impact of digital and interactive technologies such as the internet in Costa Rica. His assessment of the role and responsibilities of the media with regard to public life is that there is a striking paradox: while the media has demanded politicians and other public actors to be accountable, it rarely offers accountability for its own institutional practices.

Despite the fact that Cuba is a constant centre of attention in academia and politics, its media have often been overlooked. The preconceived idea is that the country's media is merely part of the government's propaganda apparatus, and this assumption is often used as a pretext for excluding it from discussions of the Latin American media. In Chapter 8, Juan Orlando Pérez has managed to dislodge this paradigm and instead offer us a more realistic, comprehensive and elaborated view of the complexities and contradictions that characterize the country's media systems. Such an analysis is not restricted to a discussion of US-Cuba tensions but extends to an assessment of different aspects of the media and media audiences within Cuba itself. Looking at the importance of cultural industries on the island, especially the film industry after the revolution, and the increasing presence of the internet and satellite television, the author suggests that Cuban people are far less isolated from the rest of the world than many might think. He explains that, contrary to other socialist countries in Eastern Europe or Asia, western and popular culture was never entirely banned in Cuba and that it is a dynamic and challenging presence in that nation.

In Chapter 9, Sallie Hughes explains that the national media system in Mexico continues to change at a rapid pace compared to other media systems in longer-established democracies. In the last two decades, she points out, the media in Mexico has moved from being a semi-authoritarian institution to a hybrid system exhibiting market-driven, oligarchic, propagandistic, ideological and civic elements. However, she argues that while there is now more diversity, media access remains largely unequal. Furthermore, there are many variants of authoritarian journalism that have survived as the dominant model within the government-owned television network, where newsroom personnel and direction are imposed by state governors in a propagandist fashion. She suggests that subordination in media outlets is based on quid pro quo exchanges of advertising or other financial incentives for news content rather than internalization of such norms because the authoritarian model has lost legitimacy.

Nicaragua, which was once the subject of intense interest from international news media and scholars, has now practically vanished from the front pages of newspapers and the books of academics. This is why Arturo Wallace-Salinas, in Chapter 10, offers an overview of the media as well as providing historical context. He starts by reminding us that the main characteristic of that society, as with most of Latin America, is poverty. Therefore, he argues, any analysis needs to start by acknowledging the role of the media in relation to social exclusion. He highlights the fact that the media has acted as a watchdog in relation to that which he refers to as a 'dysfunctional democracy'. By having played a decisive role in exposing corruption and denouncing the wrongdoings and limitations of the political system, the media in Nicaragua can claim, he says, to be one of the few functional democratic institutions in this small Central American country. However, he warns us that, by focusing almost exclusively on its role as watchdog and by neglecting other important public service roles, the media has limited its potential contribution to the consolidation of Nicaragua's still incipient democracy.

In Chapter 11 on Paraguay, Susana Aldana-Amabile explains that, following the transition to democracy from the Stroessner era, the media reflected a rise in public political engagement and briefly enjoyed increasing credibility. However, only ten years later there was a downturn in public confidence towards the media. She explains that as the media became more and more partisan and elites more focused on using the media to advance their own interests, Paraguayans lost their initial enthusiasm and became more sceptical. Aldana-Amabile argues that the Paraguayan media in general, and its television stations in particular, have mobilized violence, death and uncertainty about the future as a new form of social control. As a consequence, the media as a whole has fostered widespread political disengagement and apathy.

In Chapter 12, Celia Aldana-Durán provides a comprehensive analysis of the history and structure of the media in Peru. In the context of this analysis, she argues that the Peruvian media face several challenges and problems. Two of them are crucial in terms of democracy and development: one related to their capability to represent the country where they are located, and the other related to their loss of legitimacy and the need to regain it. Looking at the issue of race and equality, she provides evidence of how the media in Peru reproduces exclusion and suggests that to change this, it is necessary to intertwine democracy and development.

Andrés Cañizález and Jairo Lugo-Ocando, in Chapter 13, refer to the case of Venezuela, which has captured a great deal of attention from the international media in recent times. Its charismatic leader, President Hugo Chávez, has been at odds with most of the commercial media since he was first elected in 1998. In this analysis, it is argued that the confrontation between the commercial media and President Chávez occurred in the context of the current climate of anti-politics. This situation precedes the rise of President Chávez to power, which has been characterized by a symbiotic co-dependence on the part of those in political power and the media. Therefore, because of the nature of the media's ownership and structure, most of the commercial media have aligned with the opposition, therefore assuming an active and explicit role in politics. In this chapter, the structure and development of the media system are considered and an attempt made to provide an overview of its cultural industries.

The last chapter draws together threads and themes; however it is not intended to be a summary of preceding chapters, but a substantive contribution in its own right. The authors discuss regional integration and the possibility of a common Latin American public sphere. They consider the case of TeleSur, the new cross-government sponsored television network, to explore the possibilities and challenges brought about by initiatives such as the Andean Pact and Mercosur. Indeed, it is argued that these emerging trade blocs open up a series of questions with regard to national media systems and the possible promotion of a common sphere, since they are setting a different legal, political and economic framework. The main argument is that, because TeleSur aims to be both an instrument of asymmetrical confrontation with the USA and a means of facilitating geopolitical integration in the region, it must be understood as both a project that presupposes the existence of a common public sphere and a geopolitical element in relation to the USA. The authors argue that an analysis of TeleSur allows an understanding of the vicissitudes concerning media systems in the context of the trade agreements and new political realities in the region. The authors also believe that, by analysing this case, it is possible to get an idea of why relations with the USA are so pivotal in understanding Latin America's media systems in current times.

It is difficult to produce a single book about Latin American media systems, not only due to the diversity of themes that are involved, but mostly because of the shifting features of the region's media systems.

Indeed, what we see here are not static structures of power, but organic and dynamic bodies that change, integrate and mutate, both internally and externally, especially in relation to global phenomena as a whole. Increasingly, Latin America's media systems are intrinsically linked to global networks of telecommunication, media and advertising (Fox and Waisbrod 2002: 6). Nevertheless, it is important to contest the traditional characterizations of Latin American media systems as mere power structures based on subordination to, and dependence on, US conglomerates. Our ultimate aim is to present and analyse what we see as a very complex set of realities also linked to national media systems. Indeed, as it becomes clear throughout the book, the influence of the USA in areas such as advertising, corporate strategies, joint media ventures and ownership is nowadays as convergent as it is distinctive. Such relationships need to be re-examined on a case by case basis. Thus in areas such as telecommunications, we see the diminishing presence of US corporations, which are gradually being displaced by companies such as Telefónica of Spain.

Nevertheless, the USA still exercises a quasi-hegemonic presence in Latin America's media systems, although with different degrees of influence and power. However, and despite past speculations of direct US intervention – such as that the CIA-owned stock shares in specific media outlets in Latin America (Bernstein 1977; Gervasi 1979) – the real influence and power of the US government and corporations is today more subtle and sophisticated (Fox 1997). This is a topic that deserves a study in itself. Indeed, several authors in the past and present have examined Latin American dependence on the USA in relation to its media and cultural industries (McAnany 1984; Martín-Barbero 1993; Mattelart 1998). But that dependence is the result of the wider political context and economic framework that ultimately impacts not only on media systems in the region but on society as a whole – and in this sense, Latin America is no different from any other region of the world. Indeed, there is no evidence to suggest that US hegemony is greater or more widespread in Latin America than elsewhere.

Equally challenging to the researcher of Latin American media is the changing face of its audiences and their relationship towards media and centres of political power. The cases of Bolivia, Peru and Venezuela, for example, suggest that we can no longer consider the media as effective as a mechanism of hegemony in the traditional sense. Furthermore, the distribution of channels and the influence of foreign media corporations and correspondents in each of the Latin American countries – which has traditionally been the focus of numerous publications (Díaz Rangel 1976; Pedelty 1995) – has also undergone profound changes as the region's traditional set of relations between the public, private and international media has evolved into different forms. In addition to these elements, some of the chapters in this book have placed particular emphasis on issues that are infrequently debated in relation to the media in Latin America, namely cultural diversity and racism. Even though what we offer here is far from an elaborated study on the subject, it does highlight some of the important problems that derive from a predominantly white, male analysis of the media. Racial tensions and ethnic access and representation, not often explicitly recognized in Latin American politics (Klich and Rapoport 1997) or in media studies (Fox 2006), are at the core and not in the margins of social relations. In the same way, gender plays a pivotal role in defining much of the content and news agenda, despite the fact that, in many Latin American countries, women outnumber men by far in newsrooms and audiovisual studios. Some of the chapters have managed to incorporate this implicitly when referring to the data, while others have been more explicit, such as the case of women doing investigative journalism.

We have offered some insight into how journalism is practised within the national media systems. However, journalism in itself cannot be defined only through the nature of the media but also needs to be understood in terms of political practices and its relations towards power. Although some authors have claimed that, at an institutional level, journalism in places such as Latin America is not strongly developed as an autonomous institution with a distinctive set of professional values and practices (Hallin and Papathanassopoulos 2002: 182), the picture that emerges from this book is very different: one not only of professionalism – by any standard – but also of ethical commitment. Indeed, Latin America is among the regions with the worst record in terms of journalists killed and wounded. Neither is there any evidence that journalism across the region as a whole is practised any less rigorously than in any other part of the world. Furthermore, at least nine countries in Latin America have obligatory membership of collegial associations of journalists (Trotti and Williamson 1996: 106), which nowadays require in most cases a university degree. Even though, in many instances, this turns out to be a result of political feuds and mechanisms to control access to the media, obligatory membership of collegial associations for journalists also seems to provide a pressure group for journalists' rights against abuses by employers and government censorship (Trotti and Williamson 1996: 106).

On the whole, this book presents what we consider to be a comprehensive map of Latin America's media systems. However, because of constrains of time and space, it was not possible to include all of the countries of the region. The main reasons for our selection were editorial market prerogatives and discretional access to data. We hope that in time, with subsequent editions, we can incorporate other countries as part of a larger volume.

Notes

1   The privatization of telecommunication companies limited the ability
   to provide universal coverage, since the newly privately-owned company had to follow the profit-making logic of its shareholders and not
   the requirements and needs of the market.
2   Christopher May says that even before the dot.com crash the idea of
   a new economy was perceived by some authors as unsubstantiated
   (2002: 160).

2 THE MEDIA IN ARGENTINA: DEMOCRACY, CRISIS AND THE RECONFIGURATION OF MEDIA GROUPS

Patricia Vialey, Marcelo Belinche and Christian Tovar[1]

Two decades ago it was impossible to imagine the present configuration of Argentina's media landscape. In less then a decade, Argentina's media industries and markets have shifted from limited or no competition to an open and fierce competitive environment (Galperín 2002: 22).

Before these changes, it was difficult to imagine – given the then existing regulations in the country – a scenario in which a few groups and media companies from the private sector could produce, analyse and check circulating and rating information. However, as the media market became more transparent during the 1990s it also became more concentrated. This period was characterized in the communication field by the configuration of media groups, holdings, oligopolics and corporations that held the control and property of the media. The situation was endorsed by a legal framework that no longer put limitations on ownership concentration or vertical media integration. This was possible due to neo-liberal policies implemented during Carlos Saúl Menem's presidency (1989–99). His government's approach meant a reduction in the size of the Argentine state, deep changes in the economic model and profound transformation of culture and society in the country. The aim was to sell off the media, which was still in the hands of the state, and to make more flexible the regulatory framework for broadcasting ownership and operation.

The transformations which took place in the country during this period were supported by the international events dominating the scene: the fall of the Berlin Wall; the emergence of globalization as an ideology; the internationalization of markets; and the end of the welfare state. These events inspired what became known as the 'Washington Consensus'.[2] This was in reality a set of neo-liberal and monetarist policies which became the prescriptive recipe for economies in trouble, recommended by multilateral institutions such as the World Bank and the International Monetary Fund and strongly advocated by President Ronald Reagan in the USA and Prime Minister Margaret Thatcher in the UK. This group of policies were later implemented in Argentina as a way to achieve reform of the state, economy and society. Indeed, in Argentina the state's Reform

No. 23.696 and the Economic Emergency Laws (No. 23.697) were the legal basis that supported the reduction of companies and industries owned or managed by the state; and this of course included media outlets and telecommunications. Indeed, it meant the privatization of many industries such as the National Telecommunications Enterprise (EnTel), the railway and subway networks, the state-owned oil company Yacimientos Petrolíferos Fiscales (YPF), tha state-owned gas company Gas del Estado, the state-owned energy company Servicios Eléctricos del Gran Buenos Aires (SEGBA), and the water company Obras Sanitarias de la Nación, all of whom were given in lease to the private sector.

It was precisely the need to forge agreement with the media owners so that they would not question his neo-liberal policy that encouraged Carlos Menem's government to change and make more flexible the media and telecommunication regulatory framework. This meant new legislation for telecommunications that opened up the possibility for newspaper and magazine owners to acquire or create broadcast media. For example, in order to award television licenses for two new television channels (Channel 11 and Channel 13) in Buenos Aires (also known as the Federal District of Argentina), the government had to reform the existing laws. This was because its ownership was protected by the Broadcasting Resolution Law No. 22.285, developed by the military junta government in 1980[3] under the National Security Doctrine. This prevented private capital and foreign investors from holding shares in broadcast media. Menem's government then advanced the reform and modification of articles 43-c, 45-e, 46-a and 46-c of this law, which opened up the ownership regime, providing other means for media owners and groups to access broadcasting. The new telecommunication and media bill, known as No. 23.696, defined a list of companies and activities, by then in the hands of the state, that had to be privatized or leased to the private sector. These included several broadcasting outlets such as television channels L.S. 84, Channel 11, and L.S. 85, Channel 13, along with radio stations L.R. 3 (Radio Belgrano) and L.R. 5 (Radio Excelsior). As some authors have pointed out, the aim was to privatize every means of communication managed by the state, except the television network L. S. 82 ATC, L.R.A. 1 Radio Nacional Buenos Aires, and Radiodifusión Argentina (RAE) (short-wave radio), and transmitters that integrated the Broadcasting National Service (Belinche et al. 2004: 25). Guillermo Orozco Gómez, one of the main media researchers in Latin America, suggests that the idea to privatize the state-owned media and broadcasting spectrum was taken at the highest levels of power from the start. From 1990, the tendency to privatization in different areas of social exchange had become not only evident and growing, but also apparently irreversible: privatization was forcefully declared and imposed on the national communication systems and all information media enterprises controlled until then by the state (Orozco Gómez 1997: 45).

This new reconfiguration of the legal and political framework allowed the first multi-media groups to emerge in Argentina. This in turn allowed the owners of the newspaper *Clarín*, which is among the biggest selling titles, and the owners of Editorial Atlántida, which prints over a dozen magazines of national circulation, to get hold of Channels 13 and 11 respectively. Then, in 1992, with Law No. 24.124, which confirmed the Promotion and Protection of Reciprocal Investment Agreement with the USA signed a year before, foreign investors started to arrive in the country and buy into media. This was the case with the US Citibank Group, which entered into partnership with Telefónica de Argentina, owned by Spanish investors, and Editorial Atlántida, in order to set up a new media group. As a result of this, the new group, CEI Citicorp Holdings S.A., would become one of the main competitors of the then largest media conglomerate, Grupo Clarín, and both would come to dominate telecommunications and media in subsequent years.

The groups

From this period and until about the middle of the 1990s, the composition of telecommunications groups in Argentina was as follows. Grupo Clarín owned the *Clarín* newspaper; the sports newspaper *Olé*; Mitre AM Radio; 100 FM Radio; Top 40 FM Radio; *Elle* magazine (with Hachette, a French publishing house); *Genios* magazine; *Surf* magazine; television Channel 13; the cable television company Multicanal (which in itself owned 20 per cent of the cable company Supercanal in partnership with Grupo Uno from the region of Mendoza); the satellite company DirecTV (with Grupo Cisneros from Venezuela); the cable TV channels Todo Noticias, Volver, Magazine and TyC Sports (with Torneos y Competencias, a Carlos Avila enterprise of Telefónica de España, CEI and Liberty International); Artes Gráficas Rioplatense printing works; the DyN news agency; paper producer Papel Prensa; Cimeco Society, owner of the newspapers *La Voz del Interior* from Córdoba and *Los Andes* from Mendoza (with Grupo La Nación, owner of *La Nación* newspaper); television and cinematographic producer Pol-ka; cinematographic producer Patagonik (with Telefónica de España and Disney International); the mobile telephone company CTI and the internet provider Ciudad.

CEI-Telefónica (in which the investment fund Hicks, Muse, Tate & Furts also had shares) was composed of: Editorial Atlántida (general interest and specialized magazines such as *Gente, Billiken* and *Chacra*, among others); television channels Telefe and Channel 9 (with Prime, an Australian communication group); Continental AM radio; Hit FM Radio; television Channels 8 and 10 from Mar del Plata; television Channel 8 from Córdoba; television Channel 7 from Neuquén province; television channel 5 from Rosario (Santa Fe province); television Channel 9 from Bahía Blanca (Buenos Aires); television Channel 13 from Santa Fe; television Channel 11 from Salta province; television Channel 9 from Resistencia (Chaco province); television Channel 9 from Paraná (Entre Ríos province); cable television transmitter Cablevisión; television producer Endemol; cinematographic producer Patagonik[4] (with Grupo Clarín and Disney International); telephone company Telefónica de Argentina;

mobile telephone company Unifón; Torneos y Competencias (with businessman Carlos Avila and Liberty International); and the internet providers Advance and Terra. The rise of these two media conglomerates has meant a concentration in terms of television and radio audiences. It has also meant that those who already dominated the print market now have access to the biggest audience share in cable and satellite television, while controlling a significant part of internet provision in Argentina. It is also clear that there is not only vertical integration, but also horizontal expansion, since in many cases and areas these groups act not only as competitors but also as partners. As these groups manage to control new media outlets and the communication infrastructure, they also become more capable of shaping and defining the news agenda. They now have immense power and influence, since they are capable of imposing the topics that public opinion will debate.

In this context, over time the telecommunications niche became a fruitful field for investors, which in turn had a significant impact in reshaping the media landscape. Some of these movements were provoked by changes in the ownership structure, such as when Telefónica de España increased their investments in Latin America, becoming sole shareholders in many telecommunications companies. In other cases, these changes were the result of internal conflicts between media conglomerates, and political confrontation. A good example is the crisis faced by the CEI group in 1999, which later led to its dissolution after its chief executive officer and directors were accused of fraud. The result was that 70 per cent of the communications networks in Argentina were controlled by four telecommunications holdings: Grupo Clarín; Telefónica de Argentina; Hicks Muse; and Carlos Avila. New players also started to emerge in the late 1990s. The success of *La Primera* magazine, *BAE* newspaper and Radio 10 in the city of Buenos Aires resulted in a new competitor on the media scene: the Argentine journalist and businessman, Daniel Hadad.

The telecom groups and the *corralito*

Several elements combined to provoke the 2001 economic crisis in Argentina, informally known as the *corralito*. Indeed, in December 2001, after a prolonged period of economic instability and increasing government deficit, people began withdrawing large sums of money from their bank accounts, converting Argentinian pesos into dollars and sending them abroad. The government then enacted a set of measures that effectively froze all bank accounts for 12 months, allowing for only minor sums of cash to be withdrawn. The causes of this crisis can be traced back to the long-term effects of the neo-liberal policies carried out in Argentina during Carlos Menem's presidency, the lack of a coherent plan from the Alianza coalition, led by Fernando de la Rúa, that had been in government since 1999[5] and the deterioration of the international market, which showed important signs of recession, in particular the burst of the 'dot.com'[6] economy. This translated into a massive exodus of capital and deposits from the financial system. Over the course of 2001, the Argentine banking system lost over US $25 billion, resulting in the shutdown of international credit and a lack of cash in both public and private sectors. Faced with this situation, the Minister for the Economy at that time, Domingo Cavallo, who had been appointed by De la Rúa and who had already been in charge of the economy during 1991 and 1996 in Menem's presidency, put in place a restriction on banking deposit withdrawals, an action known in the media as *corralito*.[7]

This policy also produced a disruption of payments down the line. In fact, it had a devastating impact on an economy where an important segment of the workforce is paid in cash to avoid taxes, social security, etc. (the expression is being 'paid in the black'). The lack of cash affected almost 45 per cent of the workforce and contributed to a worsening social and political crisis. Not only did people lose their savings, but many were now not even being paid. The political effects by then had become unavoidable. Mass protests, riots and revolts against the Alianza coalition government led in the first place to the dismissal of Domingo Cavallo as Minister for the Economy, and weeks later to the resignation of President Fernando de la Rúa, who fled in a helicopter from the presidential palace. The crisis created a vacuum of power in which three successive governments resigned one after the other in a matter of weeks. It was only after Eduardo Duhalde, who had been Carlos Menem's vice-president until 1991, was appointed President of Argentina by the Parliament on 2 January 2002 that things began to improve. Initially intending to serve for only a few months until the chaotic situation could be controlled, Duhalde stayed in office for more than a year. During this time, he confirmed the default of most of the Argentine public debt. He also ended the unsustainable peg of the Argentine peso to the US dollar, which triggered inflation and massive discontent. Duhalde then led the country to new elections and was succeeded by Néstor Kirchner on 25 May 2003. During Duhalde's year in government there was widespread debate in the country about the legitimacy of traditional political leadership. These discussions called for major changes to the country's power structures and questioned who the protagonists of the economic scene should be. Duhalde's monetary policy, which meant the end of the peg to the US dollar and subsequent currency devaluation, accelerated the exodus of foreign capital from Argentine markets. This also had a significant impact on the media and telecommunications industries.

The media in Argentina were not only witnesses to this crisis, but also protagonists within it. For example, under pressure from international lenders, the government of Duhalde proposed to modify the bankruptcy Law No. 19.551. Until then, this law did not allow foreign creditors to take control of companies that were not able to fulfil their financial obligations. Modification of the law would have an important impact on many media and telecommunications companies who had filed for bankruptcy protection. In this context, some new media conglomerates saw their position and ownership under threat. For example, between 24 January and 5 February 2002, Grupo Clarín defaulted on payments of debts from Multicanal and AGEA (the Clarín newspaper publisher) for an amount of US $190 million. If the bankruptcy law – which had been put in place as a result of the 2001 crisis – had remained in its original form, Grupo Clarín and other national media groups would have had to give up a substantial part of their shares to their foreign creditors. The national media groups then launched a campaign and started to lobby the government, which was compelled to reform the new law, but with a special exception for the media companies. Reform No. 25.750, or the Cultural Goods Law, established that no foreign national or company could own more than 30 per cent of the 'cultural goods' of Argentinian companies. The media industry was included in this regulation, which allowed the media companies to resist takeovers by international creditors.

After the crisis: map and new actors

In the aftermath of the economic upheaval, many media companies went back to their projects of expansion and widening their market. In addition to this, the threat of takeover by international investors gradually diminished as Argentina was no longer a desirable place for such investors, who saw their profits fall in relation to previous decades. There was also some apprehension among potential investors created by changes in the Broadcasting Resolution Law, which made it difficult for some media companies to fulfil their obligations. The law was used by the government to re-nationalize by the back door some important media and telecommunications assets. The Broadcasting Federal Committee (COMFER in Spanish), responsible for regulating, controlling and managing the installation and functioning of radio and television transmitters in Argentina, used the law to take over Telefónica de España's assets in one of the two television channels they controlled in Buenos Aires, Channel 9, renamed afterwards as Azul TV. In the same way, the Committee took from the Mexican International Entertainment Company (CEI in Spanish) control of Del Plata, América, Aspen, Metropolitana, San Isidro Labrador, Rock & Pop, Feeling, Splendid and Libertad, all radio stations, because the Broadcasting Resolution Law forbade the ownership of more than one AM and one FM transmitter by a single company in the same area. Finally, the Azul TV's withdrawal from Telefónica led Prime Television Limited, an Australian-based media corporation, to hire JP Morgan investment bank to look for a buyer for the 50 per cent of their own shares in that channel. This favoured the creation of a new multi-media group. In the middle of 2002, a company formed by businessman Benjamin Vijnovsky (the main shareholder of the *Página/12* newspaper), Fernando Sokolowicz and Daniel Hadad became the sole owner of Channel 9 (Azul TV). Hadad benefited from this acquisition, since he owned a newspaper, *Infobae*, and two radio broadcasters, AM Radio 10 and FM Mega. With the Channel 9 (Azul TV) acquisition, the journalist and businessman strengthened his presence in the Argentine media market. The presence of Sokolowicz however was not as beneficial, since it compromised *Página/12*'s independence, which until then had been characterized by being the most progressive and left-wing newspaper. The ex-director of the newspaper, Jorge Lanata, in an interview given to *Veintitrés* magazine, described the economic operations which led to *Página/12* selling to Héctor Magnetto, one of the directors of Grupo Clarín, confirming many rumours that had been circulating until that time. Sokolowicz later sold his shares in Azul TV, leaving Hadad to search for new partners for his television project. It was then that the new incursion into the broadcasting market of the Vigil family, owners of Editorial Atlántida, one of the main magazine publishers in the country, began. They were trying to re-enter the broadcast media arena after the dissolution of the CEI consortium, of which they had been a part in the 1990s. However, internal disputes in the channel resulted in the Vigils withdrawing as protagonists in the business. Raúl Moneta was appointed at Channel 9 (Azul TV), running the Infocampo section, which dealt with agricultural management. This is a key area of media coverage in Argentina, since it represents the most important aspect of the economy. Moneta would later sell his 50 per cent share in the channel to Hadad in 2006.

While Hadad was expanding, other media business people did the same. This was the case for Grupo Clarín, which started to develop new strategies in order to become the leading media company in the country. Before the 2001 crisis, Grupo Clarín had developed supplements for each area of the city, as a way to strengthen their position in the depressed advertising market. These publications accompanied the newspaper and contained information about different areas of Buenos Aires. The strategy was successful and translated into a significant increase in newspaper sales. Afterwards, when the French firm Hachette left Argentina, the Clarín group took control of *Elle* magazine. The group also launch supplements, to be bought separately from the newspaper, which specialized in areas such as architecture, and small and medium business enterprises. In addition to the cultural magazine, Ñ, it also acquired the newspaper *La Razón* in Buenos Aires, which was relaunched as a free evening paper. The Clarín group also went into the book publishing market, creating the Tinta Fresca publishing enterprise, dedicated to books for general basic education (EGB), using experience acquired from the magazines *Jardín de Genios* and *Enseñar*, for children and teachers respectively. In this way, the group demonstrated that it had a coherent strategy to face the crisis, increasing their profit by reaching different segments of the public with distinctive products. Furthermore, although the Clarín group reached an agreement with their international partners in the satellite company DirecTV to cede its 50 per cent of shares in the subsidiary in exchange for 5 per cent from the Latin American operations, it nevertheless managed to acquire 25 per cent of its main competitor in cable TV, Cablevisión. With this acquisition, Clarín managed to obtain almost 50 per cent of the subscribers to this type of service in Argentina, Multicanal and Supercanal customers to its market. On top of this, the group added to its portafolio of cable channels Todo Noticias, Volver, TyC Sports, Magazine and Multideportes.

Grupo Clarín increased its participation in the broadcasting market in other regions in the country by acquiring channels such as Channel 12 from Córdoba and Channel 7 from Bahía Blanca (Buenos Aires). It also signed commercial and contents agreements with television Channels 6 from Bariloche (Río Negro); 10 from Tucumán; 10 from Mar del Plata (Buenos Aires); and 10 from Río Negro province, which allowed them to sell many of their programmes to other parts of the country. Indeed, in terms of content generation, the Clarín group started a partnership with Marcelo Tinelli, when the media group bought 30 per cent of *Ideas del Sur*; a television production company, then owned by Tinelli. The group also went into the mobile telecommunications business by creating CTI, in association with América Móvil, owned by the Mexican telecommunications holding TelMex, and the Grupo Techint, a multi-national holding which operates in different sectors (infrastructure, steel mills, design and assembly of industrial plants, energy and public services). The association between Grupo Techint and Grupo Clarín has also proved to be very successful in other areas. Both groups created a private mail service, Unir S.A. and a publishing and printing service, Impripost Tecnologías S.A. The group is also experimenting with other business ventures without partners. Among these, it has launched a telecommunications service for big corporations and has diversified into the organization of events and exhibitions via its new division, Vontel. It is also offering a free internet service called Fullzero and has launched a broadband provider called Ciudad Internet Flash. In addition to all this, from 2000 the group has been developing the management firm Gestión Compartida, as a centre of shared services which offers management consultancy in administration and finance, human resources, information systems and general management services. It now has a portfolio of more than 30 other companies, outside those that are part of its own holding.

There have been also major changes in other media groups that have forged new alliances, such as the America TV channel. In 2001, Carlos Avila had replaced Eduardo Eurnekian at the top of America TV management. A few months later this channel experienced financial difficulties and was unable to meet some of its obligations. Avila, who at the time was also the owner of the television rights of Argentinian football matches until 2014, tried different projects in Latin America, the USA and Asia. He also acquired the magazine *La Primera* from Hadad, and renamed it *Poder*. Avila also acquired shares in *Ámbito Financiero*, the main business newspaper, which connected him to the journalist-businessman Julio Ramos. He also invested in the internet through the Uol-Sinectis company in partnership with Jorge Fontevecchia's publishing house, Editorial Perfil SA.

After the 2001 crisis the owners of Grupo Uno from the region of Mendoza, Daniel Vila and the ex-interior minister José Luis Manzano, started managing America TV, cable television channel Supercanal, the digital television transmitter Televisión Directa al Hogar and the multi-media group La Capital, with more than 20 communications media enterprises in the provinces of Santa Fe and Entre Ríos. Vila and Manzano also entered the sports magazine business with *El Gráfico* and *AM La Red*, which up to that time had been managed by Avila via the firm TyC.

Meanwhile, and taking advantage of the fact that the main broadcasting regulator COMFER was dealing harshly with those companies and networks that were not complying with the existing legislation, the TV presenter and businessman Marcelo Tinelli decide to grasp the opportunity to buy some media outlets and get hold of broadcasting licenses. At first, he rented for his own radio station, the FM Feeling, which broadcasts throughout Buenos Aires. The station belonged until then to the Mexican consortium CIE, which wanted to leave the business but had no suitable buyer. Some months later, under Kirchner's presidency, Tinelli also acquired AM Radio Del Plata, which also belonged to the Mexican consortium.

Not all foreign investors were willing to leave the Argentinean media market after the 2001 crisis. Investors from Spain such as Telefónica did not give up completely in trying to consolidate a media project in the emerging Latin American market. Their strategy consisted of creating local brands instead of trying to globalize their own mobile brand, so that by 2005 the individual brands were absorbed and replaced by MoviStar. The company also bought other Latin subsidiaries from BellSouth, among them Movicom from Argentina. MoviStar is today one of the main mobile phone operators. It is owned by Telefónica Móviles and operates in Spain and in many Latin American countries. Among these are: Argentina (formerly Telefónica Unifón and Movicom BellSouth); Chile (formerly Telefónica Móvil and BellSouth); Colombia (formerly BellSouth); Ecuador (formerly BellSouth); El Salvador (Formerly Telefónica Móviles or Telefonica MoviStar); Guatemala (formerly Telefónica MoviStar and BellSouth); Mexico (formerly Telefónica Móviles México and Pegaso); Nicaragua (formerly BellSouth); Panama (formerly BellSouth); Peru (formerly Telefónica Móviles and BellSouth); Spain (formerly Telefónica MoviStar); Uruguay (formerly Movicom); and Venezuela (formerly Telcel-BellSouth). It also operates in other countries where Telefónica Móviles has networks under other brands, such as: Brazil (formerly under Movistar in some places, now under the Vivo brand via a joint venture with Portugal Telecom); Morocco (under Meditel Telecom brand) via a joint venture with Portugal Telecom, BMCE Bank and others; the Czech Republic (under the O2 brand); the Slovak Republic (under the O2 brand); Germany (under the O2 brand); the Republic of Ireland (under the O2 brand); and the UK (under the O2 brand). The MoviStar name has been in use in Spain since the launch of GSM services in 1995. After purchasing the BellSouth mobile operations branch in South America, the name became effective worldwide on 5 April 2005.

One of the reasons why Telefónica has remained calm despite a turbulent market is because Argentina has one of the fastest-growing mobile markets in Latin America. It has a penetration of more than

87 per cent – well above the Latin American average, trailing only Chile and a few Caribbean islands. Three operators, MoviStar, CTI Móvil and Telecom Personal, now run in close competition for market share. Nextel has a small but profitable slice of the market and there is also some competition from alternative players. In July 2007, two local cooperatives, Fecotel and Fecosur, were awarded government mobile licences. In May and July 2007 respectively, Telecom Personal and MoviStar launched Argentina's first 3G services over HSPDA networks, while Blackberry reached Argentina in 2006, and mobile banking arrived in early 2007 (Web Reports 2007b).

In more recent times, Telefónica has sold part of the more traditional media outlets (mainly but not only terrestrial broadcasters) in Argentina to concentrate on the mobile phone and telecommunications business. However, it sold them not to Argentinean investors, but to other foreign investors. Such was the case for AM Radio Continental from Buenos Aires. In 2005, with investments in the radio media, the group Prisa from Spain acquired Radio Continental. Prisa also has investments in Bolivia, Chile, Colombia and Costa Rica. With this acquisition the group, which already had wide print operations in the country, entered the Argentine broadcasting market. That year it also bought Editorial Santillana, a major publishing house that has a lucrative market all over Latin America, and other smaller publishing houses such as Aguilar, Altea, Taurus and Alfaguara. The group also went ahead with a strategy of vertical integration, buying the bookshop chain Fausto, one of the largest in the country. With this move, the group consolidated itself as one of the main cultural industries in Argentina. This strategy made sense since Argentina is one of the main publishing centres of the Spanish-speaking world, with over 50 publishing houses that compete in the international market.

Other important changes within the media, creative and cultural industries in Argentina occurred as a result of profound transformations in the advertising market. During 2005, the investment in publicity reached 4.148 million Argentinean pesos, more than double the 2,009,559,300 pesos in 2002, when the economic crisis had hit the hardest, but still far under the over 5 million of 1998. Of this investment, 42.04 per cent went to television, while 38.1 per cent went to newspapers and magazines. The report of the Argentina Association of Agencies of Publicity (AAAP 2007) indicates that in 2005 open signal television in Buenos Aires (Telefe, Channel 13, Channel 9, America TV and Channel 7) took 1,177,858,100 pesos of advertising investment against 261,282,540 pesos in relation to cable.

Overall, in the past few years the media systems in Argentina have gone through a roller-coaster, as has the rest of the country. These economic upheavals have led to important changes in the composition and structure of media ownership. This has in turn meant in some cases a new landscape in terms of ownership and in others a completely new set of media outlets. The media in Argentina has also undergone important changes in the face of globalization. All these factors have created a very distinctive scenario characterized by the post-dictatorship transition and hyperinflation in the 1980s and by neo-liberalism and financial crises in the 1990s.

Media market and consumption

Argentina is today still one of Latin America's leading media markets. The country has over 274 national and local newspapers (Brito 2005: 3), hundreds of commercial radio stations, some 42 television stations and a penetration ratio for radio of 163 receivers for every 1000 people. Cable television has developed rapidly in Argentina since the early 1990s and today the country has the largest cable penetration in Latin America, at 51 per cent compared with an overall penetration of 12 per cent for the continent. Furthermore, until a few years ago there were more people with cable television than landline telephones (Rionda 1997: 1). Cable and satellite companies now offer some 150 channels, although most of them are imported from the USA, Latin America and Europe.

One of the main reasons for the success of cable television is the wide network of fibre-optic cables, laid in the 1990s, especially in Buenos Aires where almost 40 per cent of the Argentinean population is concentrated. This is also one of the main reasons why Argentina is among the leading countries for internet access in Latin America, with 34 per cent of the population using the internet on a regular basis. However, only 70 per every 1000 people have internet access from their homes or offices, which indicates a similar trend to the rest of Latin America, where the internet is 'consumed' but not 'owned'. Furthermore, although higher than most of the rest of Latin America, Argentina's broadband penetration is nonetheless below the world average, being behind the USA, western Europe and even Chile. Since 2004, however, the number of broadband subscribers in Argentina has been rising. ADSL has consolidated its leadership, overtaking the cable modem, which used to be the main broadband technology.

Broadcasting remains the main form of media in Argentina. In the television arena, regulatory changes are in the pipeline to adopt a digital terrestrial television standard (Web Reports 2007a). The government is also promoting alternative media outlets via trade unions, universities, non-governmental organizations, cooperatives and local communities. The current penetration ratio in Argentina is some 212 television sets per every 1000 people, while there are some 650 radio receivers per every 1000 people.

The end of the crisis that began in 2001 has also meant some recovery for the print industry. According to the Instituto Verificador de Circulaciones (IVC), by 2006 sales of *Clarín* in Buenos Aires stood at 380,000 copies a day from Monday to Saturday and some 770,000 on Sundays (57 per cent of the market). *Clarín* is followed by *La Nación*, with sales of around 160,000 copies from Monday to Saturday and 250,000 on Sundays (15 per cent of the market). Other influential newspapers in the capital are *Página/12*, which is a left-leaning newspaper and *Ámbito*

Financiero, the main business newspaper that adopts an editorial style comparable to the *Financial Times* in the UK or the *Wall Street Journal* in the USA. There are numerous other newspapers in other regions of the country with very healthy circulation figures. Among these we can highlight: *La Voz del Interior* in Córdoba (over 64,000 copies a day); *La Capital* in Rosario (over 40,000 copies a day); *Los Andes* in Mendoza (over 35,000 copies a day); and *La Nueva Provincia* in Bahía Blanca (over 15,000 copies a day). In addition there are some tabloid-style newspapers that are doing particularly well, such as *Diario Popular*, with sales of over 80,000 copies a day from Monday to Saturday and over 130,000 copies on Sundays, and *Crónica*, which has a similar circulation. These two papers are considered to be sensationalist and are known to compete for the same readership, which comes mostly from the sectors at the bottom of the socioeconomic scale. *Diario Popular* is a left-leaning paper that emphasizes crime and catastrophic news, and produces supplements for the suburbs of Buenos Aires, where it is published. *Crónica* is a nationalist paper with an anti-USA and anti-British angle (particularly following the Falklands War), and is published in three daily editions. As for other capitals of the world, Argentina has also seen the emergence of free newspapers, for example *La Razón* which distributes over 98,000 copies a day, *Generación la U*, which distributes over 29,000 copies a day, *Noticias de la Calle*, which distributes over 25,000 copies a day and *Huarpe*, which distributes over 20,000 copies a day.

Other areas of the publishing business have also experienced some recovery. Magazines such as *Noticias de la Semana* (which sells on average over 47,000 copies per edition), *Caras* (over 42,000 copies), *Elle* (over 34,000 copies), *El Federal* (over 26,000 copies), *Caras y Caretas* (over 14,000 copies) and *Cosmopolitan Argentina* (over 10,000 copies) (IVC 2006) are among the best selling titles. Argentina publishes some 600 magazines. However, the 2001 crisis had a devastating effect on this market, and sales dropped by 80 per cent across the whole segment. There was a small recovery in 2003 of 5 per cent, but the area is still far from what it was in the 1990s.

In terms of book publishing, Argentina has also managed to recover some of the market share it had in the past, when the country managed to produce and sell over 70 million volumes per year in the 1990s. The 2001 crisis saw book sales fall to less than 34 million, but recently the market has experienced an upturn, with sales increasing by 50 per cent (OECD 2007). Publishers nevertheless have to deal with a reduced market and consequently have reduced their print runs to an average of 2500 copies per title as against the average of 5000 in the 1990s. Production costs are also creating strong competition in the publishing market around the world, and there are now less than 150 companies exporting books from Argentina to the rest of the Spanish-speaking world, as compared to almost twice as many in the early 1990s.

It is in the area of film where the recovery of the creative industries (in which we include all media and cultural content production) has been mostly felt. Since the end of the nineteenth century, Argentina has commercially produced for the wider audience some 2500 films. Its so-called 'golden age' was in the 1940s and 50s, when the film industry managed to produce some 50 films per year. The neo-liberal policies of the 1990s and the crisis of 2001 saw a drastic fall in the number of productions. Nevertheless, thanks to the economic recovery and more state subsidies, the country has experimented a steady recovery of the film industry. In 2003, 53 films where made, while 2004 and 2005 saw 66 and 63 films produced respectively. This decade has seen almost the same number of films produced and shown to date as the whole of the 1940s. The outlook is therefore promising, with films such as *La suerte está echada* (2005), *Un año sin amor* (2004), *Roma* (2004) and *La señal* (2007) having competed successfully to be screened by cinemas. The Argentinean cinematographic market is now much healthier, with over 35 million tickets sold in 2006. Nationally produced movies manage to take almost 10 per cent of this market, with over 3.1 million tickets sold. The number of film screens is just over 1000, after a significant fall in 2001. Film producers in Argentina have only started to receive government subsidies in recent times, but there is an increasing trend for cable television companies to co-finance the production of commercial films. We can also argue that the film industry, as in other sectors of the creative industries in Argentina, has adopted distinctive strategies in terms of production and distribution. Instead of following the model of Mexico and the USA in which many films enter the market but many also fail commercially, Argentina decided instead to copy the model of continental Europe – that is, with smaller flows and less impressive post-entry growth of successful films, but at a much more successful rate (Bartelsman *et al.* 2004).

Media economics and journalism

It is clear from this analysis that the reconfiguration of the media and telecommunication conglomerates in Argentina is a pivotal element in understanding the country's new media landscape. Argentina has replicated the experiences of other countries in deregulating the media and telecommunications, and since the early 1990s the country has developed a legal-political framework that has practically eliminated any obstacles or restraints for the creation of multi-media giants. This has become the characteristic feature of this new media landscape. Broadcasting and telecommunications have been transformed by the forces of globalization and privatization into concentrated and powerful conglomerates that insert themselves into wider international corporations (Eliades 2005).

However, it can also be said that, contrary to the 1990s, national media owners have learnt that in order to stay independent, they also need to consolidate. The Néstor Kirchner administration, which has placed emphasis on its nationalistic and left-wing credentials, has allowed media consolidation but limited foreign investment (a policy also followed by the dictatorship in the 1990s). Indeed, in May 2005, his government signed Resolution 527/05, which allowed media groups to consolidate and expand. Media and telecommunications conglomerates such as Clarín took immediate advantage of this, and in September 2006, Clarín merged its two television companies, Multicanal and Cablevisión, a move that was announced as 'the return of national capital to the leading brands of subscription TV' (Clarín 2006b).

This also meant the vertical integration and consolidation of related distribution platforms for both companies. For example, Fibertel, the leading broadband supplier, provided internet access via cable modem, and Teledigital provided further cable services. This transformed the new company into one of the biggest players in the region, with over 2,7000,000 subscribers to cable and more than 450,000 subscribers to internet of broadband (Giglio 2006). This is a distinctive and most interesting development that deserves further research.

Despite all these changes, it is not possible to say that access, plurality and variety of information has improved in the past few years. Argentina, as for the rest of the region, has come to terms with the fact that more media does not necessarily mean more opinions (Blanco and Germano 2005), something that is very problematic for independent journalism. Nevertheless, these changes have had some impact on recent developments in Argentinean journalism and its relation to power and politics. Journalism and journalists in Argentina, who have a long tradition of professionalism and independence, even during the dictatorship period and despite formidable pressures and censorship (Eltzer 1988: 120), have had to deal with important transformations in the media environment in which they work. For example, in the past the newspapers were instrumental in presenting different points of view and representing different interests in the everyday treatment of information. They were protagonists, not only in covering and interpreting reality, but also in defining meaning as 'narrators, commentators and participating in the political conflict' (Borrat 1989: 14). However, from the 1990s onwards, these actors were gradually displaced by the broadcasting media as the key players in framing public opinion. This media demands and permits a less rigorous approach to facts and events (Bourdieu 1998). Furthermore, in the light of more flexible legislation, the broadcasting media has created powerful and influential groups. These groups, no doubt, have been able to capture, select, create and use information across multi-media platforms in order to achieve goals that go beyond their own media remit. Because of this, the process of the globalization and modernization of the media in Argentina has translated into power to influence the 'daily public agenda', not so much telling people what to think, but what to think about – a sad situation that Argentina shares with others in the region.

Notes

1 This chapter reflects some of the findings of the investigation project 'Media, Politics and Power: The Configuration of Media Groups (multimedia) in the After-crisis Argentina, Period 2001–2005', directed by Marcelo Belinche, co-directed by Patricia Vialey and carried out by investigator teachers and pupils from the Media Studying and Observation Centre (CEOM in Spanish): C. Tovar, F. Niggli, G. Annuasi, R. Viñas, P. Valatti, R. Brecevich, G. Verne, M. Iparraguirre, B. Villar, N. Carmona, C. Bernal, P. Leme, L. López Silva, F. Guiot, L. Retta, M. Di Francesco and N. Simonoff.

2 The Washington Consensus, codified in 1989 by John Williamson, contained ten basic reforms: 1) fiscal discipline; 2) priority for the social cost; 3) tributary reform; 4) financial liberalization; 5) unified and competitive types of change; 6) liberalization of foreign trade; 7) opening to direct foreign investment, IED; 8) privatization of state companies; 9) deregulation; and 10) respect for property rights. See Moncayo Jiménez (2004).

3 The national reorganization process (better known as the military junta) overthrew the democratic government of Maria Estela Martinez de Perón on 24 March of 1976, and governed Argentina between 1976 and 1983. At the start, the military government was headed by the commanders of the three armed forces: Jorge Rafael Videla (army), Emilio Eduardo Massera (navy) and Orlando Ramon Agosti (air force). These commanders were replaced in 1980 by Roberto Viola, Armando Lambruschini and Omar Graffigna. They in turn were replaced during 1981 by Leopoldo Fortunato Galtieri, Basilio Lami Dozo and Jorge Isaac Anaya, who took Argentina to war against the UK over the Falklands (Malvinas) Islands. Finally, from 1982, the military government was controlled by Cristino Nicolaides, Rubén Franco and Augusto Jorge Hughes. The legacy of this period of military government was an almost complete destruction of Argentina's national industry, a massive increase in its international debt and, a repressive legacy of the so-called Guerra Sucia, which left over 30,000 being displaced or forced to disappear, according to most human rights organizations estimates (Guest 2000).

4 Patagonik has made more than 30 films including *Cenizas del paraíso*, *Una noche con sabrina love*, *Apariencias*, *Neueve reinas*, *El hijo de la novia*, *Valentín*, *Patoruzito* and *Deuda*. These films, beyond their quality and content, were strongly promoted and advertised in the media belonging to the group.

5 The Alianza por el Trabajo was an electoral coalition between Unión Cívica Radical (a centre-right political party) and FREPASO (a group of smaller political parties). The coalition was created in 1997 and won the presidential elections in 1999, under the leadership of Fernando de la Rúa. The coalition was dissolved on 20 December 2001 after the resignation of President de la Rúa following the economic crisis of that year.

6   Joseph Stiglitz, who won the Nobel prize for economics in 2001, estimates that during the crisis of 2001 the telecommunications companies generated extraordinary losses.

7   'The *corralito* was instrumented on Saturday 1st December of 2001, when the Government decided that the Argentineans could only withdraw from their banking accounts 250 pesos per week in cash. That was added to the prohibition to transfer money to the outside and the obligation to make most of the payments through debit cards, credit or checks' (Terra 2003). The Spanish word *corralito* is the diminutive form of *corral*, which means 'animal farm enclosure'; the diminutive is used in the sense of 'small enclosure' and also 'a child's playpen'. This expressive term alludes to the restrictions imposed by the measure and to the fact that the government was treating people as both animals and children.

3 THE MEDIA IN BOLIVIA: THE MARKET-DRIVEN ECONOMY, 'SHOCK THERAPY' AND THE DEMOCRACY THAT ENDED

Erick Torrico Villanueva

Democracy was restored in Bolivia on October 1982 after 18 years of almost uninterrupted authoritarian military regimes.[1] However, it would take Bolivia another three years before it started implementing the type of political and institutional reforms contemplated by the so-called Washington Consensus.[2] In August 1985, reform took the shape of an initiative to modernize political institutions and adapt them according to the requirements and designs of multilateral organizations and international cooperation agencies. This programme ran alongside the implementation of a 'Program of Structural Adjustment' designed by the World Bank and the International Monetary Fund, often known as 'shock therapy'.

That same year, after the early general elections called by President Hernán Siles Zuazo, who then led the central-leftist front of the Unidad Democrática, the struggle to define the nature of the democratic model of Bolivia was resolved in favour of the so-called 'new right', with presidential decree 21060, 'New Economic Politics'.[3] The government of Víctor Paz Estenssoro, who had been the historical leader of revolutionary nationalism and had been elected president for the fourth time, implemented a series of market-driven policies which privileged private business as the main agent of development, restricted political decision-making exclusively to those political parties that had been elected to the Parliament and limited the scope of influence of rural and urban trade unions – that until then had been very combative and active – to specific and narrow areas. In other words, in August 1985, Paz Estenssoro dismantled the bases of the nationalist and revolutionary state that he himself had created more than three decades before, and supplanted it with a neo-liberal state.

A fundamental component of this new institutional life was the call for a *negotiated democracy* – one which would derive from the agreements between political parties. These agreements to secure support for the executive would create alliances for the second round of voting for Parliament. In order to secure permanent support, the party who obtained a majority would distribute 'quotas of power' in the administration among associated parties, in what became a highly criticized practice.

The original neo-liberal framework admitted so many modifications that by 1994 it had become unrecognizable. From that year, the law of

Popular Participation modified relations between the state and local communities, offering resources to assist their demands for a basic infrastructure, health and education. The logic behind the agreements between party elites provided some stability to the adjustment programme and allowed Bolivia to become a 'market-driven democracy'. This was the case at least until April 2000, when the weaknesses of the system of consensus became evident. This took place in parallel with an accumulation of social dissatisfaction due to unfulfilled civic demands, and the regrouping of unions and social movements. Many left-wing parties failed to survive in this environment of structural adjustment, while many of their historical leaders, who otherwise would have capitalized on the increasing economic crisis and political instability, were absorbed by the lucrative 'rates of return' offered by those in power. Meanwhile, the commercial media, particularly television and print, displaced the political media, which had played an important combative role in the pre-democratic era.[4]

The new political-social framework which emerged at the end of the twentieth century ended with riots and protests that took place between February and October 2003.[5] Such open confrontation between society and state was the final straw for the system of negotiated democracy. These events represented a structural challenge capable not only of ending the democratic experiment but also threatening to break up the nation. Among the main characteristics of this period was a lack of tolerance among individuals, and active civic disobedience – although it must be said that both were probably the product of institutional weakness.

In this scenario, characterized by uncertainty and the rupture of traditional social communication channels, the place and the role of the media has again been questioned. Particular attention has been given since 2000 to the media's role in both promoting and limiting the public sphere. Since then, there has been an incipient but timid and limited debate about the role of information and communication technologies in Bolivian society.

Lack of communication between society and state

For many years in Bolivia, the state and society have lived separate lives. This lack of communication is perhaps the basic reason for structural conflict. It is a situation that expresses the dynamics of the daily politics of the country, defined by historical instability. This is not, as many outside Bolivia would believe, a recent phenomenon. Blockades – symbolic protests that have predominated in images of Bolivia across the globe in recent years – are not a new phenomenon but instead a daily experience, stemming from a structural condition that, in more than 180 years of republican history, has not been satisfactorily resolved. This structural conflict has often been either ignored or simply hidden from wider view.

Even though the re-establishment of democracy in October 1982 was characterized by both progress and setbacks, it nevertheless became the first real opportunity to highlight the limits and failures of the old state, while also revealing the impossibility of perpetually postponing a response to the demands of a complex and polyphonic society. Bolivian society does not accept its own multi-cultural complexity and hybridization. It is a society that is not properly represented by the current structure and state organization, despite many partial reforms of both, and all the signs are that the state will probably not be able to continue for much longer in its present form.

Bolivia faces an absence of communication among social actors that may be attributed to the homogenized but exclusivist nature of the state as a post-colonial construction. The form assumed by the state, which was predominantly white and elitist, was characterized by a historical absence of sympathy with the intrinsic social, cultural, linguistic and regional diversity that defines the country. Therefore, the events that took place between April 2000 and June 2004, which highlighted decisive issues, were an expression of the lack of social interaction and adequate and coherent responses to popular demands. The call for a referendum on a national assembly that could reform the constitution by president Evo Morales is an expression of that struggle.

The place and role of the media in politics and democracy therefore only makes sense if the analysis takes into account the wider picture: one that contemplates the strategic relevance of antagonistic relations between the state and society which has been the basis of the lack of communication between the state and its citizens, and that also considers the collective diversity that characterizes Bolivia as a nation. In other words, this means accepting that this lack of communication goes beyond the media and information and communication technologies: indeed, the absence of proper communication channels is an issue pertaining to the widest possible spheres of politics and culture.

Bolivia's crisis from a communication perspective

The protests and general strikes that took place between September and October 2003 marked the end of a certain way of political and institutional life in Bolivia. Until then this way of life could be characterized as a status quo that had recycled itself for a long time without substantial modifications. The previous events of February 2003, in which peasants blocked roads and organized protests across the country, had already revealed the weaknesses of the state and the impossibility of maintaining the current structure. These wake-up calls were nevertheless played down and even ignored by the main political leaders at the time because the system was unable to relate to the protesters. The overturning of the existing order was precipitated by the government's deafness together with that of the Parliament and the traditional political parties. It was also the result of a determination by the masses to overcome the state's habitual passivity. The ousting of President Gonzalo Sánchez de Lozada on 17 October 2003 also marked the end of attempts to preserve the traditional system of governance and destroyed what was left of the state model implemented in August 1985.

As a consequence, and from a political point of view, Bolivia faced a three-dimensional crisis that remains largely unresolved. The state, as a body in decomposition, could have been characterized then as unable to recognize regional or cultural diversity, as exclusive (since it only widened the existing socioeconomic gap), as corrupt, as inefficient and as a promoter of a 'capitalism of gangs'. Indeed, the type of economy that it advocated was really just a parody of so-called market-driven capitalism. Instead of being based on a transparent mechanism of economic exchanges, the use of the country's natural resources was determined broadly by deals between politicians and some national and foreign economic groups. The main economic role of the state then became merely to set up rules to ensure that these groups obtained large profits.

In this context, democracy became a mere formality and citizenship was reduced to a periodical exercising of the right to vote during electoral periods. Meanwhile, the most popular political parties, which also happened to be the most committed to major economic interests, simultaneously appeared to be the repository of popular will (at least until 2002), but without really representing this will as the 'owners' of political power. Democracy, which social struggles ensured was recovered in 1982, was then transformed, and Bolivia became a pseudo-democracy,[6] a caricature, a democracy of political parties where the voters were taken into account only as a statistical figure in elections and opinion polls.

In the same way, governance – which should ideally be based on consensus among a given society's strategic actors to manage demands and conflicts in order to reach decisions – was undermined by the shadowy arrangements and political pacts between the elites of the political parties. The whole scene resembled a 'political society of mutual aids' inclined to blackmail and concealment. The arrangements that constituted the main framework of the Bolivian political system until the end of 2003 had three detrimental effects: (a) the loss of independence of the legislature with respect to the executive; (b) widespread corruption and political impunity; and (c) an increasing gap between the values, goals and practices of the state and those of the collective. Freedom of information became another casualty of this brand of 'democracy' for the following reasons: (a) closer ties between media owners and political and economic elites; (b) the interchangeability of roles among media and political actors; (c) increasing sensationalism and 'tabloidization' of the news (emphasizing celebrity gossip, crime, eroticism and politics), encouraged by stronger competition to capture advertising revenue in the context of a declining market; and (d) open and subtle government pressures and censorship between 2002 and 2003 to shape specific news coverage by the media.

The result of what became progressively market-driven politics and its interdependence with media spaces was the privatization of the public space. Consequently, the erosion of citizenship became a basic condition of a democracy based on delegating involvement and participation. Corruption and political illegitimacy are perhaps the two aspects that best explain the loss of stability and the social disaster that in the end led to the government being elected 14 months after assuming power. However, it is also clear that this situation did not come out of the blue; instead it built up throughout 17 years of neo-liberal policies. Indeed, this crisis was the result of a prolonged and complex process, one in which the main political leaders from the government, Parliament and the traditional parties were unwilling to accept their own responsibilities and reluctant to modify their conduct and stance towards the electorate.

Based on this analysis, we might suggest that from a communication perspective that there was a profound 'disconnection' between society and the state.[7] It could also be argued that the solution to this situation would have been a strong political will to open new spaces of participation and the creation of alternative lines and channels of communication in order to pave the way for democratic renewal. Ideally, this would have led to a democracy that was based on social consensus that went beyond inter-party agendas and that could create new alternative and participative public spaces – a solution that placed intercultural and interregional communication at the core of the new social project.

After the so-called 'Gas War'[8] the government of Carlos Mesa (2003–5) came to power. This was an administration that relied on the always volatile public mood and that had no organic link with the traditional parties in Parliament. However, this government's lack of structural support and unwillingness to make radical decisions led to Mesa's resignation. The then head of the Supreme Court, Eduardo Rodríguez Veltzé, took over with the explicit mandate to call new elections. The elections of 18 December 2005 were won by the candidate for the Socialism Movement (MAS), Evo Morales Ayma.

The mass media in sight

Bolivian media spaces, known for withholding and framing communication processes, were reconfigured in the 1980s, becoming more commercialized and market-driven. The establishment of commercial television in 1984, even allowing for the legal restrictions at the time, was the first step. This was followed by a massive increase in private advertising revenue and more public-driven spending on political-electoral propaganda. All of this was possible due to economic liberalization together with a stronger role given to traditional political parties by the implementation of the decree 21060.[9] As a direct consequence, Bolivia saw substantial growth in the number of commercial media outlets.

Dozens of radio stations began to broadcast, especially on FM, and by 1990 Bolivia had almost 100 new private television channels and a significant increase in the number of newspapers (particularly daily and weekly publications). This brought about the emergence of new information services that entered the market to compete with traditional services offered by the news agency Fides, which was run by the Catholic Church.[10] The owners of the most important urban media, mainly television broadcasters, began the articulation of their company-related interests while promoting lobby and pressure groups to defend their own interests.

During the last ten years of the twentieth century, the process of media commercialization intensified with the arrival of foreign investment in television and print media. This allowed the emergence of new single and multi-media private networks with national coverage.[11] It also permitted the monopolization of publicity activities by the global advertisement companies which dominated the market.[12] In addition to this, Bolivia saw the establishment of two newspapers owned by the two biggest media conglomerates that began competing for those segments of the market that were inclined towards sensationalist news coverage. The country also witnessed the increasing presence of advertising linked to foreign capital in banking, oil, telecommunications and the beer industry as well as a growing demand for communication and media consultation, and public relations services for private companies, institutions and political parties. In this context, the appearance and growth of broadcast media outlets owned and financed by evangelicals and other religious groups should be also considered as part of the development of a privatized, commercial media.

In contrast, the situation for publicly-owned media was dire. The same period saw the disappearance of 75 per cent of broadcast media outlets owned by trade unions, public universities or the government. The national system for public broadcasting services, which was announced and frequently discussed at various levels of government, failed to materialize. Today, non-private media, especially government radio, survives at the edge of the diffusion spectrum and comes under constant pressure to stop conveying government propaganda. However, there are still a great number of radio stations that comply with what it is often called in Europe a 'public service broadcasting remit' (information, education and managing public demands), especially in rural areas. They mainly receive the support of the Catholic Church, some non-governmental organizations and occasionally rural communities of listeners. However, the formerly 'alternative' character of such broadcasting has been replaced by one that is community-centred yet fragmented. This is because these stations no longer have the opportunity to offer alternative voices capable of deconstructing, contextualizing or opposing the predominant discourses and narratives broadcast and printed by mainstream commercial outlets.

Today, although there are no firm statistics, it is considered that Bolivia has some 150 television stations including national broadcasters, local and syndicate stations. There are nearly 900 radio stations and around 50 newspapers (daily, weekly, fortnightly and monthly), although there are less than 20 journalistic sites on the internet (SITTEL 1999, 2000; Ramos 2003; Barriga 2004). Of all the media, around 84 per cent are owned by private groups. Annual investment in advertising has decreased from some US$35 million annually in the 1990s to some US$15 million in current times. The main chunk of advertising investment is absorbed by a handful of commercial and private media, which have managed to position themselves by creating vertically integrated oligopolies in the media sector, characterized by many media outlets whose ownership is concentrated in a few hands, thereby expressing fewer voices. It was in this way that market-driven democracy, established in 1985, was able to create a partnership with private media organizations. Because of this, and despite the ongoing crisis of the market-driven democratic model, changes in the structure and function of the media never threaten to make real modifications to the media's daily output. For example, the brief success of some radical and alternative publications in October 2003, which questioned the nature of the system, was met by harsh censorship, rejection and violence. Indeed, the events of October 2003, which brought forward the agendas of nationalizing the natural gas industry, setting a new written constitution and empowering local government, also generated racist and separatist sentiments in the mainstream commercial media, sentiments that democracy had managed to contain for years. All of this widened the rift between citizens and the state even though it also suggests that the dynamics of conflict could introduce unexpected modifications in the configuration and functioning of the spaces of dissemination and media networks.

What about digital Bolivia?

Even though Bolivian authorities and policy-makers have been aware of the developments in information and communication technology since 1991, they have been unwilling or unable to articulate a national project that would implement a coherent and comprehensive framework for developing their policies towards information technology in the medium and long term. Since 2000, there have been some very interesting and diverse initiatives coming from government, non-governmental organizations, academics and even the private sector. Nevertheless, most of these initiatives have lacked coordination or have failed to produce specific targets. Rather, they have tended to reflect a range of conflicting views over how to develop the role of information and communication technology in society, especially when it comes to the responsibility of the state with regard to the market's ability to satisfy the informational and educational needs of the population.

Bolivia is still far from being a full participant of the so-called 'information society'. This state of affairs has come about despite some investment in the information sector by private firms. Indeed, telecommunications, mobile technology and internet enterprises have contributed to the development of some infrastructure since 1996. One example is the investment of Telecom Italia, which owns 50 per cent of the National Enterprise of Communications and the AXS (formerly AES). This has facilitated a significant improvement of national density in the use of landlines, which now stands at 14 telephones per 100 people. Less than 2 per cent of the Bolivian population has a home or office connection to the internet (PNUD 2004: 169) and just over 5 per cent uses the internet at all (IWS 2007). Of this group, just one quarter connect using broadband, while most of the 480,000 internet users in Bolivia use a dial-up connection in private internet cafés. Almost 80 per cent of internet users are concentrated in the three main urban cities of La Paz, Cochabamba and Santa Cruz. Bolivian incursion into cyberspace has been much slower than in other countries in Latin America, and internet penetration has had an annual growth of less than 1 per cent since 2000. The degree of Bolivia's info-exclusion reflects the lack of inter-societal communication to which I have been referring throughout this chapter. Nevertheless, in the past few years Bolivia has managed to discuss, in a more comprehensive manner, the role of information and communication technologies beyond the realm of profit-making businesses. This is partly due to the creation of Plataforma CRIS-Bolivia, a branch of the Communication Rights in the Information Society initiative, which was established during the World Summit on the Information Society between 2003 and 2005[13] to promote civic society's participation in the formulation of technological policies and initiatives (CRIS 2007). This debate has provided a forum for discussing information technologies as a part of the country's overall national development strategy. Subsequently, the government Agency for Information Society Development in Bolivia (ADSIB in Spanish) promoted the formulation and design of the 'National Strategy for ICTs development'. Since its publication in 2005, this document has become the cornerstone of the new telecommunications policy (ETIC 2005).

This policy raises a number of issues, however. Even though social and non-governmental organizations have managed to introduce elements of 'realism' to the National Strategy document, the ADSIB still plans to connect all schools, universities, libraries and health centres to the internet by the year 2015 in accordance with the 'Millennium Goals' of the United Nations. By adopting this approach, the ADSIB is reproducing the techno-positivist rhetoric that has come to dominate many multilateral institutional policies. It is a rhetoric based on the notion that problems of development are merely related to connectivity. Such an assumption tends to disregard the socioeconomic determinants of poverty. Bolivia has consequently embarked on what may be understood as a 'silent debate' in which information technology policies are starting to be assessed in relation to internal inequalities, external dependencies and the democratic future. This is a significant development, considering the lack of discussion of this issue in the recent past.

By 2007 there were less than 3000 websites that were electronically published and maintained on a regular basis from Bolivia itself, and these included government and privately-sponsored, as well as personal sites. In addition, there were only three news portals exclusively created for the net that can be considered to have the characteristics of mainstream electronic journalism (www.bolpress.com, www.hoybolivia.com and www.econoticias.com). In addition to these sites, there are only a handful of websites displaying what can be considered as alternative news content. In this last sense, Bolivia is very far from exemplifying the democratization of communication and access to information by means of information and communication technologies.

Questioning the media-centred analysis

The general elections of 1985 marked the emergence of 'techno-politics' in Bolivia. It was then that political space started to be predominantly framed and defined by the media. During this period the media became not only agents of political power capable of offering airtime for political leaders, but also actors in the wider transactions of power. It was then that political campaigning was 'modernized' and started to incorporate principles and techniques of marketing and public relations to a far greater extent. These principles and techniques of political spin-doctoring would be later incorporated into government and Parliament to promote public policy and legislation. The effect was that in this 'reconstituted' democracy, mass media (especially television) became a new arena for political expression. The media modified the relationship between the authorities and the citizens (which became mediated and increasingly distant), while promoting their own strategies to increase their influence and power.

This media-centred approach to politics continued until October 2003, gaining momentum in the presidential and municipal electoral campaigns from 1989 to 2002. For example, in the eyes of the people, the media somehow displaced the legislative government and the political parties as the institution that should oversee accountability of public resources and management of public demands; the fact that the media overtly embraced and supported several candidates for local elections and the Parliament; the transformation of television into a negotiation forum for the state and civic society during the so-called 'Water War'[14] of April 2000; the fall of a government minister in 2001; the publication of opinion poll results that pre-empted the electoral results of 2002 and had an impact on the final result; and the interpretation of the events of February and October 2003 by the media, which offered its own narrative and explanation. There are many other similar examples that are symptomatic of the emergence of techno-politics in Bolivia.

However, because of the constant interventions of the media into politics, Bolivians began to change their perception of the media, which until then was widely positive. Nowadays the situation is very different. There is widespread doubt and critical questioning with regard to the media's role in shaping public opinion and defining political outcomes. The loss of legitimacy which had been characteristic of traditional politics has also started to affect the media and the media space. This was the case when people widely rejected the way the mainstream media covered the events of February and October 2003 and the local elections of 2004. It is worth noticing that it was those candidates who relied on the media for their campaigns, rather than on direct interpersonal contact with people, who came last in the electoral race, especially in those geographical areas where the crisis generated by the 'Water War' was worst felt. It is clear that these events marked a turning point for video-politics, a fundamental component of media-centred politics (techno-politics) in Bolivia. In cases in which this link between the mainstream media and certain candidates was more explicit and questionable, as with the local elections in Santa Cruz in 2004, there was a further erosion of the credibility of, and trust in, journalistic institutions. Another specific contribution to the erosion of media credibility and trust was the editorial position adopted by the media during the protests of May to June of 2005 that led to the resignation of President Mesa. This was because their agenda seemed to be mainly defined by commercial imperatives instead of the concerns of the electorate. Hence it is possible to suggest that the legitimacy of the media, with close ties to those with interests at stake, suffered as much as that of the traditional political and economic elites.

The 'democracy' that ended

The democratic system in Bolivia relied for its source of power on the exclusive nature of those inter-party agreements that sustained the system. Due to the minute difference in the numbers of votes received in the elections of 1985, 1989, 1993, 1997 and 2002, the elected political party was obliged to strike post-electoral deals. These arrangements included pacts in Parliament that would guarantee the outcomes of second-round presidential voting and a commitment to share political spaces and economic benefits of power. This pragmatic formula blurred all ideological differences between the participants: Acción Democrática Nacionalista (ADN), the Movimiento Nacionalista Revolucionario (MNR) and the Movimiento de la Izquierda Revolucionaria (MIR). This accounts for the lack of opposition to the imposition of the market-driven economic policy and the shock therapy programme. This dynamic subsequently also led to the reproduction of power structures by the same elite circles, which soon degenerated into lack of representation and widespread corruption. Corporate and individual interests were often privileged, leading to corrupt practices and nepotism. These practices simultaneously promoted a wider gap between politicians and citizens. The benefits that democracy is supposed to offer did not reach the majority of the population and opacity in politics became even worse. Some surveys and opinion polls showed that in a scale from 1 to 7, the government got 3.12, the Parliament 3.08 and political parties 2.8, all revealing very low expectations from the public towards democracy itself (Costa et al. 2003: 205). In less than 15 years (1985–2000), this form of 'negotiated' democracy accumulated all the problems that could bankrupt it: 'inefficiency, ineffectiveness, illegitimacy and instability' (Linz 1996: 36).

The media pathways of politics

While this deterioration of institutional life was taking place in the political sphere, the legitimacy of the media was also being progressively eroded to the point where there was a widespread rejection of the media, as mentioned earlier in this chapter. First, the media – especially commercial television and newspapers – determined the interpretation of political events and debates – it was invariably the media that brought political events and leaders into Bolivian living rooms both during, and outside, electoral times. Second, while politics in general, and politicians in particular, were often discredited, the media became the arena in which politics was *performed*: It made direct and explicit interventions in the process of decision-making and decision-taking; it shaped the direction of public policy; it managed conflicts; and it promoted or undermined political leaders, parties and their opponents. The trajectory followed by the media in Bolivia meant that it encountered, and perpetuated, the same problems faced by other institutions, such as political parties, at the time. Despite the fact that interaction between the political and media dimensions of public life is not only necessary but desirable, the *degree* to which this relationship became symbiotic and parasitic in the case of Bolivia – especially between certain political leaders and some television networks – led to tragic and pernicious consequences.

The triple fall of the media

The media's role was ultimately defined either by the crisis of traditional structures and the attempt of elites to hold onto power, or by social mobilization and protest, which was initially fragmented and dispersed. The media's role since 2002 was an additional factor, but a very important one, in catalysing the disintegration of the traditional social order that had characterized Bolivia since the introduction of democracy. Both the news agenda and the editorial positions assumed by the media fostered an increasing state of polarization, and very few saw any other outcome except violence. The implementation of neo-liberal hegemony in the design and instrumentation of public policy had been possible because of the weakness of the trade unions and left-wing parties and movements. These weaknesses in themselves were a result of the internal disputes and hostilities within the left together with the inability of those movements to organize an effective and coherent opposition following the restoration of democracy in 1985. This should also be understood in the broader context of the international socialist movement following the fall of the Berlin Wall and the disintegration of the Soviet bloc.[15] Therefore there was little need to coerce the population with violent repression during that period, even though this state of affairs had characterized the implementation of neo-liberal policies on previous occasions. Only on a few occasions did the government need to declare a state of emergency to control union leaders and small farmers who opposed these types of measures in order to dismantle what was left of the welfare state. After 15 years of neo-liberalism, with little sign of economic prosperity, and indeed with the intensification of extreme poverty and in the face of a much discredited political leadership, the economic and political model became unsustainable. It was then that a still very diffuse democratic alternative started to emerge.

This period was characterized by uncertainty, and the media toyed with this chaos while attempting to retain its own privileges. Confronted with the dilemma of having to cover and report the crisis of the political and economic elites – their partners in power – those in the media decided to follow two main strategies. Some media outlets discredited or ignored those social movements that led these protests, and this was generally done in a sensationalist manner.[16] On the other hand, the media frequently resorted to populist tactics in order to retain their audiences.[17] Even though these two patterns were more pronounced among the broadcast media, newspapers also followed suit. This in turn led to the overall media sector losing credibility, influence and legitimacy. A comparison of two national surveys in 1999 and 2004 shows the decline in public trust towards the media. From obtaining 5.6 in a scale of 7 in 1999 (ahead of the Catholic Church that received 5.3 that same year), public trust in the media had plummeted to 4.4 in 2004, below many other institutions (Corte Nacional Electoral 2005: 188–9).

Continuities in the characteristic lack of communication

Bolivians' relationship with the media is characterized by the lack of organic channels of communication. This situation adversely affects the structure and agents of political institutions, the diversity of cultures and regionalisms, and the ever incipient information technologies. To understand the issues more fully, it is necessary to go beyond the notion of 'political communication', since this tends to limit our understanding of the political element of communication to explicit political messages and narratives. Another important prerequisite for understanding is the need to recognize the gullibility of 'techno-optimistic' assumptions that this lack of communication together with inequalities in access to, and exchanges of, information can be overcome by increasing the number of receptors, transmitters, data storage and processing devices. The government of Carlos Mesa Gisbert instead centred its attention on the macro-demands set by the protests of October and June 2003 and by the management of a state of daily conflict (strikes, riots, protests etc.). It thus failed to develop a platform for communication that could effectively address the political system's loss of legitimacy and representativeness. The remedy would have been to establish an effective and well resourced system of communication (which existed neither then nor today) and also to create and promote social conditions for a dialogue that could allow the renewal of Bolivian democracy. In the political arena at least, the disconnection between the government and its citizens persists and continues to be expressed in three main ways.

First, *lack of communication between the government and its citizens*. This situation peaked during the attempts of Sánchez de Lozada's government to impose an incoherent, and at some times competing and contradictory, political coalition. His contact with social reality was framed and defined by a centralized and semi-authoritarian propaganda machine based on marketing and given to censorship. Even though some of this isolation was overcome by the Mesa government – in part because of its own background and experience with the media – this was accomplished in a haphazard manner. For example, the Mesa government did not address the inability of the different regions of the country to interact with each other or with the central power. Equally disappointing was the destiny of the law of 'transparency and access to public information', aimed at promoting citizens' right to access official information. Despite receiving support from the Anticorruption Presidential Delegation in May 2004, the government was unable to pass the law through Congress.

Second, *lack of communication between the Parliament and the electorate*. This state of affairs was defined by several factors: the way in which members of Parliament are elected according to closed lists in which people have to vote for parties and not by name; agreements among party elites to distribute quotas of power among themselves; a lack of independence of the legislative power from the executive; the use of seats in Parliament not to represent the constituency but to promote one's own political career in the executive or the foreign service; implicit and explicit arrangements between political parties to protect themselves from investigations into corruption; and the loss of contact between elected MPs and their constituencies after the elections. It can be suggested that the election by an individual MP's name and the establishment of local forums for discussion were measures that came to Bolivia too little and too late. Most political leaders blame the media for the loss of legitimacy without questioning their own previous conduct. Even after the events of 2003, when there was a real possibility of national reconciliation, there was a distinct lack of initiative from the political parties.

Third, *lack of communication between parties and citizens*. In part, this situation stemmed from the previous two and was reflected by the *instrumentalization* of citizens as a political commodity. Instead of representing the electorate, political parties lobbied for corporate interests. This resulted in increasing levels of social concern about the role and conduct of political parties, which was later reflected in surveys and polls. Indeed, between 1990 and 2001, the political parties managed to score only 2.8 on a scale of 7 in terms of public trust (Costa *et al.* 2003: 205). Another study undertaken in 2004 confirmed these results (Encuestas and Estudios 2004). The main political parties were widely identified by the public as the most corrupt institutions in the country. Only 0.3 per cent of the people interviewed claimed to trust them, while 26.6 per cent said that they would support getting rid of them all together (Encuestas and

Estudios 2004). These trends became evident in the elections of 2002, in which Evo Morales's party, MAS, became the second biggest party in the Congress despite being a relative newcomer. These elections also resulted in a 78 per cent change in the allocation of parliamentary seats: 33 per cent of the new MPs were small farmers and indigenous people who had never before entered formal politics. This situation was to recur in the local elections of 2004 and, ultimately, in the presidential elections of 2005, where the biggest losers were again to be the old parties of the status quo.[18]

On top of this, not only did the government of Carlos Mesa fail to address the general problems of lack of communication but he also aggravated the lack of communication between the government and its opposition. The transitory government of Rodriguez Veltzé (June 2005–January 2006) worked under vastly reduced pressure due to lower expectations on the part of the electorate. It was a government that merely concentrated on taking the country to the *next* elections. However, once the government of Evo Morales Ayma came to power in January 2006, a new set of forces emerged, shaping a new scenario in which the present government is openly confronting traditional actors, preferring supremacy to negotiated arrangements when defining public policy. It has also brought the advent of a new opposition that takes every available opportunity to question the supposed authoritarianism of the newly-established power. Media spaces are being used by the official government and its adversaries as a means of acting out this confrontation. If the electoral victory of Evo Morales initially allowed Bolivia to overcome a certain degree of non-communication between the government and the electorate, this is no longer the case. The way in which constitutional reform has been debated has tended to polarize those who enter the discussion, and those private media who oppose government proposals for reform are widening the existing gap between the state and wider society. In the meantime, such outlets are actively contributing to a new problem, namely the increasing distance between the commercial media and the government.

Today, Bolivia is facing a major reorganization of the state and its institutions. A new hegemony is emerging from the National Assembly. There are new actors and opponents on the political stage. The media will continue to be a key actor in this evolving sociopolitical process, despite the fact that most media owners have yet to grasp the real dimensions of what is happening in the country. Neither, it seems, have they learnt a great deal from the experience of the recent past. Instead, encouraged by the actions of the present government together with the lack of a coherent opposition, the media continues to be a source of sensationalism and superficial news.

Notes

1   Since 1952, four consecutive civil governments made possible impor-
    tant changes such as the nationalization of tin mines, the introduction
    of the universal vote, initial policies on land redistribution, education
    reforms to incorporate 'rural settlers to the nation' and the introduc-
    tion of central planning into the design of economic policy. However,
    these first civic governments also showed the limits of revolutionary
    nationalism that postulated the alliance of classes and rejected any
    link to socialism. The tension between nation and revolution
    increased until, in November 1964, the military took power to
    guarantee the preservation of the interests of the most conservative
    sectors of Bolivia.

2   The Washington Consensus is a term often used to describe a series of
    economic policies for developing countries proposed by Washington-
    based institutions such as the International Monetary Fund, the
    World Bank and the US Treasury Department.

3   The left, split in diverse factions, was not prepared to govern nor to
    coexist in a democracy. It had no coherent nor feasible democratic
    agenda. At the same time, the right did not have any difficulty in
    unifying its forces, presenting itself as the best technically qualified
    party to assume power and face the challenge of re-establishing order
    during the economic crisis, while addressing social demands.

4   During this time of dictatorship, private and urban newspapers, along
    with radio stations, were condescending of authoritarian governments
    despite being censored and violently repressed by them. The resistance
    and democratic fight was concentrated in union and provincial radio
    stations. Television, which was created in 1969, and the public
    university system that emerged in 1978, were also condescending of
    subsequent military rulers. Commercial television, which started in
    1984, was no different.

5   On 12 February 2003 an insurrection of low-ranking police officers
    took place. The action was directed against an increase in income tax.
    Protests at La Plaza de Armas in La Paz led to a violent confrontation
    between police officers and the military. This provoked popular anger
    towards the pro-government parties. These events left 33 people dead,
    205 wounded and several public buildings destroyed and looted.
    Peace only returned when the then president, Gonzalo Sánchez de
    Lozada, withdrew the planned tax reforms. Nevertheless, neither the
    president nor his advisers could completely understand what had
    happened and after seven months the crisis worsened. Along with
    popular demands to re-nationalize the gas and oil industries that had
    been privatized in 1995, there were specific requests not to export
    natural gas raw to the USA via a Chilean port over which Bolivia had
    a territorial dispute. Sánchez de Lozad's answer to the 'Gas War' was
    military repression in places such as the city of El Alto, which led to
    the worst massacre of Bolivian contemporary history: more than 60
    civilians were killed. The situation became unbearable and the only

way out for Sánchez de Lozad was to run away on 17 October, joined by some of his closest colleagues. Carlos Mesa Gisbert, vice-president at the time, took power in an unexpected and paradoxical process of institutional continuity.

6 This is also known as 'delegated democracy' or 'low-intensity democracy' because after voting, the elector remains at the edge of decisions. The voters' demands are managed in private, between particular elites that defend their own corporate interests through informal and illegal channels of negotiation or pressure.

7 This lack of structural communication has three different levels: government-citizenship, Parliament-citizenship and parties-citizenship.

8 The Bolivian gas conflict was a social confrontation which focused on the exploitation of the country's vast natural gas reserves. The expression can be extended to refer to the general conflict in Bolivia over the exploitation of gas resources, including the 2005 protests and the election of Evo Morales as president. Prior to these protests, Bolivia had seen a series of similar earlier protests, including the Cochabamba protests of 2000, which were against the privatization of the municipal water supply.

9 Decree 21060 was also known as the New Economic Policy (NPE in Spanish). It was based on the so-called Washington Consensus and established a shock therapy of structural reforms.

10 The news agency Fides, also known as ANF, was created in 1963 by the Catholic Church in La Paz. The news agency is run by the Jesuits and offers news services to all media outlets in the country. Today it remains a main source of independent news.

11 Investments came from the Mexican media group Televisa and the Spanish group Prisa, which has a 50 per cent share in the television network ATB, the strongest economically in the country. Televisa and Prisa own among other media outlets: the newspapers *La Razón* (La Paz), *El Nuevo Día* (Santa Cruz) and *Extra* (regional sensationalistic), the weekly *La Gaceta Jurídica*, the national magazine *Cosas* and the website Bolivia.com. The other important network, Grupo Lider, is formed from national capital and owns the newspapers *El Deber* (Santa Cruz), *Los Tiempos* (Cochabamba), *La Prensa* (La Paz), *El Correo del Sur* (Sucre), *El Potosí* (Potosí), *El Alteño* (El Alto), *El Nuevo Sur* (Tarija), *El Norte* (Montero) and *Gente* (regional sensationalistic). This group has also entered into television, with investments in the PAT network.

12 The most important firms were McCann Ericsson, Ogilvy and Mather and Gry.

13 The World Summit on the Information Society was a two-phase United Nations summit. The first phase took place in Geneva in December 2003 and the second in Tunis in November 2005. The aim of the Summit was 'to develop a common vision and understanding of the Information Society, to better understand its scope and dimensions and to draw up a strategic plan of action for successfully adapting to the new society'. It was set up to facilitate communication between

civic entities and to offer news and other information related to the CRIS campaign's efforts to ensure that communication rights were fully incorporated into the Summit's agenda and output.

14 The Water War in Bolivia, also known as the Cochabamba protests of 2000, was a series of protests that took place in Cochabamba between January and April 2000, due to the privatization of the municipal water supply. Later on, in September, the protests would extend to the capital, La Paz. The events were characterized by political rallies, riots and protests in order to reverse the decision to privatize water services and raise tariffs by up to 300 per cent. At least nine people died and hundreds were injured. The protests were a turning point in Bolivian politics.

15 La Unidad Democrática y Popular, that tried to govern from 1982 was constantly harried by union groups and also by conservative groups, and consequently called early elections.

16 In other words, emphasizing the negative elements of these movements, such as crime and sexual and political scandals.

17 Publication of any opinion, at the edge of a responsible work of edition and the reproduction of extreme questioning by media operators were characteristics of this practice.

18 The ADN, MNR and MIR reached the lowest representation in Parliament in their history.

4 THE MEDIA IN BRAZIL: AN HISTORICAL OVERVIEW OF BRAZILIAN BROADCASTING POLITICS

Olga Guedes-Bailey and
Othon F. Jambeiro Barbosa

The decision by the Brazilian government in 2006 to adopt the Japanese model of digital television demonstrated that nothing had changed in that country regarding broadcasting regulation and media politics. Notwithstanding strong opposition from grassroots organizations devoted to the 'democratization of communications', left-wing MPs and social scientists who had been researching digital technologies, the president eventually opted for the model ostensibly favoured by *Globo* Network and the other Brazilian broadcasters. Any change in the Brazilian media political environment? Certainly not. Episodes similar to the one described above represent the usual conduct of governments and broadcasters in Brazil since the 1930s, when broadcasting was first regulated by the dictator Getulio Vargas. From then on, history shows that while there have been slight differences among individual actors, the basic patterns of negotiation have remained the same for governments and broadcasters.

Brazil has been a nation state since 1822 when, with independence from the Portuguese crown, it became the Brazilian Empire. The country's political culture has since been shaped by the accumulation of absolute imperial power, domination by the political oligarchy and economic elites, the influence of government technocracy, military dictatorship, foreign influence, such as the British in the nineteenth and the early twentieth centuries, and lately economic ties with the USA, which remain strong. The resulting political culture has defined Brazil's economic, social and cultural life. In the communications sector, regulatory laws implemented by democratic governments or dictators since 1930 are the result of the different political dispositions and correlations of power within that culture.

This chapter offers a concise historical overview of the political economy of the Brazilian broadcasting sector. We will focus primarily on broadcasting, because television is economically, politically and culturally the most influential medium of communication in Brazil.[1] We argue that Brazil's broadcasting milieu has been characterized by the presence of the state in the process of media regulation, with the president exercising strong control over the licensing procedures. Although a number of changes have taken place – for instance, authorization for foreign capital to invest in the media sector (press and broadcasting up to 30 per cent and cable television subscriptions up to 49 per cent) – the government continues to dominate in this area.

As a result of the existing regulatory system, we argue, a conglomerate structure has developed within the television industry, where national networks have practically dominated all commercial television stations. This has been reflected in the programming offered to audiences, with limited choice of content, in a process of 'dumbing down' that centres on cheap and intellectually unchallenging entertainment programmes. We also discuss the Brazilian broadcasting industry and its relationship with the military dictatorship that exercised power from 1964 to 1984. We consider the foundation on which the regulation of the broadcasting industry has been built. We will further examine: the political and socioeconomic scenario in Brazil from 1930 (when the country underwent a revolution, forming the contemporary Brazilian state) until the early 1960s; the radio broadcasting industry in the early 1930s; the first years of television broadcasting; and the ideological pattern of early regulation acts that affected broadcasting in Brazil, and still do so today.

Historical roots of Brazilian television regulation

Up to the 1920s the Brazilian state consisted of regional political powers which viewed the national government's function mainly in terms of foreign relations and as a source of financial resources to be traded for regional political support. The basis for a modern state was established by the revolution of 1930,[2] that led in 1937 to the formation of the *Estado Novo* or 'New State', when Getulio Vargas, supported by military leaders, assumed dictatorial powers in a corporatist state based on a new constitution derived from European fascist models, thereby curtailing presidential elections and dissolving the Parliament. The 'New State' ideology imposed a vision of Brazil as a single unified country, with a clear nationalistic philosophy, which strengthened the state and President Vargas's (1930–45; 1951–4) powers over the legislative and judicial systems.

Under Vargas's presidency, culture became part of the state's apparatus to produce and publicize its ideology within society. The state's relationship with cultural production became multi-dimensional, including both coercive and supportive aspects: while it arrested, beat and tortured intellectuals and artists, it also frequently supported them with bureaucratic positions, donations, awards or sinecures. In consonance with the new ideology, the DIP (Press and Propaganda Department) was used to publicize the Estado Novo's image as well as implementing both systematic ideological propaganda and a policy of blocking the circulation of other ideas. The new political regime also created a national system for the control of all forms of communication. The 1937 constitution's Article 122 subordinated the press to government on the grounds that only the state was in a position to evaluate what news was or was not suitable for the country. Radio broadcasting and the press were, then, under the economic control of the system of production – both through ownership and advertising – and under the political control of the DIP. Radio broadcasting was particularly important in promoting the new nationalistic values of the *Estado Novo* and President Getuliol Vargas systematically used radio as an official device for political and ideological purposes.

In the economic sphere, Vargas started formulating the policies that would define the future development of the country. Oil, petrochemicals, metallurgy, roads and railway networks, among others, were part of Vargas's plans to modernize the country. The economy experienced strong growth and the industrial sector, intensively concentrated in South-Central Brazil, underwent a remarkable growth through internal market expansion. In fact, the industrial sector became the central issue for economic activities: labour regulation, foreign exchange mechanisms and infrastructure investments were aimed at its expansion and increased strength.

The infrastructure the *Estado Novo* installed from 1945 onwards, following the end of World War II and re-democratization of the country, allowed the Brazilian industrial sector to speed up its growth and become the most dynamic economic sector Under President Juscelino Kubitschek (1956–61). The country was opened up to foreign investment in order to modernize and diversify its systems of production, and transform its industrial technology.

Radio, which since the late 1930s had a commercial ethos, performed an influential role in the 1940s and 50s, becoming an important link between the production and consumption of goods, through advertising. Television, which started its activities in 1950, only in the 1960s replaced radio as the main advertiser of Brazilian merchandise.

Brazilian radio

The Brazilian media landscape is overwhelmingly dominated by private companies, which operate commercially, obtaining revenue from advertising and sponsorship. They have a close relationship with the government, by either supporting the main political parties or receiving favours from public agencies. The first radio broadcasting station in the country, Radio Sociedade do Rio de Janeiro (Rio de Janeiro's Society Radio), for example, made use of equipment bought by the Brazilian government for the national telegraphic service (Sampaio 1984: 96). That station, founded on 23 April 1923, was the first regular radio broadcasting transmitter in Brazil and had as its objective to 'work for the Brazilian citizens' culture and for Brazil's progress' (Sampaio 1984: 96). From 1923 onwards, several stations were established in Brazil. In 1930 there were 19 regularly operating and in 1938 their number had reached 41, mostly commercially sustained. In 1926, the most powerful station in South America –

Sociedade Radio Educadora (Educational Radio Association) was created in São Paulo. In spite of its name, it was a commercial station.

Broadcasting, radiotelegraphy and radiotelephony were then considered to be the same thing under the few laws on the subject. All of them were commercially exploited and used by the economic, intellectual and social elite. In the case of radio, the only audience for its programmes on high-brow literature, science and classical music were high society families and successful artists and intellectuals. However, with the expansion of the market for consumer goods, radio stations became commercially viable, even though audiences were still restricted to those with enough income to afford the new technology. Programming emphasized news and high culture but, as the audience expanded further into the middle and lower classes, it started shifting towards entertainment such as variety programmes and comedy with live audiences.

Consolidation of radio broadcasting was greatly advanced by two decrees: 20.047, of 1931, and 21.111, of 1932. They declared that radio was exclusively the privilege of the state, which would use it for the public good. They also established that the state might grant licences, on a temporary basis, to private companies to establish commercial channels, under a permanent system of control. Thus, through those decrees, Brazil adopted the trusteeship model of broadcasting licensing, which had already been enshrined in US legislation.

Between 1928 and 1935 the international advertising agencies J. Walter Thompson, McCann Erickson, Lintas and Standard, all from the USA, were established in Brazil. They had an important role in radio broadcasting development. They not only produced advertisements, they developed a culture of media as a commercial enterprise, thus shaping a political economy for broadcasting and the press. Capturing and distributing advertising budgets in the existing media, they pioneered a model for the functioning of broadcasting.

Other evidence of radio broadcasting consolidation was the creation of the Associação Brasileira de Rádio (Brazilian Radio Association) in 1933, which brought together the embryonic broadcasters with the objective of defending their interests. The Association was created to challenge some clauses of decrees 20.047 and 21.111, particularly those relating to the setting up of a national network with educational objectives, and to restrictions on licensing. The members of Associação Brasileira de Rádio had adopted a commercial approach to operating radio, which resulted in a dynamic and eclectic style of broadcasting along US lines, addressing the largest possible audiences and having advertising as its income source. In the late 1930s, some commercial stations had orchestras, regional bands, actors, speakers, comedians, programmers etc. Like their US counterparts, these early Brazilian broadcasters also created commercial departments to sell advertising and engage in marketing, altering their internal structures so that they could compete in a market-driven economy.

The expansion of Brazil's economic activities in the late 1930s provoked a large increase in the placement of advertising in the media. Radio became a contender for the available advertising budget. Newspapers owners came to view association with or ownership of radio stations as a goal. Pressured by economic and political conditions, radio clubs and similar bodies had by then collapsed and were substituted with commercial enterprises, several of them owned by the same economic and political groups that owned newspapers. In 1938, the first and biggest ever Brazilian commercial media conglomerate was constituted: the Diários e Emissôras Associados (Associated Dailies and Radio Broadcasters), which started operations that year with five radio stations, 12 newspapers and one magazine. About 20 years later, it owned 36 radio stations, 34 daily newspapers, one national television network with 18 stations and several magazines.

The Vargas government legacy in terms of the Brazilian media was to establish a pattern of authoritarian use of the media channels. With the fall of the Vargas government at the end of World War II, in 1945, a Constituent Assembly was elected to draft a new constitution. The 1946 constitution ended censorship and public control over the mass media and affirmed total freedom of expression. However, the state continued to exercise the right to grant radio licences, and the state-owned stations continued to operate, the main one, Radio Nacional (National Radio), sustained by both public funds and advertising, having become the most powerful Brazilian station. Private broadcasters, however, had complete freedom to compete among themselves and with 'official' stations for the growing advertising budget of the expanding industrial and commercial sectors.

Radio Nacional was for about 15 years the most important radio station in Latin America. From 1945 to 1960 it received almost 8 million letters from listeners. It was also the radio station that initiated experimental television transmissions in Latin America, in 1946. Initially set up in state capitals, radio broadcasting later expanded to the countryside and started growing quickly: in 1940 Brazil had 70 radio stations; in 1950 that figure reached 243; in 1960 there were 400; and there were about 1000 in 1970 (Caparelli 1982: 80). Radio broadcasting thus established important patterns for the television industry in Brazil: the pursuit of a mass audience; the predominance of entertainment over educational or cultural programming and of private over public ownership; and advertising support over government, public or non-commercial financing.

Television's first years: a slow start

Unlike radio, which was initially operated by clubs of amateurs, the television industry emerged in Brazil under the aegis of the commercial sector which was aiming to increase the marketing for Brazilian goods. It first developed in the richer states of Rio de Janeiro and São Paulo, and years later in other main cities. This development followed the path of capitalist expansion in Brazil, i.e. concentration of capital in the country's Central-South region, where those two states are located.

The first Brazilian television station was bought from RCA in New York in 1948. With its inauguration on 18 September 1950, Brazil became the first Latin American country, and the sixth in the world (after the UK, the USA, France, Germany and the Netherlands) to have a television broadcasting station (Federico 1982: 81). TV Tupi-Difusôra started broadcasting to roughly 500 sets in São Paulo, and, three months later, this had increased to almost 2000 sets (Caparelli 1982: 20). In 1951 a second television station was launched in Rio de Janeiro – TV Tupi do Rio de Janeiro. In the same year another was created in São Paulo – Rádio Televisão Paulista (bought by the Globo Network in the 1960s), and in 1953 TV Record de São Paulo was set up in the same city. By 1959 Brazil had six television stations and about 80,000 television sets (Caparelli 1982: 23).

The first television channels were watched by the economic and social upper classes in a few major cities, because television sets were a luxurious imported good, not affordable for ordinary people. Programming then catered for the elite with adaptations of Shakespeare and Dostoevsky, among other masterpieces, along with ballet and classical music. Later, television started adapting foreign motion pictures, and producing auditorium entertainment programmes, particularly musical ones. These programmes were produced by professionals originally from radio, whose main job was to adapt radio programmes for television.

In the late 1950s, Brazil started to produce cheaper television sets which increased the television audience in places such as Rio de Janeiro and São Paulo, where 100,000 sets were sold in the early 1960s. Television broadcasting was then performing the role of engaging the audience with the new consumer culture through advertising and entertainment. During the 1950s new television stations were opened in other regions of the country, but it was only in 1960 that television broadcasting became national, with the introduction of video recorders. The first ones were used in the inauguration of the new Brazilian capital, Brasília, on 21 April 1960. The new technology allowed for the industrialization of production and the creation of studios for programme production, concentrated in São Paulo and Rio de Janeiro. This move diminished the local character of television broadcasting and reduced the creative and production autonomy of television stations outside those industrial centres.

In 1962, approximately 34 television stations had already been licensed, and most of them were operating. That same year, after nearly nine years of political negotiations, the National Telecommunications Code became law. It established the basic conditions for a radical transformation within the telecommunications and television industries in Brazil. For the first time, general guidelines were set up for the sector. The Code represented an important landmark in Brazilian communications, imposing a structure upon and legally organizing telecommunications services.

The development of the television industry in the 1960s was the result of the economic development under the Kubitschek government, the two communication regulatory acts (the National Telecommunications Code in 1962 and the Broadcasting Services Regulatory Act in 1963), and, from 1964 onwards, the 'friendly' interference of the military dictatorship. Subsequently, the broadcasting industry held different functions since radio turned into a regional medium catering for segmented audiences while television develop into a national medium to reach the national mass market. The concept of the audience in the ethos of the new arrangement was that of 'consumer' rather than 'citizen'.

Media regulation

The discussion on Brazilian history has so far shown the enduring presence of an interventionist state in the social, political, cultural and economic spheres. Although present for a long time in Brazilian history, this tradition became crystallized in the *Estado Novo* political system and nationalistic ideology. Such nationalistic and state-led visions of the country were challenged from the 1960s onwards, when the process of capitalist modernization intensified in Brazil, with the consequent internationalization of its home market, including its cultural market: foreign music on radio, and films and entertainment programmes on television were outstanding examples of that process. The development of capitalism in Brazil created a national market for cultural products, especially under the Juscelino Kubitschek government (1956–60), during which time the communication and culture industry expanded remarkably. Although challenged, the state remained in control of the radio and television industries, through its power to grant licences and supervise the broadcasting and telecommunications services.

The current television industry policy-making and implementation processes are embedded with the characteristics of the first regulatory acts on Brazilian broadcasting services (decrees 20.047 of 27 May 1931 and 21.111 of 1 March 1932), which reflected the state's ideology of the *Estado Novo*. The regulation of the Brazilian television industry has nationalistic roots, which have restricted the participation of foreigners.[3] The consolidation of radio broadcasting as a social and economic activity paralleled the triumphant 1930 revolution, and this may help to explain the revolutionaries' nationalistic vision of broadcasting. Decrees 20.047 and 21.111 considered broadcasting to be of *national interest*, and therefore subject to state control. These decrees are perhaps a historical landmark, since they set up the basis from which nationalistic ideologies have influenced policy-making on broadcasting in Brazil. Those ideologies were projected into many of the future legal provisions of the National Telecommunications Code, the Broadcasting Regulatory Act, and correlated legislation. The main areas of these provisions relating to the television industry are: (a) preference, in the presidential decision, for applicants who present the highest percentage of Brazilian-made equipment for their television stations; (b) preference, in the presidential decision, for applicants who present the highest percentage of time in their daily programming for Brazilian issues, authors and artists; (c) agreements between television stations and foreign companies or organizations are prohibited; (d) television stations are not allowed to have representatives of foreign organizations involved in their administrative activities; (e) television stations cannot have foreign employees, shareholders, directors or managers. The *Estado Novo* understood broadcasting as a service of public interest, and therefore to be protected and regulated by the state. This perhaps explains the attributed 'educational purposes' in decrees 20.047 and 21.111. However, the educational principles of broadcasting were not effectively defined by the government. Moreover, the legislation opened television up to 'decent' private Brazilian enterprises, setting the basis for the current system of state power over concessions through the trusteeship model, to attend to private interests. Since then, all subsequent governments have failed to make broadcasters comply with the original educational objectives. As a consequence, commercial instead of public television has been overwhelmingly predominant. In fact, broadcasting industry regulation has been notoriously designed around private companies' demands to expand consumer markets. This has been reflected in the reform of the *Código Brasileiro de Telecomunicações* of 2007, which established a generous 25 per cent of programming time for advertising. In addition, the flexible rules on programme content allow broadcasters to pursue successful low-cost programme genres, which attract viewers and avoid issues that are more complex. The regulation also favours private companies by establishing a market reserve for commercial broadcasting; non-commercial radio and television are not allowed to take any form of advertising or sponsorship.

The concept of centralization was introduced in the legislation of the decrees of the 1930s. It presented ideas on national networks and national programmes – both to be controlled by the federal government. This meant that the state would centralize not only the licensing process but also broadcast a national programme and implement a national telecommunications network. The system of centralization was influential in the drafting of the 1963 Broadcasting Services Regulatory Act, which set up the president of the republic as the licensing power for radio and television stations. It also assigned the president and the minister of communication the power to manage the licensing and controlling processes in the broadcasting industry. Recent constitutional provisions have put presidential decrees on broadcasting licensing under review by Parliament, but up to now this has not generated significant disagreements between the two powers. The problem lies in the fact that most Brazilian parliamentarians have received – or have personal, economic or political links with those who have received – presidential licences to enable them to operate radio and television channels, and therefore are beneficiaries of the system. Finally, although the DIP (Press and Propaganda Official Department) was suppressed in 1945, political control over radio and television services is still a prerogative of the president. Historical examples of exercising that controlling power were Getulio Vargas's and Janio Quadros's decrees, which changed the licences' validity period from ten to three years. A more recent illustration was the use by President Sarney of broadcasting licences: he granted concessions for radio and television channels to parliamentarians, in exchange for a longer term of office.

The military dictatorship and the broadcasting system

In the late 1950s Brazil underwent a fertile period of development under the Juscelino Kubitschek government, and after he left in 1961 the country endured a period of political turbulence, which culminated in the 1964 military *coup d'état*. The military had the support of centre and right-wing parties, most of the middle and upper classes, the Catholic Church, businessmen – particularly those linked to foreign capital – and financial organizations. During the 20 years they were in power, the system of broadcasting was managed through the National Security Doctrine. This meant an increase in capitalist development and the development of a political system based on public order and economic growth, including a state interventionist ethos that would affect all sectors of society. In the communication arena, the role of the media was to support the military ideology. Broadcasting was considered a private activity and reserved exclusively for Brazilians, particularly those individuals and groups supporting the government. Licensing was essentially a question of ideological agreement and economic and financial viability. A national infrastructure for telecommunications services to be used by broadcasting networks would be implemented to support national integration, to generate a mass market for national goods, to disseminate the military ideology and to generate economic and financial stability in the television industry. The military government directly invested in the country's infrastructure and basic industries, in order to create a national consumer goods market. The new economic policy welcomed foreign capital, which invested heavily in the most dynamic and profitable sectors of the Brazilian economy, such as the chemical, mechanical, automotive, electro-electronic and cultural industries.

The cultural sphere was seen as important to national development, so cultural production was stimulated as a means of national integration, but at the same time maintained under state control. The military created several state organizations to deal with areas of cultural production, and among them were: Embratel (Brazilian Telecommunications Enterprise); the Federal Council for Culture; the National Council for Tourism; Embratur (Brazilian Tourism Enterprise); the National Institute for Cinema; the Ministry of Communications; Embrafilme (Brazilian Enterprise for Motion Pictures); Funarte (National Foundation for Arts); the National Centre for Cultural Reference; Radiobrás (Brazilian Broadcasting Enterprise); Concine (National Council for Motion Pictures); Secretary for the National Heritage; and the Pro-Heritage Foundation.

In the economic sphere, the so-called 'economic miracle' was based on strong government intervention, oligopoly in certain sectors, and internationalization of the economy, which resulted in an extremely unequal society. The regime was kept in power by a systematic and brutal smashing of all forms of political opposition. The psycho-social control of the population was exercised through massive use of the media, particularly television, use of an extensive network of intelligence services, widespread censorship, the reduction of civil rights, and the control of labour and political organizations.

Despite this, the structural changes introduced by the military government in the telecommunications sector, particularly the building up of a modern infrastructure for national and international telecommunication services, constituted a decisive factor in the development of the broadcasting industry in Brazil. The military government also developed a series of initiatives aimed at improving the communications sector, ranging from enhancing the system of concession and increasing national production of television sets to setting up schemes of low interest loans for the public to purchase such sets, and expanding the advertising budget, both directly and through state-controlled companies.

Although they invested in the telecommunications sector, the military also enacted laws and decrees through which they favoured private investment. In 1968, for example, they issued decree-law 486, which exempted equipment and spare parts for the installation and maintenance of radio and television stations from import taxes, under the condition that they were imported directly and exclusively by the licensees. Analysing the factors shaping the Brazilian television industry, McAnany (1984: 220) argues that the rapid provision of television sets was critical to its growth. Thus, both the relatively lower cost of a set and the 1968 law implementing long-term credit for television set purchases were decisive for the development of the industry. McAnany also emphasizes the importance of microwave links for transmission,[4] regarded by the military government as crucial to national networking and the selling of advertising. This was a substantial stimulus not only for local but also for transnational businesses to invest heavily in television from the beginning of the 1970s onwards. The rapid increase in television advertising showed a 700 per cent growth in television expenditure from 1969 to 1978 and must have accounted almost entirely for the large advertising growth in general (McAnany 1984: 221).

Straubhaar (1989a: 236) suggests that the development of a general telecommunications system was a high priority for the military government because:

They saw it as vital for economic development, but also for national security and winning popular support. Broadcasting, especially in more remote regions, would help reinforce a sense of national identity by carrying news of government development efforts and other messages. The military governments also wanted a national television system to support the market economy, coinciding with, if not driven by, commercial elite interests.

Consolidating national networking

The growth of the Brazilian television industry was therefore an integral part of the changes the country experienced in the 1960s. In other words, television development in Brazil paralleled capital concentration, the internationalization of the internal market, and the geographic convergence of industrial production in the Central-South region of the country. Moreover, the economic policy of the military regime, aimed at creating a national mass market for industrialized products, was reinforced by the television industry's national spread through the national telecommunications network. Television became established as an industrial and commercial activity and as an important seller of goods and ideas (and military ideology), particularly via advertising and news programmes.

In 1969, Embratel introduced national, direct television broadcasting with the first television centre, which made possible the interconnection of television stations with the National System of Telecommunications. The Brazilian system of television broadcasting was then organized and structured in networks consisting of a few stations which broadcast a main signal that would be re-transmitted locally by affiliated stations. A remarkable example of that epoch was the emergence of the Globo Network. As a result of the network system, the television industry changed its programming, intensifying the use of the production centres in South Brazil. Thus, based on the social, economic, and cultural patterns of Rio de Janeiro and Sao Paulo, the industry sought to unify, under those urban patterns, the heterogeneous national television audiences. Television networks produced programmes for mass appeal, in order to reach broad general audiences, particularly in the middle and lower classes. They created or imported programmes that would sell popular goods (e.g. soap, tobacco, textiles, food, and electrical appliances). Advertisements for products aimed at the elites moved to magazines and newspapers. The Brazilian television industry soon found that their audience preferred domestically produced programmes (e.g. soap operas, variety shows and comedies) to imported ones (mainly from the USA). They then invested firmly in programme production. As a consequence, in the decade of 1972–82 the percentage of television programmes imported into Brazil declined from 60 to 39 per cent (Rogers and Antola 1985: 24). In 1979, for example, 48 per cent of television programmes were imported and 34 per cent were produced at a national level, the residue coming from the regional and local levels. In 1982 only 22 per cent of viewing time was dedicated to foreign programmes, which were then relegated to non-prime time slots as cheap fillers (Straubhaar 1989a: 240). In 1988, the Globo Network, which already had a majority audience share, produced 80 per cent of its programming, therefore only importing or buying 20 per cent of its content from independent producers (Festa and Santoro 1991: 183).[5]

To improve the quality of the industry, in 1972 the Brazilian government introduced colour to national television. The PAL-M system, with 525 lines, a variant of NTSC/PAL, was chosen. In the same year, the first colour television sets became available in the market, mainly to the upper classes because of their prohibitive cost. By the beginning of the 1980s there were more than 100 television stations functioning (12 of them government owned), and about 20 million television sets in Brazilian households. Thus, stimulated by the government – which also held by far the biggest advertising budget in the country – the Brazilian television industry accelerated its consolidation as the strongest national cultural industry, oriented to entertain the audience and to make a huge profit. Influenced by the commercial television values of the USA, and encouraged by the new competitive environment, the Brazilian television industry improved its profit-making mechanisms, and produced and distributed low-content quality programmes on an industrial scale, designed to attract the largest possible audiences and encourage sales to advertisers. In this way, it also emerged as the primary nationwide purveyor of news and information for mass audiences, forcing the radio industry to provide for local and regional interests.

A decisive factor in the strengthening of the television industry was the growth of the global national advertising budget and the establishment of advertising as a lucrative activity in the services sector. That process started in the 1920s and 30s, when foreign and national advertising agencies first directed their attention to social and economic elites, through newspapers and magazines. It then increased in the 1940s, when advertising reached radio and its large numbers of consumers. It expanded even more in the 1950s, at the climax of the radio era, when advertising agencies were dynamically shaping new lifestyles and cultural practices, as well as encouraging mass consumption of industrialized goods. In the mid-1960s, advertisers finally realized the potential of television for advertising.

In the 1960s, the growth of capitalist relations in Brazil, and the country's transformation into an urbanized and industrialized society, created not only a national bourgeois class, but also a new and large middle class, whose economic power, cultural tastes and lifestyle made it a mass consumer for the emerging culture industry, including television. A new Brazilian consumer culture emerged, supported by the communications industry. The field then underwent substantial change, particularly through the imposition of market imperatives on the production of cultural goods.

The television industry was steadily flourishing while (or because of) developing a profitable political articulation of interests with the military government. On the one hand, television broadcasters had the support of the state to reach a national audience, and new legislation – the Telecommunications National Code and the Broadcasting Services Regulatory Act – privileged their private interests, thus aligning them with the military powers. On the other hand, the state assumed a clear role as regulator, supervisor and heavy-handed intervener in the sector with the support of the television broadcasters. Television became the mass medium to publicize and shape ideas and moral, political and cultural values, and to support the productive system through advertising. Thus, beyond having regulated the industry through the Broadcasting Regulatory Act, consolidating its role as the television licensing power, the state also became both its censor and its main advertiser. The military dictatorship could therefore fulfil its role as the defender of both the interests of economic elites (by supporting the television industry to expand the consumer market) and itself (by controlling television content and advertising the government's positive achievements).

At least three factors seem to have been essential in the development of the television industry in Brazil during the military regime. They are: the need to expand the national market for industrial goods; the government's need for political and ideological control over the country; and the government's need for uniformity in the management of a huge country. The dictatorship had the support of the television industry for two main reasons. First, they would not receive the same support from the print media given the traditions of a free press in Brazilian culture. Newspapers were linked to regional political articulations and interests. Although most of them were supporting the regime, it would be difficult, expensive and uncertain to ask them to give up their regional interests and build a national press. Moreover, Brazil had at that time a population of which 35 per cent were illiterate. Second, the regime had a great amount of power over television broadcasters, given that they depended on the government to maintain their businesses. Furthermore, television programmes could reach everybody in the country, including illiterates. In addition, a positive aspect was that television services would inevitably benefit from the building up of the national telecommunications system.

Conclusions

The analysis presented here suggests that there is a political thread that explains the continuities in the political economy of the Brazilian broadcasting industry. We would like to highlight two important aspects of that narrative. The first is that Brazil has historically been a strong example of using the trusteeship model to benefit private interests. In fact, since the 1930s, broadcasters have been exploiting radio and television as private tools for profit and political power. Further, there has been a lack of technical, legal, conceptual and financial conditions for non-commercial broadcasting stations to operate regularly. The second aspect underpinning the contemporary structuring of the broadcasting industry is the American influence in the political, cultural and economic processes of Brazil. For example, the Brazilian government used the American Broadcast Act, with its emphasis on presidential control of regulation, as a template to produce the Brazilian Broadcasting Regulatory Act. The aim was to establish in Brazil a liberal-democratic television system similar to the American one, but adapted to the authoritarian and elitist traditions of Brazilian social, economic and political structures. That meant setting up a predominantly commercial model of television broadcasting able to sell material and symbolic products, through advertising and programming, as well as educational state television (not a public service in the European sense), directly supported by government budgets, to 'educate' and provide skills to allow people to integrate into the national market. However, educational radio and television stations have never received appropriate financial support from any government.

The historical overview presented suggests that the actual structure and practices of the Brazilian television industry are a direct result of the submission of the state and the media regulatory bodies to the economic elite, broadcasters and politicians, and their political, ideological and economic interests. That is why continuity, which translates into commercial, national media conglomerates and a lack of an adequate public service, has been the main feature of the Brazilian television regulatory system, where changes only occur by strict permission or hard political struggle.

To conclude, we would like to point out that the regulatory system of Brazilian television undermines contemporary liberal theories of the media, which suggest the disempowerment of the nation state in the decision-making process of media regulation due to the influence of transnational media conglomerates. These organizations would be the new definers of national media regulation according to the dynamics and interests of international markets. Or to put it another way, rather than the state and other domestic groups and institutions, multi-national corporations would be the main source for regulation of internal media markets. Our discussion illustrates that this logic has not yet been adopted in Brazil. Contrary to global trends of a borderless media market, the Brazilian state continues to be central to decision-making, implementation and control of the regulation process of the media system. So far, there is no indication that international developments have weakened the state or internal politics, or diversified domestic interests. Moreover, the Brazilian government's power is even stronger than before: for instance, the president's and Parliament's powers for intervening in the sector are a constitutional matter and not just a subject for ordinary law, as was the case until 1988. Therefore, the regulation of the television industry, including the television licensing process, remains controlled by the state.

However, we are aware that the contemporary media landscape is a changing space. For instance, if we take into account the opening of the cable television and the press and broadcasting market to foreign capital, we could suggest that the new Brazilian regulatory structure seems to be moving to redefine the conceptual bases from which it performs its role. The questions perhaps are to what extent will the system change to attend to transnational corporations' demands, and to what degree the Brazilian state is prepared to enter the powerful global media market. The answers remain to be seen.

Notes

1   In general, Brazilian printed mainstream media are part of print media conglomerates or media conglomerates that include broadcasting and press. For example, the biggest conglomerate of print media belongs to Abril Press, which has 69.3 per cent of the magazine market and 14 per cent of the television channels by subscription, with the help of foreign capital. The four biggest television networks – Globo, Record, SBT and Bandeirantes – are owned by only six private groups (Egypt and Osorio 2002).

2   Before the *Estado Novo* started in 1937, the country underwent a revolution in 1930, with a temporary government between 1930–4. From 1934 to 1937 there was a 'constitutional' government which elected Getulio Vargas for the presidency.

3   Only recently, through the Constitutional Amendment 36 (28 May 2002), newspapers and broadcasters have been permitted to receive up to 30 per cent of foreign capital. However, foreign investors cannot exercise any control over editorial alignment. Before this, the Cable television Law, enacted in 1995, had permitted up to 49 per cent of foreign capital in the constitution of enterprises operating television TV services. Satellite services, including television, are permitted up to 100 per cent of foreign capital.

4   The development of radio frequency (RF) technology has permitted the use of microwave links as the major channel for long distance communication. The use of microwave links has major advantages over cabling systems.

5   According to the 1993 *Brazilian Media Yearbook* (Grupo de Mídea 1993) that tendency has not changed significantly in subsequent years. During that year, the four national television networks had about 70 per cent of their programming filled by domestically-produced programmes.

5 THE MEDIA IN CHILE: THE RESTORATION OF DEMOCRACY AND THE SUBSEQUENT CONCENTRATION OF MEDIA OWNERSHIP

Gustavo González-Rodríguez

May 2006 was a landmark for the Chilean media in two respects. On 3 May a 'Strategic Alliance' was formed between the La Araucania society, which is a subsidiary of the company *El Mercurio*, and the newspaper *El Sur* from Concepción, the third most important city in the country, located 515 kilometres south of Santiago and an important centre for industry and forestry. *El Sur* is one of the few truly regional newspapers in Chile, founded on 15 November 1882. By means of this alliance, *El Sur* became part of *El Mercurio*, the network that reigns supreme over print media outlets located in the major Chilean cities, from Arica on the northern boundary with Peru to the archipelago of Chiloé, some 1200 kilometres south of Santiago. The second landmark was the workers' strike at *Diario Siete* on 17 May. *Diario Siete* is an independent newspaper managed by the well known journalist Mónica González[1] and controlled by a society headed by the former Christian Democrat minister Genaro Arriagada. It had been in existence for only one and a half years, having been formed when *Siete mas Siete* magazine accepted a merger with Consorcio Periodístico de Chile S.A. (Copesa), thereby becoming a newspaper. According to Genaro Arriaga and Mónica González, the agreement was that *Copesa* would be in charge of the printing, distribution and advertising of the medium and not interfere in the paper's editorial line. On 9 June however, Arriagada announced the paper's closure. *Diario Siete* therefore followed the fate of its three predecessors: *Fortín Mapocho*, *La Época* and *El Metropolitano*. *Diario Siete*, becoming the fourth thwarted daily press project since the restoration of democracy in 1990.

Despite this, the closure of *Diario Siete* did not affect Copesa's position as the second biggest owner of the press in Chile, with a concentration of its power in the capital and the Santiago-based newspapers of *La Tercera*, *La Cuarta* and *La Hora*. *La Hora* is a free newspaper with two daily editions. Together with the El Mercurio group, Copesa has installed a media duopoly in Chile, whereby two dominant companies control the print run, the greatest share of readers and almost the entire advertising portfolio. This state of affairs is best described as a duopoly, since, while Copesa and El Mercurio operate a two-headed monopoly, it is also fair to say that the papers owned by these groups manifest a uniformity of political-ideological projects, editorial lines, styles and news coverage.

Where Pinochet failed democracy succeeded

The restoration of democracy began on 11 March 1990. One of its greatest contradictions, however, lies precisely in the acceleration of concentrated ownership. Although this process has been taking place worldwide, this period saw the destruction of the dynamic alternative press that sprang up in the 1980s in opposition to Pinochet's dictatorship. 'What Pinochet did not achieve, democracy did' is a phrase that, through constant reiteration, is now widely used to express pessimism over the impoverishment of the mass media's structure, which has submitted to the powerful dominance of the market that, from the outset, contaminated the politics of the 'Concentration of Parties for Democracy'.[2]

A similar situation prevails in free access terrestrial television. Chile first came to this medium by means of particular legislation that was approved towards the end of Eduardo Frei Montalva's government (1964–70). This legislation handed ownership and channel management to universities and the state. However, Pinochet's dictatorship opened the system up to private ownership, both foreign and local, while state television was forced to finance itself, thereby ascribing the same to the commercial canons of private channels as to the so-called university television. As with the press, the programming of terrestrial television leaves little space for diversity or indeed for the imagination, besides a small selection of specialist channels of a cultural orientation but with minute audiences. News programmes are uniform, being transmitted at similar times on the four main channels, and reflecting the same news priorities and the same ways of capturing audiences. They are high on sensationalism and football, with little international coverage and a paucity of cultural or scientific themes. This mode of journalism may be identified as, and confused with, 'info-entertainment'. Banality, easy jokes and opinionated styles predominate in 'informative' programmes of all varieties, where television celebrities, footballers and politicians parade the screens in search of fame. This celebrity-ridden, or 'show-biz' television, has recently exploded into Chile's press. It is a phenomenon that accurately reveals, within its own codes, a certain underworld that has surfaced to dispel the repressive moral conservatism that governed Chilean public life during the dictatorship and emanated from the Catholic hierarchy with regard to issues pertaining to family, marriage and sexuality.[3]

As with Chile's press, there has been a progressive decline in the diversity of the television programmes on offer. This tendency is even more pronounced in the magazine market. While many magazines are targeted at particular audience segments with higher incomes, those dedicated to culture and politics have more or less disappeared. The year 2005 saw the disappearance, for example, of Chile's two most prestigious independent cultural publications, *Plan B* and *Rocinante*, which were the country's leading examples of political and denunciatory journalism. *Rocinante* and *Plan B* have now been consigned to the 'cemetery' of earlier magazines that were closed during the 1990s. As with Chile's newspapers, these magazines marked an era of opposition to Pinochet's dictatorship, and included *Cauce, Apsi, Análisis* and, later, *Hoy*. Joining these were others that had appeared at the beginning of the 1990s, notably *Página Abierta* and *Los Tiempos*.

Investigative journalism past and present

The democratic magazines and newspapers that appeared during the last decade of Pinochet's dictatorship were the professional bastion of women who made their mark in Chilean investigative journalism. Prominent examples of these journalists were Mónica González, Patricia Verdugo[4] and María Olivia Mönckeberg. To these might also be added Alejandra Matus, who had the dubious privilege of being the first Chilean citizen to be exiled under the democratic regime when, in 1999, she sought asylum in the USA as a result of judicial persecution as a consequence of her publication *The Black Book of Chilean Justice* (Matus 1999). She was only able to return to Chile in 2001.[5]

It has been María Olivia Mönckeberg, however, who has perhaps driven the transformation of the themes of investigative journalism that focused primarily on crimes against humanity during the dictatorship. In more recent years, Mönckeberg has published books reflecting probing and well documented enquiries regarding the so-called 'factious' powers which either originated, or were fortified, under Pinochet's dictatorship and that retain some influence in Chile today.[6] Investigative journalism in Chile usually takes the form of books, although its influence is also evident in the print media and on television, where there have been occasional attempts to probe more deeply into certain events or processes and thereby occasion some accusations that have caused a public commotion. However, the abuse – or overuse – of resources such as hidden cameras, together with the tendency of journalism-as-policing, led to the violation of certain ethical considerations in a scramble for spectacular revelations. This phenomenon is termed 'rotten meat' journalism by Argentineans, whereby sensationalism is disguised as investigative journalism.

Both the press and television companies claim to have considerable public influence, setting the agenda for discussion. Even so, their audience does not trust, sometimes understandably, the professional rigour of these media and gives more serious consideration to the radio, perhaps because it is a more genuinely interactive medium. Nevertheless, radio stations also reflect a concentration of ownership. Traditional radio stations have tended to disappear as consortiums have migrated to transnational business entertainment chains. Between them, the Consorcio Radial Chile, which belongs to the Spanish group Prisa and the Colombian group Caracol have acquired many of Chile's major FM stations. Their major rival is Ibero-American Radio Chile, which belongs to the Claxon group, whose main shareholder is the Venezuelan tycoon Gustavo Cisneros, one of the richest men in the world. In terrestrial television, the Claxon group also owned the channel Chilevisión until it was acquired in 2005 by Chilean millionaire Sebastián Piñera, who also owns the airline Lan-Chile in addition to many other businesses. Piñera was the right-wing presidential candidate who lost to the current president Michelle Bachelet in the general elections of January 2006. The Mexican group Televisa owns 37.4 per cent of the channel Megavisión's shares, while the conservative Chilean businessman Ricardo Claro controls the remaining 62.6 per cent. Finally, the channel La Red is fully owned by the Mexican tycoon Ángel González.

Chilevisión's licence is, strictly speaking, the property of the University of Chile, the country's main public higher education institution. However, it had to get rid of the licence due to the financial problems that are commonly associated with public education system in Chile. Of the terrestrial channels with national coverage, the only one managed by a university is the television corporation of the Catholic University, better known as Channel 13 due to its frequency in Santiago. The only national network is Televisión Nacional de Chile (TVN). But according to a law passed by the Television National Council in 1992 and negotiated carefully between the two large political coalitions,[7] public television cannot receive money from the state, and is instead forced to finance itself by mimicking the techniques used by private channels and attracting advertising revenue. A similar fate befell Channel 13, which was only notionally a university channel and whose Catholic ethos conditions some aspects of its editorial policy, especially on so-called 'ethical' themes. The Catholic channel and Megavisión have systematically boycotted the Ministry of Health campaigns for AIDS prevention because they disagree with the use of condoms, and they have strongly opposed divorce laws. They also have well-known conservative priests as presenters.

Market concentration has also had an effect on the diversification of broadcasting media. Not only in open terrestrial television, which is still by far the most watched in Chile, but also in cable television, which was supposed to open up additional spaces. This was perhaps illustrated by the project of the youth channel Rock and Pop, which started in the mid-1990s but only managed to survive until 1999. Its innovative proposal did not manage to attract the necessary advertising support, even though the channel was owned by the Compañía Chilena de Telecomunicaciones, a local group that also owns Radio Cooperativa, the main radio station of the country.

Another deficit in the media system in Chile is the limited space for the development of community radio or popular radio, which in official terminology were defined as radio stations of minimum coverage, according to a law enacted during the government of Patricio Aylwin, after a campaign by ARCHI (the Association of Chilean Radio Broadcasters) to root out 'pirate' stations. That law greatly complicated the application system to obtain temporary frequency licences, which in the metropolitan region (Santiago) implies having a transmission power of only 1 kilowatt, in turn implying only a coverage of 'four blocks'. The law prevented community radio stations from any possibility of obtaining resources through advertising space, under the argument that they are 'non-profit' entities, with a particular application of the concept. 'Non-profit' should mean that the management of a channel of minimum coverage should not make any profit from it, but should not deny them the possibility of generating the necessary income to invest in the development of the medium itself.

While the licences for the radio stations of minimum coverage are only for three years, in traditional radio broadcasting they last 25 years. Furthermore, even if on paper these small stations appear independent, in practice they are part of powerful radio networks. Investors are willing to pay very high prices for FM stations in a market that is clearly saturated, because these stations come with a licence. In this way, alternative radio projects also become segregated and forced, in the best of cases, to remain as medium-wave channels, without any possibility of accessing the mass audience of FM. This has happened with radio stations such as *Radio Tierra*, linked to feminist groups and social organizations, and Radio Nuevo Mundo, which is close to the Communist Party.

The curious absence of the state

A lack of pluralism crosses the entire media spectrum in Chile and is a result of a system which was articulated during the dictatorship and has been consolidated under the democratic governments that have applied in this field a *laissez faire* approach that Pinochet did not have. The military regime attached to neo-liberalism's hindquarters the discourse of the absence of the state. However, in Chile's history there is not another period in which the government has had so much control over the media, either directly or indirectly. The conditions imposed by the dictatorship contrast with the previous diversity, characterized during a great part of the twentieth century by the connection between the written media and the radio with the political parties or great ideological currents. As Guillermo Sunkel and Esteban Geoffrey have pointed out, in fact, up to 1973 each relevant party of the political system owned directly a newspaper or magazine, or was linked to one (Sunkel and Esteban 2001). From 11 September 1973, the date of the cruel coup against Salvador Allende, the dictatorship led the way for the future duopoly of El Mercurio and Copesa, with the closure of all newspapers linked to Allende's Unidad Popular (UP) party, such as *El Siglo*, and to the Communist Party (*Ultima Hora* and *Puro Chile*), and the Socialist Party (*Clarín*, a popular tabloid). Very soon, the turn would come for *La Prensa*, linked to the Christian Democrat Party.

El Mercurio and Copesa subordinated to the dictatorship due to their ideological affinity, but also because of financial restraints. Both consortia ran the risk of bankruptcy, in the same way as many other companies carried away by the crisis brought on by external debt that affected all Latin America from 1982, but were saved by generous credits given by the Banco del Estado (State Bank) that, because of continuous refinancing, were never paid back to the bank whose possessions belong to the Chilean people. The state lost at least $27 million in favour of El Mercurio, while the operations regarding Copesa allowed the group to be finally acquired by business conglomerates enriched under the dictatorship and linked to the Unión Demócrata Independiente (UDI), a conservative political party created to legitimize and provide political structure to the dictatorship of Augusto Pinochet. This party paid a mere $7 million for this group.

The dictatorship also had control over the television channels that, up to then, were still owned by the universities, through the so-called delegate-principals (generally military people) in those universities. It used Televisión Nacional de Chile (TVN), owned by the state, in an unrestricted way as a vehicle of political propaganda for the regime, and created Radio Nacional, a network of channels with coverage in all the Chilean territory and international frequencies, in an effort to counteract the programmes condemning Pinochet's government produced by Radio Moscú, Radio Habana and other information instruments for the exiled.

Radio Nacional was created based upon Radio Corporación, a channel acquired by the Socialist Party under Allende's government, which was closed after the coup, as well as all the rest of the radio stations that identified with the left, particularly Radio Magallanes, owned by the Communist Party. Because of the strict laws imposed by the state of emergency, even the channels that had maintained a certain independence from the regime, like Cooperativa and Chilena (owned by Santiago's archbishopric), had to submit themselves to censorship and often applied self-censorship in order to maintain their existence. Radio Balmaceda, of the Christian Democracy that won the first dictatorship debates, as well as the newspaper La Prensa, also ended up closing. Orbe, a national information agency, was another of the instruments of disinformation and manipulation used by the military regime, having also the support of the Chilean branch of the UPI (United Press International) agency while the rest of the international agencies maintained certain informative independence, although with caution to protect their journalists.

Once democracy was re-established, Patricio Aylwin's government decided to rescue freedom of speech by appealing to the market as a regulatory element. It ended up by getting rid of all of Radio Nacional's stations, as they were economically non-feasible. Orbe returned to private hands and an attempt to create a new state agency was cancelled shortly after its launch. As a result, the only media to remain in the hands of the state were TVN and La Nación, which publishes the newspaper of the same name, and the Diario Oficial, the gazette in which motions, decrees, laws and other state-related issues are published.

The phrase 'the best communication policy is not having a communication policy at all' is attributed to the sociologist Eugenio Tironi, first secretary of culture and communication in Aylwin's administration. As a result of this neo-liberal approach, the state withdrew from ownership of radio stations and news agencies. It also meant that the government ceased advertising in emerging independent media, such as *Analysis* and *Apsi* magazines, which contributed to the consolidation of *El Mercurio* and Copesa, which already controlled the media market. The constitutional platform left by the dictatorship and which oversaw the reinstallation of democracy was an almost perfect work of political engineering, with ties that preserved for a long time the impunity of human rights violators, starting with Pinochet himself, the role of the army as guarantors of a new institutionalization and an economic model that recognized the market as its great chief. The new structure of legislative power, based on a binomial system, brought a long life to the authoritarian enclaves that have not yet entirely disappeared despite the profound constitutional reforms that president Ricardo Lagos (2000–6) managed to enact in the final phase of his mandate, in September 2005.[8]

After an extensive legislative transaction, it was only on 4 June 2001 that a new press law was promulgated which partially dismantled the repressive dictatorship's legal apparatus which limited the journalistic practice of attacking the 'abuses of advertising'. From the point of view of human rights legislation there were partial advances with the re-establishment of the freedom of speech, and legislation that eliminated the previous censorship and reduced the military justice faculties, which had had almost absolute powers during the dictatorship. The most evident case of censorship was the ban of the film *The Last Temptation of Christ*, made by US director Martin Scorsese. The censorship of the film was first applied by the dictatorship, which also prohibited some 500 other films. However, once democracy was re-established, the High Court gave in to the conservative pressures of the Catholic hierarchy and renewed the ban. A group of lawyers then took the case to the Inter-American Human Rights Court, which, on 5 February 2001 issued a condemnatory sentence against the Chilean government (Zúñiga 2006).

The conflict surrounding Scorsese's film was one of numerous controversies that showed, from the first years of the re-establishment of democracy, the limitations to the freedom of speech and press that came from a group of decrees and laws that protected the ruling powers from the scrutiny of the media and the public, as pointed out in a report by Human Rights Watch (2006) published in 1998. This report was almost a premonition of things to come. A year later, as mentioned earlier, Alejandra Matus was forced to go into exile. Indeed, the then president of the High Court of Justice, Servando Jordán, used a provision in the National Security Law, which was set by the dictatorship, to confiscate her book and persecute the author.

Liberal capitalism without competition

The complex set of restrictions imposed on journalistic practices during these 16 years of re-establishment of democracy contrast with the absolute market freedom in the media system that ended by annulling, nearly completely, the typical competition of economic liberalism. The most illustrative example is that of the press. After the closure of *Diario Siete*, Chile had 57 newspapers, of which 9 had national circulation, 46 were local and 2 were free. Currently, the national newspapers are *El Mercurio*, *Las Últimas Noticias* and *La Segunda*, owned by *El Mercurio*. *La Tercera* and *La Cuarta* belong to Copesa. Meanwhile, Empresa Periodística La Nación, partially owned by the state, publishes the dailies *La Nación* and *Diario Oficial*. The list is completed with *Estrategia* and *El Diario Financiero*, which are inclined towards economic and business content. *Estrategia*, which began as a magazine, belongs to the Gestión group, which is linked to various business sectors. *El Diario Financiero*, created by a group of journalists towards the end of the dictatorship, changed hands several times until being acquired by Ricardo Claro, the conservative businessman who is also the main shareholder of the channel Megavisión. *Publimetro*, the main free newspaper, is the only daily written media operating with foreign funds. It is owned by the holding Modern Times Group (MTG), which has similar publications in many cities around the world, mainly where there are underground (metro) services, although in Chile, apart from Santiago, it also circulates in Valparaiso, Viña del Mar, Rancagua, Talcahuano and Concepción. The other free newspaper is *La Hora*, owned by Copesa, with a morning and an afternoon edition that circulates mainly in Santiago and Valparaíso. The group El Mercurio, owned by the Edwards family, has four different societies under its wings, allowing it to possess newspapers throughout the country and confirming it as the biggest press conglomerate.

The company El Mercurio SAP owns *El Mercurio* and *Las Últimas Noticias*, both morning newspapers of national distribution, and *La Segunda* which is an evening newspaper.

The group El Norte S.A. owns eight newspapers: *La Estrella de Arica*, *La Estrella de Iquique*, *El Mercurio de Antofagasta*, *La Estrella del Norte*, *El Mercurio de Calama*, *La Estrella del Loa*, *La Prensa de Tocopilla* and *El Diario de Atacama*.

El Mercurio de Valparaíso S.A.P. is owner of the newspapers *El Mercurio de Valparaíso*,[9] *La Estrella de Valparaíso* and *El Líder de San Antonio*.

The group Araucanía S.A. controls the newspapers *El Diario Austral de Temuco*, *Renacer de Arauco*, *Renacer de Angol*, *El Diario Austral de Valdivia*, *El Diario Austral de Osorno*, *El Llanquihue de Puerto Montt*, *La Estrella de Chiloe* and *El Sur de Concepción y Crónica*.

El Mercurio also owns many associated newspapers, such as *La Prensa de Curicó* and *El Centro de Talcia*, giving it almost monopolistic power over all the regional and local media structures in Chile. The Araucanía group obtaining *El Sur* was the finishing stroke for one of the last bastions of the local press and made evident the unceasing expansion of the 'Edwards clan', who have also acquired, in recent times, the newspaper *El Diario de Atacama* (in April 2004), and launched *La Estrella de Chiloé* in July 2005.

The acquisition of *El Sur* allowed the Edwards clan to settle in Concepción, one of the last big cities in which they are not present by owning a medium, because in the southern part of the country, in the port-city of Punta Arenas, *El Magallanes*, which belongs to a local group, still survives, while *La Prensa Austral*, from the same city is associated with El Mercurio. In Chillán, 400 kilometres south of the capital, there is also the newspaper *La Discusión*, which has been managed since 1976 by the University of Concepción. But apart from these two cities, the Edwards family dominate the media in Santiago, Valparaíso and Concepción, the main urban concentrations of the country as well as in other centres of demographic expansion since the 1970s such as Temuco, Antofagasta, Iquique, Copiapó and Calama y Valdivia.

Contrary to *El Mercurio*, Copesa constitutes a more decentralized media conglomarate from the point of view of the distribution of its shares. From Santiago it is hoping to gain influence with the national newspapers instead of creating branches in the regions and provinces. Two business groups which already control three companies each, appear (on paper) as owners of 96 per cent of Copesa's shares. The common referent of both is Alvaro Sahié, a businessman who became rich during Pinochet's dictatorship and also has a financial business as the main shareholder of CorpBanca. A political affinity with UDI is evident through Sahié and other directors of the companies that form part of Copesa, such as Sergio de Castro or Miguel Angel Poduje, who were ministers during the dictatorship.

Copesa's case is different from El Mercurio's, not only because of the fact that Copesa was formed by a group of businessmen that haven't been traditionally linked with the communications market but who had links with the military regime, as pointed out by the investigators Osvaldo Corrales and Juan Sandoval (Corrales and Sandoval 2005). The 'flagship' of the group is the newspaper *La Tercera*, which began to circulate on 7 July 1950, as an evening edition of *La Hora*.[10] Since 1949, under the government of Gabriel González Videla (1946–52), of the Radical Party, the publishing business of these media has been identified with the family of Agustín and Germán Picó Cañas, businessmen of that same party. Under the dictatorship, in 1987, their heir, Germán Picó Domínguez, sold part of the shares to Álvaro Sahié, to finally get rid of Copesa in 1991, when Poduje and other businessmen with past links to the dictatorship past joined the company.

Apart from *La Tercera*, this consortium also has *La Cuarta*, which is its second newspaper of national coverage. Created in 1984, this paper sought to fill the gap left by the closure of *Clarín* after the coup of 11 September 1973. *Clarín* was a sensationalistic newspaper that described itself as 'popular' and that defined a period in Chilean journalism from 1954 by the originality of its language.[11] The newspaper

Puro Chile, created by the Communist Party in 1969, followed the same style and was also closed by the dictatorship. As second head of the duopoly, Copesa established in Chile MTG and its free newspaper *Publimetro*, and on 7 March 2000 launched *La Hora*, to which it added *La Hora de la Tarde*, also free, as an evening edition.

The arrival of MTG in Chile threatened the established newspapers, which are grouped in a National Association of the Press (ANP). As a result, the ANP launched a lawsuit against the association between MTG and the international conglomerate, Metro S.A., which would involve the distribution of *Publimetro* in urban railway stations, a key market for publishers. The Supreme Court of Justice accepted the request of the ANP lawyers, and as a result free newspapers cannot be distributed inside train stations, only outside. MTG was nevertheless able to install its product, which has managed to compete with *El Mercurio* and Copesa for a chunk of the advertising market. However, its influence is minor in terms of the generation of news agenda, because of the characteristics of its own journalistic proposal, which is concentrated on informative notes for fast reading and targets mainly commuters.

The journalistic group *La Nación* is a closed limited liability company, in which the state owns 69.3 per cent of the shares, allowing the government to control the board of directors and to appoint the administrative managers, as well as the director, and other important positions in the newspaper. The counterweight of this media to the duopoly of *El Mercurio* and Copesa is minimal and, although it contributes by considering facts or themes ignored by the traditional press, it has not been able to get rid of the stigma of being a 'government newspaper', which reduces its credibility. Since the re-establishment of democracy, this business has tried to expand. It created a subsidiary that, in 1991, began to publish the newspaper *El Nortino*, a supplement inside *Iquique*, which survived little more than a decade. In the end, the official newspaper continues to be a great source of resources for *La Nación* that also sells printing services to several magazines and other publications.

Diario Financiero and *Estrategia*, the last in the list of national newspapers, are typical examples of the segmentation of the journalistic market. Both joined with some delay the international wave of media specializing in the economy. *Estrategia*, which began to circulate in 1978 as a weekly newspaper, became a daily edition near the end of the dictatorship, to compete with the emerging *Diario Financiero*. But the competition was relative, because they were both newspapers specializing in business issues, with a market fundamentally concentrated in the business community.

Winning readers or consumers?

In Chile, most publications seem to seek readers rather than promote a political or ideological agenda, as they identify themselves with a neo-liberal economic model. *El Mercurio* and Copesa also subscribe to this model. Thus, the confrontation of ideas is diluted in the domain of 'ideological monopoly', a notion put forward by Corrales and Sandoval (2005: 2). For these authors,

> a characteristic of the national business is its high level of ideological uniformity. Economically it is expressed in a high level of commitment with the neo-liberal model and culturally with a strong conservatism. In this way, when they act as advertisers, they use advertising investment as a tool to strengthen those media that are more related to them, introducing a distortion in the market which makes difficult the emergence of other expressions.

The increasing dependence of the media on advertising revenue is a result in some respects of the decreasing numbers of readers, a phenomenon that affects newspapers worldwide. This phenomenon, alongside increasing concentration of ownership, has redefined the news agenda in the country. Thus, the press and terrestrial television enter a game of categorization, with censorship and self-censorship, but also of practising certain factious powers. These powers allow them to impose on the public agenda themes that do not necessarily correspond to the real concerns of society, but to the interests of the dominant elites. In this way, the media produces exclusions in accordance with the inequalities present in a country that has one of the worst income distributions in Latin America.

It is interesting that the main point of the competition between El Mercurio and Copesa is a dispute over the ABC1 segment. This segment corresponds to people of high income in Chile, according to the categories of consumers created by the advertising agencies that identify the segments C2, C3 and D as lower strata. This same categorization is applied in the analysis of People Meter, a system of instant measurement of television audiences, financed mostly by the advertising agencies themselves. When Copesa associated with Genaro Arriagada to create the *Diario Siete* newspaper, it was because it wanted to expand its presence in the ABC1 market. Copesa believed that this medium would attract readers identifying with the governing moderate left coalition. This strategy was not successful and the consortium, on the contrary, maintains a solid demand in the strata C2, C3 and D with the newspaper *La Cuarta*. However, these groups do not have a high purchasing capacity, so most of the advertising that Copesa receives goes to *La Tercera*.

Advertising investment in Chile represents 0.64 per cent of the gross domestic product (GDP) and rose in 2004 to $602 million, according to the Chilean Association of Advertising Agencies (Achap).[12] In 2003, the investment was $499 million. In 2004, terrestrial television received 49 per cent of advertising, and the daily press 29.5 per cent. In third place was the radio, with 8.3 per cent, followed by the public way, with 6.7 per cent. Subsequently, magazines grasped 3.5 per cent, cable television 1.7 per cent, online media 1.1 per cent and, finally, the cinema, 0.3 per cent. According to reports in the magazine *ANDA* (National Association of Advertisers),[13] the newspaper *El Mercurio* received, in

2004, 15.21 per cent of advertising investment, *La Tercera* 4.55 per cent, *Las Últimas Noticias* 2.04 per cent, *Publimetro* 1.99 per cent, *El Diario Financiero* 1.38 per cent, *La Segunda* 0.91 per cent, *La Cuarta* 0.73 per cent, *La Hora* 0.32 per cent, *La Hora de la Tarde* 0.32 per cent and *La Nación* 0.30 per cent.

The Edwards group, with its three newspapers (*El Mercurio*, *Las Últimas Noticias* and *La Segunda*) takes around 60 per cent of advertising investment in the press, exceeding by far that of Copesa, that with *La Tercera*, *La Cuarta* and the two editions of *La Hora* attracts 20 per cent of the market share.[14] *Estrategia*, with 6.8 per cent, *Publimetro* (6.5 per cent) and *El Diario Financiero* (4.9 per cent) are well positioned in the advertising market, while *La Nación* has access to barely 1.2 per cent of the market.

A state that does not generate pluralism or diversity

The closing of *Diario Siete* generated some debate in the lower chamber of the Congress about the allocation of state advertising. This had been condemned since the start of the democratic transition as a discriminatory practice towards journalists and directors of independent media. The government and its companies hire advertising with the same criteria as private enterprises, favouring in this way the hegemony of the duopoly or 'ideological monopoly'. In the last edition of the cultural magazine *Rocinante*, its director, Faride Zerán, indicated as the cause of the closure the poor state of advertising. Left-wing magazines such as *Punto Final* and *El Periodista*, as well as the weekly magazine *El Siglo*, of the Communist Party, have also unsuccessfully demanded advertising from the public sector.

Ricardo Lagos Weber, son of the former president, Ricardo Lagos, and chief of staff during Michelle Bachelet's government, was also responsible for communication and media affairs. He believed that the state should make its advertising investment according to the circulation and ratings of the media, therefore following traditional market-driven criteria. This approach prevented the left-wing government from directly allocating advertising, and this contributed to the emergence and expansion of alternative media outlets, which could express different political and ideological views. A system of subsidies, alternative to that of advertising, is not acceptable either in this mercantilist atmosphere. Thus, pluralism and democracy lose. The voices excluded from the media system are not only those of the left-wing groups, but also those of other sectors, among them the sexual minorities. The newspaper *Opus Gay*,[15] of the Movement of Homosexual Liberation and Integration, has managed to launch five printed editions since its creation in 2001, with a good circulation, but sales covered less than 40 per cent of the costs. Due to lack of advertising, *Opus Gay* had to disappear as a printed medium and return to internet, like the majority of alternative media in Chile.

The state contributes 6 per cent of the total advertising investment in Chile. A study of by Observatory of Media-Fucatel,[16] based on government ministry data, autonomous state companies and public services, confirmed that *El Mercurio* is the greatest receiver of government advertising, with 41 per cent from the ministries and 32 per cent from public companies in 2005. For Copesa, *La Tercera* has a participation of 11 per cent and 15 per cent respectively, while *La Cuarta* receives 20 per cent of ministerial advertising and 11 per cent from public companies. In this case, *La Nación*, with 14 per cent of advertising from the ministries and 1 per cent from public companies, has a better deal than that of private business. The criteria of allocation of the business and state advertising guidelines do not correspond to the media circulation indexes, whose verification is in the hands, since 2003, of a system created by the National Press Association, the National Association of Advertisers and the Chilean Association of Advertising Agencies, based on periodic audits from the transnational consultant KPMG (Klynveld Pet Marwick Goerdeler). However, not all the media have agreed to participate in this system, the report of which, for the second semester of 2005, established the following circulation averages for the daily press: *El Mercurio*, 150,363 copies; *La Cuarta*, 136,503; *La Nación*, 6122; *La Tercera*, 124,034, *Las Últimas Noticias*, 143,999; *La Segunda*, 33,246; *Publimetro*, 84,711; *La Hora*, 96,000 and *La Hora de la Tarde*, 22,000 copies.

Regarding magazines, Copesa heads the ranking of the weekly magazines with the 71,581 copies of *Qué Pasa*. The same consortium produces every 15 days 71,354 copies of the female magazine *Paula* that is delivered free to the subscribers of *La Tercera*. Nevertheless, the great phenomenon of the Chilean press is the fortnightly magazine *The Clinic*, which began to circulate in 1999. This magazine adopted its name from the London hospital where the former dictator Augusto Pinochet was placed under arrest on 16 October 1998. With a transgressor style and irreverent language, this magazine has the special merit of having remained in the market thanks to its circulation, with average sales of 49,741 copies every 15 days, according to KPMG's report. *The Clinic* is not only a humorous magazine but covers urban issues, celebrity profiles, literature and films, popular gastronomy and social history. This magazine has become the best Chilean exponent of so-called 'narrative journalism'. From its pages, many people became famous, like Andrea Lagos, one of the best young journalists of these days, graduate of the School of Journalism of the University of Chile. Alejandra Delgado and Sebastián Foncea, from the same school, have been shortlisted for the Foundation of New Journalism prize of Gabriel Garcia Márquez, along with Verónica Torres, also a recent graduate of the University of Chile.

Although analyses of the quality, influence and business tendencies of the media industry tend to be focused in the press, it is also true that the great vehicle of information and entertainment for Chileans is television, and especially free access or terrestrial television. Reports from the National Council of Television (CNTV) indicate that the free access television is the source from which 80.8 per cent of Chileans obtain information on what happens in their city, 83.8 per cent on what occurs in Chile as a whole, and 74.9 per cent on world news. These indexes, from the year 2005,[17] show a progressive advance of the television medium, proportional to the loss of influence of the press. CNTV's own statistics and studies and those of the advertising agencies confirm that the groups C2, C3 and D are those that dedicate more hours to terrestrial television, while ABC1 emigrate constantly toward the paid television, either satellite or cable. Nevertheless, the contents of television advertising[18] are oriented, as in the press, to the segment ABC1, although programming is seeking to become more 'popular', with constant resort, even in the news programmes, to sensationalism and scandal, which are replacing cultural and international information, as has already been indicated. These orientations, influenced by the schizophrenia of the instant audience measurements of the People Meter, are a result, without doubt, of the dependence on advertising, with all the negative consequences that brings in terms of self-censorship and concealment of certain themes or facts. The power of advertisers has meant that the strikes of the unions of the Spanish transnational Telefónica did not become news, and nor did standstills in some large stores that are also first line contributors to advertising revenue.

It is unfair, nevertheless, to attribute the impoverishment of the news, and of television programming in general, to audiences from lower income strata. CNTV's last survey indicates that between 2002 and 2005, while television was winning more audiences, the percentage of Chileans that declared satisfaction with that medium descended from 54.4 to 40.3 per cent. In the particular case of the news programmes, the causes of public dissatisfaction indicate that there is an excess of news from Santiago and little from the rest of the country, as well as an overemphasis on the exploitation of human pain, too much information on crime, and strong political bias. It is also indicated that there are certain news stories that are intentionally not reported, that there is superficiality in the presentation of the information and that the time dedicated to football is excessive. Regarding themes, 72.4 per cent of Chileans consider environmental themes to be insufficiently covered. They also identify as insufficient the coverage of local or community matters (68.2 per cent), of science and technology (71.2 per cent) and of art and culture (73.8 per cent). On the other hand, they see as excessive the coverage of politics and government issues (66.6 per cent), football (40.2 per cent), police matters and delinquency (40.2 per cent).

Other relevant data from the CNTV surveys refers to the treatment of the different social sectors. Chileans consider as the most favoured actors (presented better than they are) political parties, television and 'show-biz' celebrities, government authorities, businessmen, the Catholic Church and the army. On the other hand, as more underprivileged actors, the indigenous people, the elderly, the workers, youth and the adolescents, the disabled, homosexuals and foreigners of neighbouring countries (particularly Bolivian and Peruvian emigrants) are seen to be presented in a poor light. Perhaps this is the greatest criticism of the characteristics of the mass media system in Chile that, for the sake of monopolistic concentration has established the rules for the re-establishment of democracy under the 'ideological monopoly' of neo-liberalism, and as a result falls far short of pluralism and equity, responding as it does to the interests of the dominant sectors, rather than those of citizens and society.

Notes

1   Mónica González is recognized as one of the best Chilean journalists, especially for her investigations into the violation of human rights and corruption under Augusto Pinochet's government (1973–90), for which she went to prison on two occasions. She is the author of the books *Bomb in a Street of Palermo* (with Edwin Harrington as co-author, 1986), *Chile Between Yes and No* (with Florencia Varas as co-author, 1988), *The Secrets of the Joint Command* (with Héctor Contreras as co-author, 1989) and *The Conspiracy: The Thousand and One Days of the Coup* (2000).

2   A conglomeration of parties of the centre and left under the name of Concentration of Parties for the NO, which headed the campaign to overthrow Pinochet in the presidential plebiscite of 5 October 1998, and acquired its current name in the electoral campaign of 1989. It has ruled with presidents Patricio Aylwin (1990–4) and Eduardo Frei Ruiz-Tagle (1994–2000), both Christian Democrats, and later with socialists Ricardo Lagos (2000–6) and Michelle Bachelet (2006–today). The parties that form the consensus (agreement pact) are the Socialist Party, the Christian Democratic Party, the Party for Democracy and the Radical Social-democratic Party.

3   It is not a minor fact that in Chile, it was only in 2004, 14 years after the re-establishment of democracy, the Parliament passed a law on divorce. Chile was the second-last western democracy to pass a law on divorce (it still does not exist in Malta), despite the fact that from the mid-1990s, surveys indicated that more than 70 per cent of the population supported such a law.

4   Patricia Verdugo, holder of the National Award for Journalism 1997, has written many journalistic books, especially about human rights: *An Open Wound* (1979), André of La Victoria (1984), *The Paws of the Puma* (1985), *Burnt Alive* (1986), *Operation 20th Century* (with Carmen Hertz as co-author, 1990), *Times of Bright Days* (1990), *Conversations with Nemesio Antúnez* (1995), *Secret Interference* (1998), *Bucarest 187* (1999), *Evidence in View* (2000), *The Enigma of Machu Picchu* (2001) and *How the USA Aborted the UP Project* (2003).

5   Alejandra Matus is also the author of *Crime with Punishment* (together with Francisco Artaza, 1996) and of *Long-lasting Injustice* (2002).

6 Mönckeberg published in 2001 *The Plundering of Economic Groups to the Chilean State*, in 2003 *The Opus Dei Empire in Chile* and in 2005 *The Privatization of the Universities: A Story of Money, Power and Influence*. She was also co-author of *Crime Under State of Siege* (1986).

7 Besides the Concertación de Partidos por la Democracia, there is also Alianza por Chile, that unites two parties: Unión Demócrata Independiente (UDI) and Partido Renovación Nacional (PRN). Thanks to the binominal system for legislative elections, only the Concertación and the Alianza parties are represented in Parliament and the Senate. The smaller groups such as the communists, the ecologists and the humanists have not managed to gain a place in Parliament.

8 These reforms restored the president's ability to remove people from high military command. They also eliminated the designated senators, reduced the previously powerful National Security Council to the role of adviser and reduced the powers of the Constitutional Tribunal. But not many other essential reforms were achieved, neither the change of the binominal system nor the constitutional recognition of the indigenous people.

9 The oldest newspaper in Chile. It also claims to be the oldest paper published in the Spanish language. It was founded on 12 September 1827 by liberal journalist Pedro Félix Vicuña, who afterwards became senator and representative in the Parliament. In 1880 this newspaper was acquired by Agustín Edwards Ross, who initiated the 'dynasty'. His son, Agustín Edwards McClure, founded El Mercurio de Santiago on 1 June 1900.

10 Strictly speaking, the original name of the newspaper was The Third One of The Hour, because it was the third edition. It was founded on 25 June 1935 by the Radical Party, that later would be identified with social democracy. The paper disappeared on 31 May 1951, although the name was kept and permitted Copesa to create a free newspaper to compete with Publimetro.

11 Diozel Pérez, former features editor-in-chief for Clarín, had the mission of creating La Cuarta, for which he hired Alberto Gamboa, director of Clarín in 1973 and political prisoner during the dictatorship. Pérez is still director of La Cuarta, while Gamboa went on to other journalistic projects.

12 See http://www.achap.cl.

13 See http://www.anda.cl.

14 Copesa also edits the weekly magazine Qué Pasa, which has the highest number of readers in its category and which receives the highest percentage of advertising investment in the magazine sector.

15 The conservative Catholic prelacy of Opus Dei attacked from the beginning the newspaper Opus Gay and even tried to prevent the use of that name with the argument that it caused offence to the followers of that religious group. Nevertheless, the Chilean courts rejected a lawsuit from Opus Dei in 2004.

16 Analysis of the Distribution of Advertising in State owned Compa-
    nies, 2004 and 2005. Media Observatory-Fucatel, Santiago, May
    2006. Available at http://www.observatoriofucatel.cl.
17 National Survey CNTV, 2005, available at http://www.cntv.cl.
18 According to ANDA, free-access television takes 56.27 per cent of the
    'advertising cake', a percentage that in 2004 was divided into
    17.6 per cent for the Catholic University Television Corporation,
    15.67 per cent for Megavisión and 13.07 per cent for Televisión
    Nacional. They are followed by Chilevisión, with 4.81 per cent; La
    Red, with 4.61 per cent and, lastly, the Catholic University of
    Valparaíso Channel, with 0.52 per cent.

6 THE MEDIA IN COLOMBIA: BEYOND VIOLENCE AND A MARKET-DRIVEN ECONOMY

Jorge Iván Bonilla, V. and
Ancízar Narváez Montoya

It is a founding principle of the liberal tradition that there is a 'fourth power'. This 'fourth power' emanates from civil society, being essentially non-governmental and autonomous to the extent that it curbs the abuses and excesses of official governmental rule. Some refer to this as the 'public opinion tribunal', the principal forum of which is the mass media, the chief function of which is to oversee – and even challenge – the public powers of the state. It is charged with the task of informing the public in a truthful, impartial and independent manner, in order to furnish citizens with the required information to make informed judgements (Habermas 1994: 212). This concept of the media was defined by two historical events: firstly, there was the appearance of the official press alongside the independent and bourgeois press. The official press came in the form of royal gazettes that were inextricably linked to absolutist power so as to defend the privileges of the clergy and the elite (Habermas 1994: 60). Secondly, the left wing press – or 'radical press' as it was known in the nineteenth century – strongly identified with the urban proletarian masses (Curran 1981: 241).

The itinerary of the modern mass media resembles a pendulum: it swings from assisting civil society to exercise its right to freedom of expression and to fight for independence and visibility in the public sphere, to being an instrument of governance that is firmly in the hands of the political and economic establishment. It is the latter scenario that best characterizes the mass media's momentum at present. Colombia's mass media has not escaped this dynamic and its journalistic and informative tradition is inscribed within the nation's political and cultural history, which is characterized by weak state institutions, an exclusive two-party political system and a strong Catholic legacy. Colombia has a total population of approximately 44 million inhabitants whose country has a history of recurring cultural and political upheaval. Its weak state institutions have required a permanent resort to force in order to resolve controversies. This tendency was apparent in the nineteenth century, when Colombia lived through 13 civil wars, a legacy that can be seen in the present internal armed conflict which has lasted more than 50 years. Paramilitary private armies, drug dealers and insurgent guerrillas are all participants in this struggle since all challenge the sovereignty of the state together with the country's vast national territories. In 1849, the Liberal and Conservative Parties were founded and Colombian politics have been characterized by an exclusive two-party system ever since. These parties entrenched a fundamental conflict over issues such as slavery, land ownership and the union or separation of Church and state. However, since the bi-partisan 'National Front' agreement of 1957, these parties have practically transformed into a state party that systematically excludes any alternatives. This can be seen today with the majority of support accruing to President Alvaro Uribe. Finally, the Spanish cultural legacy has ensured the building of a national identity out of the Catholic religion and the Spanish language. This has been at the expense of the Amerindian and Afro-descendant traditions, which have been both despised and persecuted as alien agents. It has also been at the expense of the enlightenment (positivist) tradition, which is reflected in the illiteracy index of nearly 9 per cent, as revealed recently by the 2005 population census, and in the growing influence of the Church on state decisions that violate citizens' civil rights.

Press, power and politics in the configuration of the nation

From the appearance of the first printed work to be published regularly, the *Newspaper Journal of the City of Santa Fe de Bogotá* on 9 February 1791, the Colombian press has been linked to the changing expressions of political power. From the very beginning, political parties and leaders quickly found their own newspaper spaces from which to promote their doctrines and ideological positions. On the other hand, the press has also assisted the staging of a symbolic representation of power, whereby battles have been played out for the nation's future direction. It is no coincidence that most heads of state over the past 120 years have practised journalism and consider themselves as 'men of the press' (Santos 1989: 118). This accounts for the censorship to which the press has long been subjected, together with the string of incarcerations, threats, assassinations and periods of exile suffered by Colombian journalists at the hands of local, regional and national authorities. This power has been exerted both with and without legal backing.

Given this scenario it is possible to distinguish four stages in the evolution of Colombia's written journalism: the colonial press, the revolutionary press, the doctrinarian-partisan press and the current press. The colonial press, which operated under the protection of the Spanish colonial government; it arrived in 1737. However, it lasted until the pre-independence movements of 1808. This coincided with the incipient formation of early 'reader societies' that were subject to monarchic rule, whose main exponent was the *Papel Periódico de la ciudad de Sante Fe de Bogotá* (1791–7). This paper was founded by the Cuban editor, Manuel del Socorro Rodríguez, who was a personal friend of the Viceroy Ezpeleta.

The revolutionary phase of the Colombian press began with the weekly newspaper *Nuevo Reino de Granada* (1808), founded by Manuel del Socorro Rodríguez and edited by Francisco José de Caldas. This phase saw the rise of true intellectual adventures that provided the foundation for the modern imagination with the unveiling of new political referents for the sovereign state (Uribe and Álvarez 1985). The loose pages and leaflets of this print media were used as political and ideological vehicles for promoting the ideas around a new nation of citizens. At this time, the following publications appeared: *La Constitución Feliz* of Manuel del Socorro Rodríguez, *Diario Político de Santa Fe de Bogotá* of Joaquín Camacho and Francisco José de Caldas, *La Bagatela* of Antonio Nariño and *Argos Americano* of José Fernández Madrid.

It was between 1819 and 1900 that contemporary Colombian journalism began. This was the phase in which the current press model emerged. This (family-run) model was characteristic of the second half of the nineteenth century and the first half of the twentieth, and it was politically dogmatic and ideologically doctrinarian. The press went along with the prevailing political ideology, whether federalist or centralist, Freemason or Catholic, Bolivirian or Santanderist, nationalist or unionist, to do with movements or sects. Riven with political divisions from the very outset, the newly-formed 'societies of ideas' played a fundamental role in transforming newspapers into the most important discursive arena of public life that was central to the formation of an electoral and partisan public rather than of a Colombian citizenry (Uribe and Álvarez 1985: xi).

As argued by Martín-Barbero and Rey, the Colombian press is heir to a deeply doctrinal, militant and partisan journalistic model, having been: 'inserted into the 20th century as a manifestation of a society more rural than urban, [having] barely enter[ed] into modernity'. The press, they argue 'fluctuat[es] between institutional drag' and support for 'risky movements for [political] change' (Martín-Barbero and Rey 1997: 14). The processes of political-cultural secularization and of economic modernization brought some transformations, mainly from the second half of the twentieth century. Journalism gradually moved from a family business structure – which even today is not an uncharacteristic structural model – to one in which ownership was concentrated in the hands of financial, economic or multi-media groups, or of journalists-turned-businessmen. This certainly impacted on the management of the news as well as on the renewal of the broadcasting technologies. It also affected conceptions of the readers' industry and market as well as that of national radio and television audiences. On the other hand, the US model of information production was to be more forcefully encouraged by the arrival of topical journalism in the editing room together with the first generation of university-educated journalists. This news structure was less doctrinarian and politically dogmatic and was closer to the objectivity model (Santos 1989: 129).

In this way, the Colombian press was to leave behind the days of intellectual ventures, scarce economic prospects and an ephemeral outlook. Despite the diversity of its publications, the press was to undergo a major process of reorganization from the 1960s onwards. Print journalism became a profitable economic activity that was concentrated on a very few titles, implying the paring down of information choices and a greater concentration of newspaper ownership. Conversely this also made newspapers a more precarious business venture, as demonstrated by a recent investigation (Vallejo 2006: 390–412). From the 167 newspapers founded in Colombia between 1880 and 1980, only around 35 still exist, of which four are published by the same publishing house as the newspaper *El Tiempo* (*Boyacá 7 días, El Llano 7 días, Tolima 7 días* and *Hoy*) and one by *El Colombiano* (*La Chiva*). This is made clear in Table 6.1.

Table 6.1 Colombian newspapers, 1927–2006

Department/region	1927	1985	2006
Antioquia	5	2	3
Atlántico	5	3	2
Bolivar	4	1	1
Boyacá y Meta	0	1	2
Caldas, Risaralda and Quindio	3	3	4
Córdoba and Sucre	0	0	2
Cauca	0	1	1
Bogotá D.C.	10	7	8
Magdalena	2	2	2
Nariño	1	2	1
Santander	2	4	1
Norte de Santander	2	2	1
Tolima and Huila	0	1	4
Valle	3	4	3
Total	37	33	35

Source: based on *El periodismo en Colombia, 1886–1986* and *Asociación Nacional de Diarios de Colombia, ANDIARIOS*

The current composition of national written journalism consists of around 80 current news magazines together with sports, gossip and celebrity magazines and culture and entertainment publications, which have experienced a recent boom in sales thanks to the arrival of foreign publishing houses in the country. Table 6.2 defines the current structure of the so-called national 'reference press', which is characterized by the existence of a significant number of newspapers and magazines published in Bogota. These are linked to the families of presidents of the republic and to economic groups of considerable influence in the country's governance. Related to these are the regional newspapers, which also enjoy some close economic and political links (Herrán 1991).

Table 6.2 Main newspapers and magazines in the country at present

Name of publication	Date founded	Description	Ownership
El Espectador	1887	Liberal newspaper, initially published in Medellín. Since 1915 published in Bogotá. It was a journal until 1999. Since then it has become a weekly paper.	Owned by the Cano family until 1997 when it was purchased by the Santodomingo Group.
El Tiempo	1911	Liberal newspaper, published in Bogotá.	Owned by the Santos family, head of the El Tiempo Publishing House, the ninth economic group in the country. Several members of this family have been linked to government for many generations.
El Colombiano	1912	Conservative newspaper, published in Medellín.	Owned by the Gómez Martínez family, linked to regional and national power through senators, ministers, governors and mayors.
Revista Cromos	1916	Weekly variety magazine, published in Bogotá.	Purchased in 1996 by the Santodomingo Group.
Vanguardia Liberal	1919	Liberal newspaper, published in Bucaramanga.	Owned by the Propiedad Galvis Ramírez family.

Name of publication	Date founded	Description	Ownership
El País	1919	Conservative newspaper, published in Cali.	Owned by the Lloreda family, linked to national and regional political power.
La Patria	1921	Conservative newspaper, voice of the coffee growers, published in Manizales.	Owned by the Restrepo family, linked to regional power of the Caldas departments.
El Heraldo	1933	Liberal newspaper published in Barranquilla. First paper of the Caribbean Coast with influence in seven departments.	Owned by the Fernández and Pumarejo families, linked to the regional power of the Colombian Caribbean coast.
El Siglo	1936	Conservative newspaper, published in Bogotá.	Founded by former Colombian president Laureano Gómez and inherited by the Gómez Hurtado family.
Revista Semana	1946	Weekly current affairs magazine, published in Bogotá.	Founded by Colombian ex-president Alberto Lleras Camargo. Closed in 1961 and re-founded by the family of ex-president López Michelsen in 1982.
La República	1954	Conservative newspaper, published in Bogotá.	Founded by ex-president Marianao Ospina Pérez. It is currently owned by the newspaper El Colombiano, from Medellín that purchased it at the end of the 1990s.

Name of publication	Date founded	Description	Ownership
Voz Proletaria	1963	Weekly paper of the Colombian Communist Party, published in Bogotá.	It survives with economic difficulties as the voice of this political organization.
El Espacio	1965	Sensational events newspaper, published in Bogotá	Founded and owned by the Ardila Casamijana family, one of whose members is the current governor of the Cundinamarca department.
La Tarde	1975	Liberal newspaper, published in Pereira.	Founded and controlled by the family of Colombian ex-president Cesar Gaviria Trujillo.
El Mundo	1979	Liberal newspaper, published in Medellín.	Owned by the Gaviria family. Directed by the current governor of Antioquia department's father.
Revista Cambio	1993	Weekly current affairs magazine, published in Bogotá.	Founded by Gabriel García Márquez and a group of Colombian journalists as a franchise from the Spanish magazine Cambio. In 2006 it was purchased by El Tiempo Publishing House.

Source: based on Herrán (1991) and Vallejo (2006)

What, then, is the market for readers of the country's main newspapers and magazines? The penetration of the press in Colombia is 26.6 per cent, that is to say, it reaches only 3,658,000 people (in round figures, see Table 6.3). Thirty-five newspapers are required to supply that demand. This includes the regional papers, leaving aside monthly and weekly newspapers, among which are some opposition newspapers such as the Communist Party's weekly *Semanario Voz*. This suggests that, if we only take newspapers into account, the average press readership barely reaches 112,150 people.

Table 6.3 Newspapers, reading and control

Name	Ownership	Circulation	%
El Tiempo	El Tiempo Publishers	1,265,000	9.2
El Espectador	Santodomingo Group	783,750	5.7
El Espacio	J. Ardila C. & Co.	426,250	3.1
Hoy	El Tiempo Publishers	385,000	2.8
El Heraldo	El Heraldo Ltd.	275,000	2.0
El País	El País S.A.	261,250	1.9
El Colombiano	El Colombiano Ltd. S.A.	261,250	1.9
Total		3,657,500	26.6

Source: based on the *General Media Study 2002-II*

Newspapers' main competition is neither the television nor the radio but other print media such as journalistic magazines and graphic design publications. In Colombia, independent magazines that are not circulated alongside newspapers have a far wider circulation, reaching 40.3 per cent of potential press audiences, a percentage that equates to 5,541,000 people. Eighty recognized titles meet this demand, which amounts to some 69,262 magazine readers on average. However, the figures shown in Table 6.4 suggest that there is a sort of oligopoly consisting of a small number of publications, indicating that the business is by no means profitable for all and that their existence bows to other kinds of interests.

Table 6.4 Magazines, reading and control

Name	Ownership	Circulation	%
Semana	Semana Publications	942,900	06.9
Cromos	Santodomingo Group	529,300	03.8
Dinero	Dinero Publications	248,100	01.8
Cambio	El Tiempo Publishers	226,000	01.6
Gerente		39,900	00.3
Others (75 more titles)		3,555,050	25.9
Total		5,541,250	40.3

Source: based on the *General Media Study 2005-II*

The radio: the modernization project and its integration into the market

In Colombia, the historic development of the radio is framed by the process of modernization, initiated in the 1920s and accelerating during the 1940s. In contrast to the press, radio ownership revealed an alternative manifestation of power, which, although still linked to politics, was more defined by the private, commercial nature ascribed to this medium from the outset. The radio integrated a regionally fragmented nation, which had been divided not only by the civil wars and precarious governance, but also by the country's mountainous terrain. With greater spontaneity and agility, the radio quickly became highly popular since the medium was able to find the technological link that facilitated the circulation of national, regional and local expression, mainly through music and popular drama, comedy and humour (Martín-Barbero and Rey 1997: 15).

To speak of the evolution of the radio in Colombia is to understand the medium's role in the nation's regional integration. This has been achieved by an altogether different means than the route followed by the press, since it has involved a greater decentralization of broadcasting as well as listening practices, a decentralization beyond the boundaries of the capital city. Table 6.5 shows the trans-regional reach of the medium, which has been consolidated by a system of 'linkage' that has permitted the creation of programmes with wide coverage and national audiences (CAB 2003: 169–86).

Table 6.5 Commercial radio stations (AM and FM) by regions in Colombia, 2002

Region	Number of stations
Antioquia	170
Atlántico	54
Bolívar	40
Boyacá	75
Caldas	40
Cesar	28
Cauca	37
Bogotá D.C.	32
Santander	71
Norte de Santander	21
Tolima	22
Valle	77

Source: Convenio Andrés Bello (2003: 174)

Radio in Colombia has embarked on a number of odysseys. One of these is related to the rising intention of the Colombian state to make this medium an ally in the civilizing project of the nation. This was exactly what was intended with the creation, in September 1929, of the state-owned radio station H.J.N., whose fundamental objective was to use its programming to transmit education, civic instruction and culture to the illiterate masses of a basically illiterate country. This civilizing project was lent greater force from 1940, with the opening of Radiodifusora Nacional at a time when 46 per cent of the population over 7 years was illiterate. This event renewed official interest in spearheading 'national culture' by means of the radio (Castellanos 2001: 330–434).

The second great journey of the radio in Colombia relates to its early connection with wealthy economic groups. This connection ensured the financial support for the required technological innovations but also secured a flow of advertising revenue to its programmes (Castellanos 2001: 256).

These groups gradually began to exert control over a large number of radio stations either by buying their broadcast rights or by opening new radio stations in different locations across the country. This allowed for a concentration of ownership in two oligarchies: Cadena Radial Colombi-ana (Caracol), established in 1948, and Radio Cadena Nacional (RCN), established in 1949. In the shadow of these, other radio stations have emerged and consolidated, such as Todelar, Super, Melodía, Organización Radial Olímpica and Colmundo Radio, although this has happened on a smaller scale. This growth has depended on the ability to network with the traditional powerful economic elites, which have lately felt threatened by the competition of new players such as the Spanish business consor-tium Prisa. Indeed, in 2000, Prisa acquired the majority of Caracol Radio shares as part of its interest in expanding into Latin American markets by means of its company Grupo Latino de Radio (GLR).

The third journey undertaken by the medium relates to the narratives and programming proposals that would make unprecedented connections between the local and the national. As Martín-Barbero and Rey (1997: 15) point out:

during these years, Colombian radio experimented with a genre that began, little by little, to shape its own creation: comedy programmes that ridiculed customs and in some cases even politics; radio soaps that took love or adventure stories to people's homes, anticipating a form of popular drama that later evolved into television melodrama; news programmes that mixed local and national perceptions of the news; live broadcasts that freed themselves from the restrictions of the written text by shaping an impression of live coverage of events; advice columns in which the people could talk about taboo subjects not yet tackled, indeed at times strenuously avoided, by the teach-ings and explanations of formal education.

The fourth route followed by the radio pertains to the medium's technological innovations that enabled it to compete for listeners and advertisers. The arrival of satellite and FM in the 1980s widened programming horizons. Besides having more extensive coverage, programming began to diversify thanks to the possibility of obtaining satellite information and to the availability of a different frequency to AM. This promoted the expansion of more diverse programming together with the subdivision of audiences as a marketing strategy and the establishment of radio stations that specialized in diverse themes such as music, sports and news. Although this practice was nothing new, having been established in the 1960s, it became characteristic of the market in the 1980s. In this way, Caracol and RCN, in the hands of the Santodomingo and Ardila Lülle groups respectively, together with Cadena Todelar, saw in radio the opportunity to advertise their businesses. With this in mind, they skilfully managed their marketing strategies in ways that lent the medium greater support. Caracol and RCN became internationalized and integrated with global systems of information, and with radial businesses in other countries. Caracol, for example, established links with Emisora Líder of Miami, while RCN linked up with other radio stations across the continent.

In this respect, radio in Colombia has seen considerable growth. From 589 radio licences issued in 1991 by the Department of Communications (409 in AM and 180 in FM), the issuing of licenses increased to 867 in 1998 (442 in AM and 425 in FM). According to figures from this department, which is responsible for regulating the legislative framework of radio in Colombia (Ministerio de Comunicaciones 2004), the number of radio stations grew noticeably in 2004. This growth was mainly in FM radio stations, which reached a total of 2115 (920 in AM and 1195 in FM), which were classified as commercial, community and public interest stations. Seventy per cent of these are concentrated in urban areas. Currently, 98.5 per cent of homes receive AM and 97.5 per cent FM (see Table 6.6).

Table 6.6 Radio stations by mode

Mode	AM	FM
Commercial	399	257
Public interest	61	106
Communitarian	460	832
Total	920	1,195

Source: Ministry of Communications of Colombia (2004)

In this context, it is worth emphasizing the long route taken by community radio stations, a route that has been negotiated by collective groups and social organizations as well as by the Catholic Church. All this has taken place in the framework of a process that has served as a mechanism to fortify civic participation and the democratization of ownership, although many radio stations are in precarious financial situations. Similarly, public interest radio stations stand out, operated by the government, mayoral offices, universities, municipal institutes, public libraries and even the police (police and army). At present the military has a radio network – Cadena Radial del Ejército Nacional – which includes 32 radio stations throughout the country, which is used as an ally against the counter-insurgent war taking place in Colombia.

Of the existing radio stations in 2002, 171 were linked to eight large radio networks. In spite of this apparent variety, however, the control of the oligopoly is evident (Convenio Andrés Bello 2003: 178). Of the radio networks, 54 (32 per cent) belong to Caracol, while 66 (38.6 per cent) belong to RCN. These two groups control almost 70 per cent of the affiliated radio networks and more than 18 per cent of non-affiliated commercial radio. Worse still is the control of the advertising market, the main source of funding for commercial radio. By 2002, Caracol received 40.8 per cent and RCN 39.6 per cent of all radio advertisement revenue: in all, with barely less than 20 per cent of the commercial radio stations, these two groups control 80 per cent of the advertising market.

The figures in Table 6.7 are also significant. The majority of the 20 most listened-to stations in the country are controlled by the two biggest radio networks of Colombia – that is to say, by two business groups and a Spanish media group. It should be added that the radio stations (Caracol AM and RCN Bogotá AM) are the main informative stations of the two networks. However, their sports, informative and variety production is replicated on AM frequencies in several cities throughout the country: in the case of RCN, 84 AM frequencies in 56 cities, and in that of Caracol, with a basic frequency in AM, in 22 cities.

Table 6.7 Radio, audience and control

Name	Owned by	Audience	%
Caracol Tropicana Estéreo FM 0157	Prisa-Santodomingo	814,000	5.92
Caracol La Vallenata FM 0164	Prisa-Santodomingo	594,000	4.32
Caracol Radioactiva	Prisa-Santodomingo	393,250	2.86
RCN Amor Estereo	Ardila Lülle	352,000	2.56
Oxígeno FM		349,250	2.54
Caracol AM	Prisa-Santodomingo	306,625	2.23
RCN La Mega	Ardila Lülle	291,500	2.12

Name	Owned by	Audience	%
Caracol La Vallenata FM 0464	Prisa-Santodomingo	288,750	2.10
RCN Radio Uno	Ardila Lülle	283,250	2.06
Radio Recuerdos		273,625	1.99
Caracol Tropicana Estéreo FM 0757	Prisa-Santodomingo	251,625	1.83
Súper Estación	Super	246,125	1.79
Caracol Los 40 principales	Prisa-Santodomingo	233,750	1.70
RCN Rumba Estéreo	Ardila Lülle	255,500	1.64
Caracol La Vallenata FM 0764	Prisa-Santodomingo	220,000	1.60
Caracol FM 0181	Prisa-Santodomingo	215,875	1.57
Caracol Radio Reloj	Prisa-Santodomingo	203,500	1.48
La Voz de Colombia		188,375	1.37
Caracol AM	Prisa-Santodomingo	187,000	1.36
RCN Bogotá AM	Ardila Lülle	185,625	1.35

Source: based on General Media Study 2005-II. To calculate the radio audience, Convenio Andrés Bello (2003: 167–86).

Here the evidence is conclusive: of the top 20 stations within the country in terms of audience share, 11 are controlled by the Prisa-Santodomingo group, with almost 27 per cent of the audience share, and five are controlled by the Organization Ardila Lülle, with almost 10 per cent of the total national audience (see Table 6.8). The remaining 98 per cent of radio stations (155 network radio stations and 640 commercial radio stations) have barely 65 per cent of the audience. The two groups, which represent 2 per cent of the stations, have more than 36 per cent of the audience when only the first 20 stations are considered.

Table 6.8 Radio, control and audience by economic group

Name	Owned by	Audience	%
Oxígeno FM		349,250	2.54
Radio Recuerdos		273,625	1.99
Súper Estación	Super	246,125	1.79
La Voz de Colombia		188,375	1.37
RCN Amor Estereo	Ardila Lülle	352,000	2.56
RCN La Mega	Ardila Lülle	291,500	2.12
RCN Radio Uno	Ardila Lülle	283,250	2.06

Name	Owned by	Audience	%
RCN Rumba Estéreo	Ardila Lülle	255,500	1.64
RCN Bogotá AM	Ardila Lülle	185,625	1.35
Caracol Tropicana Estéreo FM 0157	Prisa-Santodomingo	814,000	5.92
Caracol La Vallenata FM 0164	Prisa-Santodomingo	594,000	4.32
Caracol Radioactiva	Prisa-Santodomingo	393,250	2.86
Caracol AM	Prisa-Santodomingo	306,625	2.23
Caracol La Vallenata FM 0464	Prisa-Santodomingo	288,750	2.10
Caracol Tropicana Estéreo FM 0757	Prisa-Santodomingo	251,625	1.83
Caracol Los 40 principales	Prisa-Santodomingo	233,750	1.70
Caracol La Vallenata FM 0764	Prisa-Santodomingo	220,000	1.60
Caracol FM 0181	Prisa-Santodomingo	215,875	1.57
Caracol Radio Reloj	Prisa-Santodomingo	203,500	1.48
Caracol AM	Prisa-Santodomingo	187,000	1.36

Source: based on *General Media Study 2005-II.* To calculate the radio audience, Convenio Andrés Bello (2003: 167–86).

Television: the market and its audiences

Television in Colombia began as a state project on 13 June 1954. The first television programme established the style and structure of programming in forthcoming years. A greeting from the then president of the nation, General Gustavo Rojas Pinilla, who was celebrating a year of government that day, was followed by the international newscast *Tele News*, then a classical music concert, a documentary film, a live adaptation of a traditional story of national customs, the presentation of a funny sketch and of a folkloric dance, all broadcast by the technical services of Televisora Nacional, a company assigned to the Information and Press Bureau of the Presidency of the Republic (Rey 2002: 118).

Since then, national television has undergone several stages of change. The first phase corresponds to the creation of the Televisora National (1954–64), which initially started as only one channel with a particular kind of programming. There were television dramas that used images from works of national and international literature. There was news in a cinema format and there were the first educational programmes, made by personnel who had migrated from radio to television production.

Subsequently, a dual programming structure emerged: a commercial one and an educational one. This coincided with the advent of television advertising, which soon established itself as a profitable strategy that would soon begin to define the type of programmes that were offered to the general public (Vizcaíno 1999: 475–80).

The second significant moment for television in Colombia was the creation of the Colombian Institute of Radio and Television, INRAVISIÓN (1964–2004). In 1964, the year of its creation, this network covered virtually the entire country. Due to the scarcity of economic resources, the government was unable to invest in television and this situation led to the opening of the first bid for the commercial exploitation of, and investment in, the service. This later became known as the 'mixed' system of Colombian television, which established a type of regulated market that would last for more than 30 years (Herrán 1991: 172). This led to a form of national programming that had inflexible schedules, jealously guarded screen allocations, own styles of production and genres that attracted large audiences and established soap operas as the national television staple. During this phase, the cultural channel (known today as Señal Colombia) was established. 1985 saw the rise of regional television channels.

The third phase corresponds with the establishment, and development, of private concession, which began to operate in June 1998 after the passing of Laws 182 (1995), 336 (1996) and 335 (1997). This has led to a genuine transformation of the Colombian television industry, especially with regard to production, which has responded to a new spate of alliances with television businesses with stakes in the Hispanic market of the USA. This is the case with Telemundo and Univisión. The structure of programming itself, including screen quotas that in prime time account for 70 per cent of the national production, is being adapted to television ratings and market demands, which are increasingly more a criterion for planning television programming and schedules. Two private channels, Caracol Televisión and RCN Televisión, have arisen, both part of powerful economic groups with interests in the beer market, in aviation, telecommunications, the energy, textile, food and other production industries and in the financial markets.

There are currently two private national terrestrial channels operating in Colombia. These are RCN Televisión and Caracol Televisión. In addition there are seven public regional channels located on the islands of San Andrés and Providencia (Tele Islas), the Caribbean coast (Tele Caribe), the region of North Santander and the border with Venezuela (Televisión Regional de Oriente, TRO), the central coffee region (Tele Café), Antioquia (Tele Antioquia), the central zone and the old national territories (TV Andina-Canal 13), the Pacific coast (Tele Pacífico), and Canal Capital in Bogotá. Besides this, there is a third national commercial terrestrial channel (Channel 1), which is programmed by private concessionaires who rent the channel frequency from the state. To these we might add a public interest, cultural and educational channel called Señal Colombia and another named Señal Colombia Institucional, which nowadays broadcasts congressional sessions, information about government acts and, in short, political propaganda emerging from various state entities. Equally, there is only one private channel of local coverage (CityTV), which is operated by the Casa Editorial El Tiempo. This list does not include the large number of non-profit local community television channels (probably more than 300), or the university channels, which have been formed by university consortiums operating from three regions of the country: Antioquia, Atlántico and Valle.

In spite of the apparent range of viewing options, the reality for audiences, and – correspondingly – for business and influence, is very different. The television licence that started in 1998 not only allowed the creation of two private channels with national coverage (RCN and Caracol) and a local channel in Bogotá (CityTV) but also supported the growth of the private television business. The concesion of new broadcasting licences coincided with an increase of audiences for these channels (see Table 6.9). In these concessions, the private channels also have the advantage of having their own guidclincs (Bonilla and González 2004: 46–57) in three senses: firstly, the advertising expense goes from one of the group's businesses to fortify the income of another business of the same group. In this way, the group Ardila Lülle, owner of RCN, controls 46 businesses (Silva 2003: 216–18) and 3.7 per cent of gross domestic product (GDP), the Santodomingo group, owner of Caracol TV, controls 88 businesses (Silva 2003: 115–19) and, therefore, 10.9 per cent of GDP. Secondly, the private television channels charge lower rates to businesses within the same economic group. Thirdly, since this own-discount lowers the projected income of concessionary contract media businesses, they are in a position to sue the state for income 'not received', and in this way they increase their profits at the expense of the public purse. In other words, not only does the state allow them to profit from a public service, but it also provides them and their business alliances with financial support (see Table 6.9).

Table 6.9 Television audience and control

Name	Owned by	Audience	%
RCN	Ardila Lülle	12,278,750	89.3
Caracol	Grupo Santodomingo	12,072,500	87.8
City TV	Casa Editorial El Tiempo	3,355,000	24.5
Canal 1	Concesión	2,681,000	19.5
Señal Colombia	Público Nacional	2,337,500	17.0
Canal 13	Público Regional	1,512,500	11.0
Tele Caribe	Público Regional	1,223,750	8.9
Tele Pacífico	Público Regional	1,155,000	8.4

Name	Owned by	Audience	%
Tele Antioquia	Público Regional	1,141,250	8.3
Canal Capital	Público Regional	1,127,500	8.2
Canal A	Público Nacional	893,750	6.5
Tele Café	Público Regional	398,750	2.9

Source: based on the *General Media Study 2005-II*

The figures in Table 6.9 have a more sinister appearance: besides the existence in Colombia of media monopolies such as the Casa Editorial El Tiempo, there are no restraints on the horizontal integration of media capital with other economic sectors. The most powerful economic alliances also own the most influential media outlets due both to the size of their audiences and because of their advertising revenue (see Table 6.10).

Table 6.10 General overview of the media according to audience

Medium	Name	Owned by	Audience	%
TV	RCN	Ardila Lülle	12,278,750	89.30
TV	Caracol	Grupo Santodomingo	12,072,500	87.30
TV	City TV	Casa Editorial El Tiempo	3,355,000	24.50
TV	Canal 1	Concesión	2,681,250	19.50
Prensa	El Tiempo	Casa Editorial El Tiempo	1,265,000	09.20
Internet	El Tiempo	Casa Editorial El Tiempo	1,134,700	08.20
Revistas	Semana	Publicaciones Semana	942,900	06.90
Radio	Caracol Tropicana Estéreo FM 0157	Prisa-Santodomingo	814,000	05.92
Prensa	El Espectador	Santodomingo	783,750	05.70
Radio	Caracol La Vallenata FM 0164	Prisa-Santodomingo	594,000	04.32
Revistas	Cromos	Grupo Santodomingo	529,300	03.80
Prensa	El Espacio	J. Ardila C. & Cia	426,250	03.10
Radio	Caracol Radioactiva	Prisa-Santodomingo	393,250	02.86
Prensa	Hoy	Casa Editorial El Tiempo	385,000	02.80

Medium	Name	Owned by	Audience	%
Radio	RCN Amor Estereo	Ardila Lülle	352,000	02.56
Radio	Oxígeno FM		349,250	02.54
Radio	Caracol AM	Prisa-Santodomingo	306,625	02.23
Radio	RCN La Mega	Ardila Lülle	291,500	02.12
Radio	Caracol La Vallenata FM 0464	Prisa-Santodomingo	288,750	02.10
Radio	RCN Radio Uno	Ardila Lülle	283,250	02.06
Prensa	El Heraldo	El Heraldo Ltd	275,000	02.00
Radio	Radio Recuerdos		273,625	01.99
Prensa	El Colombiano	El Colombiano Ltd & Cia	261,250	01.90
Prensa	El País	El País S.A.	261,250	01.90
Revistas	Dinero	Publicaciones Dinero	248,100	01.80
Internet	El Espectador	Grupo Santodomingo	232,200	01.70
Revistas	Cambio	Casa Editorial El Tiempo	226,000	01.60
Internet	Portafolio	Casa Editorial El Tiempo	199,000	01.40
Internet	El Colombiano	El Colombiano Ltd & Cia	181,300	01.30
Internet	El Heraldo	El Heraldo Ltd	123,600	00.90
Internet	El País	El País S.A.	120,500	00.90
Internet	El Diario Deportivo		86,100	00.60
Internet	La República	El Colombiano Ltd & Cia	70,500	00.50
Revistas	Gerente		39,900	00.30
Internet	Vanguardia Liberal	Galvis Ramírez y Cía	48,100	00.30
Internet	El Espacio	J. Ardila C. & Cia	46,700	00.30

Source: based on *General Media Study 2005-II*. To calculate radio audience, Convenio Andrés Bello (2003: 167–86).

This scenario reveals that media, political and economic power are essentially one and the same to the extent that the media identify with the same political project that defines corporate interests. This is what has allowed the media to develop a virtual monopoly. On the one hand, they operate information and entertainment businesses that are perpetually subject to the rating demands, with all that implies. On the other, they are businesses actively defending a political project that can guarantee their development as businesses and even as monopolies. In the final analysis, the news agenda is deeply compromised by the political ambitions of some of the most powerful economic elites in the country; ultimately they are an integral part of the corporate framework (see Table 6.11).

Table 6.11 General overview of the media according to ownership and control

Medium	Name	Owned by	Audience	%
Radio	Oxígeno FM		349,250	02.54
Press	El Heraldo	El Heraldo Ltd	275,000	02.00
Radio	Radio Recuerdos		273,625	01.99
Internet	El Heraldo	El Heraldo Ltd	123,600	00.90
Internet	El Diario Deportivo		86,100	00.60
Magazines	Gerente		39,900	00.30
TV	RCN	Ardila Lülle	12,278,750	89.30
Radio	RCN Amor Estereo	Ardila Lülle	352,000	02.56
Radio	RCN La Mega	Ardila Lülle	291,500	02.12
Radio	RCN Radio Uno	Ardila Lülle	283,250	02.06
TV	City TV	Casa Editorial El Tiempo	3,355,000	24.50
Press	El Tiempo	Casa Editorial El Tiempo	1,265,000	09.20
Internet	El Tiempo	Casa Editorial El Tiempo	1,134,700	08.20
Press	Hoy	Casa Editorial El Tiempo	385,000	02.80
Magazines	Cambio	Casa Editorial El Tiempo	226,000	01.60
Internet	Portafolio	Casa Editorial El Tiempo	199,000	01.40
TV	Canal 1	Concesión	2,681,250	19.50

Medium	Name	Owned by	Audience	%
Press	El Colombiano	El Colombiano Ltd & Cia	261,250	01.90
Internet	El Colombiano	El Colombiano Ltd & Cia	181,300	01.30
Internet	La República	El Colombiano Ltd & Cia	70,500	00.50
Press	El País	El País S.A.	261,250	01.90
Internet	El País	El País S.A.	120,500	00.90
Internet	Vanguardia Liberal	Galvis Ramírez y Cía	48,100	00.30
Press	El Espacio	J. Ardila C. & Cia	426,250	03.10
Internet	El Espacio	J. Ardila C. & Cia	46,700	00.30
Radio	Caracol Tropicana Estéreo FM 0157	Prisa-Santodomingo	814,000	05.92
Radio	Caracol La Vallenata FM 0164	Prisa-Santodomingo	594,000	04.32
Radio	Caracol Radioactiva	Prisa-Santodomingo	393,250	02.86
Radio	Caracol AM	Prisa-Santodomingo	306,625	02.23
Radio	Caracol La Vallenata FM 0464	Prisa-Santodomingo	288,750	02.10
Magazines	Dinero	Publicaciones Dinero	248,100	01.80
Magazines	Semana	Publicaciones Semana	942,900	06.90
TV	Caracol	Grupo Santodomingo	12,072,500	87.30
Press	El Espectador	Grupo Santodomingo	783,750	05.70
Magazines	Cromos	Grupo Santodomingo	529,300	03.80
Internet	El Espectador	Grupo Santodomingo	232,200	01.70

Source: based on *General Media Study 2005-II*. To calculate radio audience, Convenio Andrés Bello (2003: 167–86).

Violence against journalists: censorship, war and politics

Moving on from the question of ownership structures, we turn to another characteristic of the mass media in Colombia, whereby journalism is caught in the crossfire of armed actors in the conflict: journalists are both 'targets' and 'victims' of this conflict. Why does this occur? For journalists, the answer to this question has two main facets. In the first place, there is a theory that journalists are at risk not only because of constant threats and intimidation, but also because of the lack of an umbrella organization that can defend them and promote professional solidarity. There is a belief that the main reason journalists become victims – additional victims – of the armed conflict is that they are poorly educated professionals with 'mixed' labour links (editorial chiefs, public relations officers and collaborators) that they generally establish with different seats of power in the regions dominated and disputed by the 'warlords': from corrupt politicians and soldiers, to the paramilitary, guerrillas and organized common criminals.

According to reports by the Fundación para la Libertad de Prensa (FLIP), 40 journalists were murdered in the country between 1995 and 2005 because of their profession (see Table 6.12). In the regions more affected by the conflict, freedom of the press is precarious, either due to intimidation and murder, which have silenced many voices, or due to self-censorship. According to a study carried out by the think-tank Medios para la Paz (2004), 65 per cent of journalists in 24 intermediate cities and areas of influence of the armed conflict report that they have been intimidated, while 32 per cent report that they have not been intimidated. When asked about their intimidation, 19 per cent answered that it came from unknown people, 13 per cent blamed the guerrilla group Revolutionary Armed Forces of Colombia (FARC), 11 per cent blamed the paramilitaries, 3 per cent the regular armed forces and the National Liberation Army (ELN) equally, while 4 per cent preferred not to answer the question.

This data coincides with previous research carried out by the pro-freedom of expression NGO FLIP (Fundación para la Libertad de Prensa) regarding the question of who threatens the press in Colombia. According to them, there is always difficulty in determining the authors of murders and threats against journalists within a framework of generalized impunity that causes the journalists to encounter trouble, not only when publishing the information they collect, but also when they do not always manage to identify and repel the pressures to which they are subjected. This is despite the efforts of the national government, which, on 10 August 2000, established the Program for the Protection of Journalists and Social Communicators, in order to guarantee the safety of journalists at risk – many institutions of the Colombian state, the Office of the High Commissioner of the United Nations for Refugees and some journalists' organizations are part of this programme.

Table 6.12 Violations of the freedom of the press, 2002–5

Type	2002	2003	2004	2005
Murder	3	5	1	2
Murder during coverage	1	1	0	0
Injured during coverage	0	1	0	2
Threatening	75	55	39	64
Abduction	12	11	0	1
Exile	No data	7	5	6
Inhuman or degrading treatment	13	5	17	15
Obstruction of journalistic work	3	8	19	6
Total	107*	93*	81*	96*

Source: Foundation for the Freedom of Press (*Fundación para la Libertad de Prensa*)
*The same journalist could suffer more than one violation

Given this situation, is it possible to ask the media to develop a national cultural project? Given the way they are constrained by economic logic of a market-driven economy and limited by a form of self-censorship that reflects the conditions of reporting in a context of generalized violence. One would think not, yet, as in other cases, the media has an emerging national project, but this is not necessarily that of democracy and self determination. It is one where economic capital can flourish within the framework of free speech under certain legal protections. However, in practice, that freedom of speech is being eroded on several different fronts.

7 THE MEDIA IN COSTA RICA: MANY MEDIA, SCARCE COMMUNICATION

Carlos Sandoval-García

This chapter offers an overview on the media institutions in Costa Rica.[1] Its starting point is to consider the media as part of wider processes of urbanization, literacy and secularization in Costa Rican society. Then the chapter moves on to the current situation, looking at three key dimensions: media ownership, offerings and audiences. A main tendency in terms of ownership has been the formation of oligopolies in the television, advertising and printed media sectors. Media programming is characterized by a situation in which homogeneity rules over diversity in content and cultural forms. While distribution of printed media audiences depends upon income and literacy, these factors do not seem to affect television audiences' habits in the same way. The last section of the chapter explores access to the internet, in which Costa Rica exhibits one of the highest indicators of connectivity in Latin America. The chapter ends by showing the paradox that while the media has been demanding politicians and other public actors be accountable for their acts, especially those regarding corruption, the media itself is rarely accountable for its own institutional practices.

Historical background

The first printing press arrived in Costa Rica in 1830, a few years later than in El Salvador (1824) and Honduras (1829). Guatemala, as the colonial capital of the region, introduced it in 1660. The first Costa Rican newspaper, whose title was *Noticiero Universal,* dates back to 1833 (Molina and Fumero 1997: 136).

In Costa Rica, literacy was a precondition for the expansion of the printing industry during the period between 1890 and 1950. Based on the analysis of data provided by the census, Iván Molina (1997: 33) has noted that towards the end of the twentieth century 51.6 per cent of the urban population was able to read and write. Meanwhile, 23.2 per cent of the rural population had this capacity. The census of 1950 reported that 91.9 per cent of the urban population was in command of writing and reading, and 71.5 per cent of rural population held these capacities (p. 44).

Between 1880 and 1914, 87.6 per cent of the press was printed in the capital San José. Although books and pamphlets were published by a government press, newspapers were printed in private printing houses, most of them owned by foreigners who had recently arrived in the country (Molina and Fumero 1997: 137, 140). Between 1908 and 1919, the newspaper *La Información* published up to 15,000 copies daily. The four main newspapers printed up to 47,000 copies daily in a country inhabited by 430,000 people (Vega 1995: 18).

Towards the end of the nineteenth century, the press experienced a number of institutional changes. For instance, the news as a journalistic genre appeared in the 1870s as part of wider changes that included the introduction of the telegraph in 1869 that linked Costa Rican journalism to political events abroad. Advertising in newspapers increased in the 1890s when the amount of space devoted to it reached 37 per cent. In 1915, news agencies began to provide information to the Costa Rican newspapers (Vega 1995: 11, 12, forthcoming). After 1902, there was more political liberty and an increase in literacy made possible the flourishing of the press (Molina and Fumero 1997: 148).

Radio began in Costa Rica in the 1920s, when Amando Céspedes and Fidel Tristán explored the possibilities of transmission. A decade later, the radio grew considerably and the government enacted regulations (Flores and Gardela 1983: 17–19). Listening to radio programmes enhanced people's sense of time – early morning news broadcasts prompted the wake-ups of thousands of school children. In the evenings, soap operas became family entertainment. New short-wave frequencies were also keenly sought at this time (Flores and Gardela 1983: 20).

The emergence of the newspaper *La Nación* in 1946 was the main institutional change in the Costa Rican press during the second part of the twentieth century. *La Nación* was established in the context of the political conflicts experienced in Costa Rica in the 1940s. At first it was an ally of the opposition forces that fought the fraud orchestrated by the government, but then it distanced itself from these forces, which would soon become Liberación Nacional, the party that consolidated after the 1948 civil war. *La Nación* supports conservative ideologies and, throughout the last two decades, has been the main supporter of neo-liberal reforms in Costa Rica. *La Nación*, as its name suggests, aims to unite the people and speak on their behalf (Sandoval 2004: 27).

Meanwhile, the first attempt to establish television in Costa Rica took place in 1954 when José Figueres, the historical leader of Liberación Nacional, the party that emerged as a winning force post-1948, insisted it had to be a public service (Vega 1987: 55). This initiative was soon deemed to be monopolistic by those interested in launching the service as a private business, in a context characterized by Cold War ideologies that emerged after World War II. Liberación Nacional even attempted to allocate the television service as part of the University of Costa Rica, the main higher education institution, but the university's authorities did not carry out the proposal. In the end, the Supreme Court favoured the thesis that claimed that the television industry had to be in the private sector and transmissions began by 1959 (Vega 1987: 62). Canal 7 was the first television station to transmit its signal in Costa Rica and remains the corporation with the highest audience.

In 1972, the recently created Ministry of Culture established the Centro de Producción Cinematográfica (Centre for Film Production), which aimed to produce documentaries on topical social issues. A new generation of film-makers began their work at the Centre, but in 1978 it was closed down as the government's response to documentaries that highlighted controversial issues. Years later, most of the producers of these documentaries became well known advertisers. In 1975, after several attempts to have access to a television channel, Liberación Nacional inaugurated a state-managed radio and television system called Sistema Nacional de Radio y Televisión (SINART), which gained support from the Spanish government. Initially, SINART was conceived as an extension of a recently established Universidad Estatal a Distancia, a state-funded open university whose work required audiovisual materials. Rather than a public service orientated towards educational goals, SINART has to date been more of a state channel, often misused as a resource of propaganda by a number of governments (Sandoval 1991).

The 1980s saw the growth of radio and television frequencies. FM radio stations increased considerably and a similar trend took place in the case of television, where UHF channels and, later, cable frequencies offered much greater choice in a very short time. Currently, and depending on the region of the country, there are 20 free access television channels, and, on average, cable services provide around 60 channels.

Between 1963 and 1973 the number of households with a television grew from 6.6 to 41.2 per cent of the population respectively. In 1984, 86.4 per cent of households reported to have a television and at the beginning of the twenty-first century there is a television set in practically every Costa Rican household. Official figures report that 12.5 per cent of households have access to cable television (Molina 2003: 15, 17). An important number of households share cable connections with neighbours, without permission from providers, in order to avoid payment of licence fees.

Media institutions are part of wider processes of modernization in Costa Rican society. Towards the mid-twentieth century, Costa Rica was still a rural society, with about two thirds of the population living in the countryside and a third living in the cities. In contrast, Iván Molina notes that throughout the 1960s Costa Rica experienced an urban expansion without precedent. A hundred new public institutions were created between 1948 and 1980 and thousands of new jobs became available. Between 1960 and 1980 transportation systems grew and provided better access to San José. About half of the population lives in the central area of the country, which is 2 per cent of the country's total territory. In 1977, about 500,000 (almost a quarter of the total population) people commuted from the surroundings of San José to the city centre. Cars became a constant in the urban landscape and the ratio of people to cars fell from 11 per car in 1985 to 6 per car in 2000. The urban population grew from 33.5 per cent of the total in 1950 to 59 per cent in 2000, when the last census was carried out (Molina 2002: 4, 5, 8, 58, 86–7, 90). Within this context, cinema perhaps reveals better than any other institution the great cultural change taking place. Established as the main entertainment in many towns and communities, especially after the 1950s, during the mid-1980s the number of cinemas began to decline considerably. Between 1983 and 1988, for instance, the number decreased from 132 to 59 (Sandoval and Al-Ghassani 1987: 74). Currently, most surviving cinemas are located within shopping malls.

Overall, while the political change in Costa Rican society orientated its institutions towards a sort of social democratic welfare state in which insurance, health, electricity, telecommunications and higher education were among the key sectors (Edelman 2005), cultural policy – the sphere to which the media belongs – advocated conservative perspectives. This is a major paradox of Costa Rican society, in that while key institutions have made possible the access of vast majorities to key services, media and other institutions related to the cultural sector have been left behind.

The weakness of cultural policies has diminished the possibility of having a wider public sphere voicing opposition to projects that have debilitated welfare institutions in recent decades. The various media, especially *La Nación*, have adopted a recalcitrant view under which it is almost impossible to find any positive news on the public sector. The neo-conservative approach seems to be that the public sector is synonymous with corruption and therefore if the public sector is reduced, corruption will decrease. Recent developments associated with new technologies such as cable television or the internet does not seem to challenge this paradox.

Media offer: the commodification of a public service

Between 1990 and 2003, the Costa Rican population increased from 3,050,556 to 4,169,730. Most of them (59 per cent) live in urban areas, life expectancy has increased and the childhood mortality rate has decreased. Although the United Nations Human Development Index has recently ranked Costa Rica as a country of high human development (UNDP 2007), in the past few years Costa Rica has nevertheless experienced a deterioration of its living standards. Indeed, between 1990 and 2005, the Costa Rican Human Development Index fell from 0.916 to 0.838, resulting in a decline from position 28 in 1990 to position 47 in 2005 (PNUD 2005: 563).

During the last 25 years, the style of development in Costa Rica has experienced drastic changes: public investment has decreased and currently it has not recovered to the levels reported in 1980. An undermining of public services such as education and health has become an everyday experience for those citizens who do not have access to private facilities. Despite the fact that Costa Rica, together with Uruguay, shows one of the less unequal income distributions in Latin America, the most unequal world region, the income gap has been increasing since 1998. The Gini index increased from 0.412 in 2000 to 0.425 in 2003 (PEN 2004: 96).

This gap between the higher income ranks and the lowest income sectors has been widening and even economic growth has had little impact on poverty reduction (PEN 2004: 121). New forms of capital accumulation, especially associated with the financial sector, exportable products and tourism, are among the main contributing factors to the widening of inequalities (Robinson 2003: 147–294).

Costa Rica is a country where neo-liberal projects have been facing great resistance. In 2000, major social protests prompted the then president to withdraw a law that intended to privatize the Instituto Costarricense of Electricidad, the institution responsible for electricity and telecommunications (Solís 2002).

Up to mid-2006, Costa Rica and Panama were the only Central American countries where a free trade agreement with the USA had not been ratified by Parliament.

In this context, the various media are crucial institutions, both in terms of the ways in which they are organized and from the point of view of the ideologies they promote. Table 7.1 offers some figures on the media system in Costa Rica, and it can be seen that overall similarities rule over differences within the different media institutions. In the case of the press and television, oligopolies are the most salient tendency of the sector (Sandoval 1996: 23). The La Nación media group includes the newspapers *La Nación*, *Al Día* and *El Financiero*, as well as a printing division and investments in newspapers of other Central American countries. The Extra group owns *Diario Extra*, a sensationalist newspaper, as well as *La Prensa Libre*, the oldest Costa Rican newspaper, which following severe decline was taken over by the Extra media group, which also owns a radio station and a television channel.

Table 7.1 Costa Rica: number of media institutions in 1999

Media	Total	National coverage	Total coverage
Newspapers [1]	37	9	29
Radio stations[2]	101	57	44
TV channels[3]	19	17	2
Internet[4]	1	1	–

Source: UNDP (1999)

[1] Three out of nine national newspapers are weeklies. *La Nación* and *Al Día*, two of the national newspapers, have regional editions.
[2] This number includes radio stations affiliated to the Cámara Nacional de Radio (CANARA) and to the Asociación Costarricense de Radiodifusoras. Additionally, this estimate includes about 19 community radio stations which are not affiliated to the former organizations.
[3] Cable channels are not considered.
[4] Radiográfica Costarricense (RACSA), a public institution, which together with the Instituto Costarricense de Electricidad, is the provider of internet access in the country.

Televisora de Costa Rica is the owner of Canal 7, the first television channel in Costa Rica, as well as of Cable Tica, the country's main cable provider. The other main company is REPRETEL, which controls Channels 4, 6 and 11, and belongs to a media group based in Mexico. Both Televisora de Costa Rica and REPRETEL claim to be competitors, but their programming seems to indicate that similarities rule over differences, both in terms of fictional programmes and factual ones.

The advertising industry has experienced a huge expansion during the last two decades in Costa Rica. The number of advertising agencies increased from 37 in 1987 to 60 in 1994, but in 2005 the number decreased to 32. The main agencies have established links with international agencies in charge of designing the corporate image of goods and services that arrive in Costa Rica and many other Latin American countries, in a context characterized by tax reduction policies. Thus, Baptten, Barton, Durstin and Osborn (BBDQ), McCann Erickson, Lintas Worldwide, Grey, Foote, Cone and Belding, and Ogilvy and Thompson, among others, become familiar names within the advertising industry in Costa Rica (Sandoval 1996: 38).

Throughout the 1990s, advertising expenditure experienced an increase, not only because firms invested more in advertising but also because the costs of purchasing space in the press and time on television increased at a greater rate than of inflation. According to Media Gurú (formely Servicios Publicitarios Computadorizados), a pioneering monitoring agency, between 1990 and 1994, advertising in television grew 166 per cent, but 109 per cent of this increase was due to the increase in the price of television time. Similarly, expenditure in the case of the press grew 136 per cent, but 108 per cent was the consequence of the increased cost of advertising space (Sandoval 1996: 18). This tendency has meant that only corporate firms can cope with such increases, such as those connected with the automotive industry, higher education and financial services. The losers are middle-range industries that cannot keep the pace of what has been called 'corporative communication'.

According to Media Gurú data, advertising is highly concentrated in the press and television. In 2003, television and the press received 36.8 and 31.9 per cent of the total advertising budget respectively. In the same year, radio stations gathered 14.9 per cent. Importantly, other media grew from 5.6 per cent in 1999 to 16.4 per cent in 2003. In 2003, within the press, *La Nación* and *Al Día* concentrated nearly 82.26 per cent of the total advertising expenditure. Meanwhile, Televisora de Costa Rica and REPRETEL (Channels 6 and 11) controlled 90 per cent of the advertising, the main source of revenues in privately-funded media. Television advertising is concentrated in the areas of news (25.3 per cent), films (19.6 per cent) and soap operas (19.6 per cent), which make up 64.2 per cent of the total advertising budget invested in television. However, such a high proportion of spending in news programmes does not mean an improvement in the quality, form or content of the news. Quite the opposite, in fact: competition for audiences and advertising has *impoverished* the offer.

The radio shows an incipient process of concentration but clearly less defined than the press and television. Individually, Canal 7 and *La Nación* are the two media institutions which recruit the most advertisements – for instance, in 2003, they obtained 78.8 and 45.7 per cent of the total spending respectively. Advertising agencies also show a process of concentration. In 2003, for example, the top five advertisement agencies managed 42.5 per cent of the total budget; meanwhile the top 10 managed 61.5 per cent of all advertisement expenditure in the country. This concentration reduces opportunities for thousands of students who decide to choose advertising studies in higher education, a course offered by a myriad of tiny private universities that have populated the country in recent years (Sandoval 1996).

Media audience

A recent survey conducted on behalf of the United Nations Development Program asked people which were their main sources of information regarding the main issues of the day in Costa Rica. As shown in Table 7.2, television tops the preferences with 55.8 per cent from a sample of 4054 questionnaires. Printed media is the second source with 29 per cent. In third place comes radio stations with 12.9 per cent. Within television, Channels 6 and 7 concentrate most of the audience, with 47.4 and 43.8 percent respectively. Despite the great number of available channels, most of the audience concentrates around those that pioneered the television audience in Costa Rica. Only 3.4 per cent of respondents did not mention television as a source of information.

Table 7.2 Where do people get information regarding the country's problems?

Sources	Number	%
Television	2,262	55.8
Newspapers	1,177	29.0
Radio	524	12.9
Friends	59	1.5
None	10	0.2
Other sources	15	0.4
NA/NR	7	0.2
Total	4,054	100.00

Source: Fonseca and Sandoval (2006: 9–11)

Regarding the press, two daily newspapers, *La Nación* and *Extra*, concentrate most of the audience. While *Extra* is the favourite source for 25.1 per cent of surveyed people, *La Nación* occupies the second position with 24.2 per cent. A third daily, *Al Día*, comes third with 9.8 per cent. As was mentioned earlier, *La Nación* and *Al Día* belong to the same media group. *Extra* is a sensationalist newspaper whose audience is greater among those readers with less education and with a rural background, as shown in Table 7.3. Inversely, *La Nación* attracts its readers from people with a more formal education, and most of them have an urban background. *Extra* began its activities in 1979 and with half the years of existence of *La Nación* got practically the same level of readership. Currently, *Extra* has become a media group that includes a radio station and a television channel.

The importance of *La Nación* is not only related to quantitative indicators of readership, but it also refers to its capacity for translating its symbolic power into the agenda of the public sphere, influencing the political class, the rest of the media and the general public. *La Nación* speaks on behalf of the nation, especially through what Robert Stam termed 'the regime of the fictive we' (quoted in Morley 2000: 185). The 'we', especially in editorials, is a sort of inclusive actor, able to choose the best political decision for the future of the country (Sandoval 2004, 2006).

Table 7.3 Most frequent newspaper used as source of information (by sex and place of residence)

	Sex		Place of residence		Total
	Male	*Female*	*Urban*	*Rural*	
None	34.6	44.9	35.5	46.2	39.8
Extra	29.0	21.2	26.8	22.5	25.1
La Nación	24.3	24.1	28.3	17.9	24.2
Al Día	10.9	8.6	8.2	12.3	9.8
Others	1.2	1.2	1.3	1.0	1.0
ND	0.1	0.0	0.0	0.1	0.0
Total of cases	(1,197)	(1,205)	(1,447)	(955)	(2,402)
Total	100	100	100	100	100

Source: PNUD *Encuesta Nacional de Seguridad* (2004)

The use of the 'regime of the fictive we' has been especially notorious in the ways in which *La Nación* frames issues such as the negotiations of the Central American Free Trade Agreement (CAFTA). The CAFTA is assumed to be advantageous for the national interest, which is defined according to *La Nación*'s views. 'National interest' is naturalized as a prerogative of *La Nación*. Interestingly, *Extra* does not address its audience in the same way; its narratives are less organized in prescriptive terms.

But as is indicated in Table 7.3, the most striking figure in the case of printed media is given by the number of people who do not read any newspaper at all. Almost 40 per cent of those surveyed reported that they do not read a newspaper. Among those, 34.6 per cent are men and 44.9 per cent are women. These figures are even more striking when we take into consideration the fact that current literacy in Costa Rica is around 90 per cent (primary school completed) (PEN 2004: 405) and differences between women and men are not particularly significant. Rather than a consequence of literacy differences between men and women, these figures are more likely to indicate the ways in which men and women locate themselves regarding current events. While *La Nación*'s audience does not show a sharp contrast along gender lines, among *Extra*'s readership the gap between men and women is significant (7.8 per cent). Politics and the media are still a male arena and this tendency increases among those with less literacy.

Rural people read 10.7 per cent less than in those living in urban areas. This contrast is more dramatic in the case of *La Nación*, whose readership diminishes more than *Extra*'s in rural areas. Being a newspaper especially read by the middle classes, *La Nación* is less present in rural areas where income distribution makes it more difficult to attain a middle-class way of life.

In the case of television, about 91.8 per cent of viewers choose Channels 6 and 7. Among Costa Ricans, the preference for Channel 7 is 6.8 per cent higher than that for Channel 6, as indicated in Table 7.4. Channel 7 is more favoured by men and in urban areas. In rural areas both channels are popular. Interestingly, among migrants, most of which have a Nicaraguan background, Channel 6 shows a higher preference, which might be a consequence of a more popular mode of address with which they feel more familiar.

Table 7.4 Television channels employed to get information (according to sex, place of residence and nationality)

Channel	Sex		Location		Nationality		Total
	Men	Women	Urban	Rural	Costa Rican	Foreigner	
7	50.6	44.1	48.4	45.9	49.1	35.8	47.4
6	41.2	46.5	41.6	47.2	42.3	54.3	43.8
None	3.2	3.6	3.9	2.6	3.1	5.1	3.4
11	2.5	4.2	3.9	2.5	3.5	2.2	3.4

Other	2.6	1.6	2.5	1.5	1.4	2.2	1.7
NS/NR	0.2	0.0	0.0	0.2	0.0	0.3	0.1
Total	1,197	1,205	1,447	955	2,089	313	2,402

Source: PNUD (2004)

In contrast to the case of newspapers, the percentage of surveyed people who reported that they do not watch television is very low. The survey does not show a sharp gender contrast in terms of newspaper consumption, while place of residence (which signals economic position) has a lower impact on newspaper readership than is the case with television.

On the other hand, a comparison of audience reach versus advertising expenditure shows that media exposure does not correlate to advertising expenditure; in other words, the traditional mechanisms used in many countries to allocate advertisement expenditure such as 'cost per million' (CPM) are not strictly applied in Costa Rica. For instance, La Nación is read by a quarter of the population but receives three quarters of the advertising located in the press; Canal 7 exhibits a similar pattern since it is watched by about 47.4 per cent of the viewing public but receives around 78.8 per cent of the advertising on television. This contrast might indicate that the audience of La Nación and Canal 7 combines sectors with more purchasing power and more political influence, but it also shows that what is not promoted by either La Nación and Canal 7 does not get recognition.

The media construction of fear

One of the most striking conclusions of recent studies on citizen insecurity is the imbalance between the actual risk of being the victim of an attack and the perception of risk (Glassner 1999). The PNUD's report on national insecurity in Costa Rica (2005b) shows that, according to a national survey, one out of four people has been the victim of a family assault in the last 12 months. However, these real threats to personal security were not prioritized by the respondents, who tended instead to perceive being robbed by strangers as a more threatening risk. Indeed, when the same respondents were asked about patrimonial insecurity (theft or damage to material goods), half of them considered that these type of assaults were the most prominent threat. Therefore, there is an important imbalance between actual risk and perception of risk.

This sense of risk is not a consequence of any single factor; it is in fact a result of multi-dimensional aspects. One of these is the possible correlation between media exposure and the perception of insecurity. The main findings suggest that exposure to crime news in the press does not cultivate strong perceptions of insecurity in real life. But watching television crime news does have an impact in terms of perception of risk and insecurity. In fact, heavy viewers of television crime news report a higher sense of insecurity than low viewers of crime news, as shown in Table 7.5: the sense of insecurity increases by 11.7 per cent among heavy viewers. Inversely, the sense of insecurity decreases by the same percentage among those who are not heavy viewers of crime news. This is a familiar conclusion for cultivation theory, associated with George Gerbner and his colleagues (1996), but what is interesting in the case of Costa Rica is that for the first time there are quantitative data that confirm that the media play an important role in the formation of perceptions. This opens up challenges in terms of the accountability of media institutions, a topic which is scarcely discussed.

Table 7.5 Exposure to television crime news and perception of insecurity

Perception of insecurity	Watch crime news on television				Yes/No average
	Yes		No		
	Number	Percentage	Number	Percentage	
Few or nothing secure	1,778	78.3	60	66.7	11.7
Very secure or secure	492	21.7	30	33.3	–11.7
Total	2,270	100.0	90	100.0	

Source: Sandoval and Fonseca (2006: 18)

The centrality of television crime news for the construction of a sense of insecurity has to be understood in the context of an increase of crime news items in television news programming. Recent research (Sandoval and Fonseca 2006) shows that crime news constituted 24 per cent of the prime time edition of *Telenoticias*, the news programme of Canal 7. Crime news was followed by advertising with 24 per cent and sport with 15 per cent. Overall, national news, which includes politics and education among other topics, only took 18 per cent of the edition, and international news got scarcely 4 per cent. The sample for this research was taken from January 2004, when the Costa Rican government and the other governments of Central America were negotiating a free trade agreement with the US government. Despite the fact that a major political and economic issue was taking place, crime news kept the lead in terms of time devoted in the prime time edition. Media representatives usually claim that they offer what is interesting for the audience but they never ask the audience what their needs are. They presume they are able to talk on behalf of the people's interests.

If the low level of readership of newspapers is combined with the emphasis of television news on crime, the result is a society where the number of media institutions has increased but the possibilities of getting information regarding key issues are scarce. This produces a thin public sphere and a political culture in which discussion and debate are often unfamiliar. For example, the intense and polarized debates regarding the implementation of the Central America Free Trade Agreement (CAFTA) have not translated into an increase in information available to the public in the mainstream media.

Public assessment of media performance

In 1999, the UNDP undertook an assessment of the state of democracy in Costa Rica. One of the topics explored was the confidence Costa Ricans had in the media. Table 7.6 indicates that confidence in the media is generally positive. Most opinions show 'some' or 'much' confidence in the media. Confidence is higher among men than women, and income seems to influence people's perception of the media: those with less income show higher confidence. Inversely, the upper middle classes and the upper class have less confidence. Though the survey associated confidence with income, educational level probably has a decisive influence on confidence, being also a strong predictor of income.

Table 7.6 Confidence in the media, according to sex and socioeconomic level

	Total	Sex		Socioeconomic level		
		Male	Female	LC/LMC	MMC	UMC/ IIC[1/]
Much	24.5	28.1	21.0	24.1	26.4	20.3
Something	43.9	42.2	45.5	43.6	42.6	48.0
Nothing	7.4	7.0	7.8	9.7	5.9	6.2
Total	100.0	100.0	100.0	100.0	100.0	100.0
N:	1,618	806	812	629	728	261

Source: UNDP

[1] LC/LMC low class/low-middle class, MMC middle-middle class, MHC/HC upper middle class/high class

The same report estimated the amount of time and space devoted weekly by Costa Rica's media to public debate. The results are summarized in Table 7.7 and show that the press devoted a tiny 3.9 per cent of its pages to readers' opinions. Meanwhile, radio and television devote only 1.7 and 1 per cent respectively to airing the public's concerns. In others words, the increase of radio and television channels in recent decades has not widened dialogue and debate in Costa Rican society. This is particularly important because public debate is nowadays associated with the media, but the media do not seem to be interested in opening up new ways of engaging in public discussion. The paradox is that in a modern, complex society, opportunities for debate and dialogue are more restricted when they should be less.

The historical perspective advanced early in this chapter now becomes crucial for understanding this impoverished public sphere. Reformist political forces undertook a number of reforms during the 1940s and 50s, but cultural policies did not have priority in their agenda. Education, health and electricity became widely available, but the public sphere remained largely untouched. Ironically, it is from this reduced public sphere that neo-liberal forces have been undermining the legitimacy of the institutions shaped by reformist governments.

Table 7.7 Costa Rica: estimation of the offer of spaces of opinion weekly, according to type of media

Type of media	Total space/time	Opinion space/ time	%
Newspapers	2,100 pages	83 pages	3.9
TV	1,677 hours	30 hours	1.7
Radio	14,000 hours	145 hours	1.0

Source: UNDP

Respondents were asked if they knew sections of the press and pro-grammes, in the case of radio and television, in which topics considered important nationally were discussed. Nearly two thirds (65 per cent) answered that they were aware of such spaces, as shown in Table 7.8. Overall, the higher the economic income and the educational background, the more people were aware of spaces for debate in the media (UNDP 1999: 401). However, when they were asked if they had denounced an issue through the media, only 5.4 per cent said they had done so. Men and women reported similar answers, 7.3 and 7.6 per cent, respectively. Denouncements increase among the better off: while only 2.1 per cent of people from a low class or low middle class have denounced issues in the media, 12.9 per cent of the upper middle class or upper class have used the media to make their views public. Responses from urban people and rural people show a sharp contrast. About 7.5 per cent of urban people have made public their concerns, but only 2.8 per cent of people from a rural background have done so (UNDP 1999: 425). Not surprisingly, urban people from higher ranks of society feel more authorized to make public their concerns. As Pierre Bourdieu ([1979] 1999: 418) noted in the case of France, those in power perceive themselves as subjects of politics, while those disempowered feel themselves as objects of political decisions undertaken by others.

Table 7.8 People who have denounced an issue through the media, according to sex, socioeconomic level and place of residence

Denounces	Total	Sex		Socioeconomic level			Location	
		Men	Women	LC/ LMC	MMC	UMC/ HC[1]	Urban	Rural
Yes	5.4	7.3	7.6	2.1	5.6	12.9	7.5	2.8
No	94.6	92.7	96.4	97.9	94.4	87.1	92.5	97.2
N:	1,618	806	812	629	728	261	908	710

Source: UNDP

[1] LC/LMC low class/low-middle class, MMC middle-middle class, HMC/HC upper middle class/high class.

Overall, both in terms of space and time available for participation, the media offer very restricted opportunities for citizenship, and this is particularly the case in rural areas, since it is believed that citizenship, rather than being a right, is still an urban privilege. In recent years, both politicians and academics have made public their concerns regarding the implications of an increase in non-participation in the last three general elections in Costa Rica (Raventós *et al.* 2004). But what is often missing is the recognition that participation and engagement in public debates is very scarce. People are accustomed to discussing issues informally in the street, in public places or in more private domains, but their voices are often missing in more formalized venues such as the media. In this context, it not surprising that people feel alienated from politics.

A main conclusion of the UNDP's report is that 'the media have "self appointed" (and function as such) as non-elected representatives of the citizenry' (1999: 385). The report also concluded that the media are not accountable for their own institutional practices, profiles and decisions. Despite the fact that the media as a whole has publicized 'accountability' as a key term for contemporary politics, the irony is that the media is seldom accountable for its own institutional practices. Information and communication are public services, and media accountability is a challenge for Costa Rican society (UNDP 1999: 406).

The internet and beyond

Access to the internet in Costa Rica has improved in recent years. According to a survey carried out twice a year by Radiográfica Costarricense, one of the two public providers of the service, the number of households with a personal computer rose from 14 per cent in 2001 to 29 per cent in 2004 and to 34 per cent in 2005. The survey has a standard sample of 1200 respondents. This means that the number doubled in five years. Among those households with computers, about half access the internet through a phone connection. Thus nearly 15 per cent of households in Costa Rica have access to the internet. It is estimated that two members of the family take advantage of the service, which gives an approximate number of 300,000 users. Other ways of accessing the internet are through internet cafés, whose number has increased in Costa Rica, and connections at workplaces. One of the largest ISP providers in Costa Rica, RACSA, estimates that about 3 million emails are sent daily (RACSA 2007).

In 2004, according to estimates made by the International Union of Telecommunications, after Chile, Uruguay and Argentina, Costa Rica came fourth in Latin America in terms of accessibility (RACSA 2006). This outcome is especially interesting because Uruguay and Costa Rica are the only Latin American countries where electricity and telecommunications belong to the public sector. In other words, privatization is not a precondition for improving connectivity, as neo-liberal fundamentalism has been presuming during the last few decades.

Nonetheless, it is not easy to give estimation of how many people really have access to the internet because there are obvious overlaps between those who get access domestically, in internet cafés and at workplaces. Importantly, the surveys show that formal education, gender and place of residence make an important difference in terms of access. Thus those with higher education, especially men living in urban areas, have more probability of being connected. This conclusion confirms what international research on the 'digital divide' has shown in different contexts (Cuneo 2002).

Beyond accessibility, little is known about internet uses and practices. Of particular importance is to explore the extent to which technological developments such as the internet may threaten the agenda-setting position of journalists and media institutions. An example from the last Costa Rican general election could offer an insight into the importance of the internet as a new dimension of the public sphere. At the beginning of the campaign, the former president and candidate Óscar Arias was well ahead in the polls. The amount of money spent by him and his party was much higher than his main rival. However, at the end, he won by only 1 per cent. This apparent anomaly has sparked much debate. Especially relevant in this context was the opposition of the younger generation to Arias and his policies. Their views seemed to have been circulating through in the internet, which for many young people had become the main way to network. For example, a few months before the election, a photo composition compared Arias with the infamous Mr Burns, the character from *The Simpsons*, about which the official propaganda had hardly anything to say.

Overall, a main challenge for Costa Rican society is the extent to which technological change could contribute towards a more inclusive public sphere and political culture. During the last two decades, the nation has replaced society as the frame upon which to discuss the future.

To reverse this tendency will be impossible unless media institutions recognize themselves that they must be accountable for their own decisions.

Note

1 I must thank José F. Correa, Ignacio Siles and Patricia Vega for allowing me access to the outcomes of their own research, which has enabled me to grasp some peculiarities of the media in Costa Rica. Bridget Hayden generously improved my idiosyncratic English.

8 THE MEDIA IN CASTRO'S CUBA: EVERY WORD COUNTS

Juan Orlando Pérez

On the morning of 12 May 1960, the good people of Havana read the most extraordinary headline in *Diario de la Marina*, Cuba's oldest newspaper. It was a confession, a *mea culpa*: 'After one hundred and twenty eight years at the service of the worst ideas, *Diario de la Marina* is for the first time published for the people, under revolutionary direction and rid of any lies against Cuba' (León Enrique 1975: 167). It was a decisive moment in the history of Cuban journalism. The day before, the publishers of *la Marina*, the Rivero family, had refused to print a *coletilla* inserted at the last minute by the journalists and graphic workers. The *coletillas* were little notes in response to editorial columns and news stories that the newspapers' workers considered malicious or defamatory against Fidel Castro's revolutionary government. They first appeared in the autumn of 1959, published by Committees for the Freedom of the Press, on which revolutionary journalists sat with graphic workers. Newspaper publishers reluctantly tolerated the *coletillas* for a while, but by the spring of 1960 the Rivero family had had enough. When they refused to print the last *coletilla*, the National Federation of Graphic Workers took over the newspaper. The publishers appealed to the courts but the National College of Journalists challenged this in court arguing that the journalists and workers had looked to 'the defence of the national interest, and to protect the conquests of the Revolution, which has brought to us total sovereignty and has laid the basis for the transformation of our political and social life according to the wishes of our people' (León Enrique 1975: 168). On 27 May the court decided in favour of the College. But the people of Havana did not wait for the verdict, and symbolically buried the newspaper that had once opposed Cuban independence and celebrated the deaths of national heroes José Martí and Antonio Maceo. The funeral procession began in the newspaper's offices and ended at the University of Havana, epicentre of revolutionary agitation: 'It was the happiest burial that ever happened in Cuba. People ... sang and danced' (Marrero 1999: 85). The Rivero family quickly left the country. It was the end of an era.

When Fulgencio Batista, who had ruled Cuba for six bloody years, abandoned the country in the early hours of 1 January 1959, there were 16 national daily newspapers circulating in a small island of approximately 6 million inhabitants. In February 1959, the Ministry of Labour reported 117 companies of 'terrestrial newspapers' and 56 of 'radio and TV newspapers' (León Enrique 1975: 150–1). Even Fidel Castro was impressed:

> There were in our country great resources of communication ... we had developed television, radio, the press ... in some cases, they were too developed. I think the number of radio stations in the country was 156; the number of newspapers was also high, and there were several television stations, among them two national.
> (Núñez Machín 1983: 46–7)

Cuba was the first country in Latin America with a public radio station (1922) and the third with television (1950), after Mexico and Brazil. By 1958, Cuban radio and television companies were exporting tapes and scripts to more than ten Latin American countries (Castro 1975: 130). Cuba was also the fourth country in the region to have a professional school of journalism, in 1942, after Argentina, Mexico and Brazil. When Castro's guerrillas arrived in Havana, there were six professional schools of journalism across the country, graduating 200 students every year (Rodríguez Neyra 1983: 21).

The history of Cuban journalism had begun around 1764, shortly after the end of the brief English occupation of Havana, when the Spanish authorities allowed the circulation of *La Gaceta*, the first ever newspaper on the island. In the course of over 200 years, Cuban journalists struggled under Spanish rule and post-colonial dictatorships, but enjoyed periods of relative openness and freedom in 1812–14, 1820–3, 1869 and 1878–96 (Portuondo 1965), and after the inauguration of the Republic, between 1902 and 1929, and between 1940–52. The National College of Journalists had been founded in 1943, after a National Congress of Journalists, three years before, that proclaimed journalism 'a liberal profession dedicated to inform and orientate the public opinion, to look over the public activities of the inhabitants of a region and to disseminate the culture among the people of a country', and called for the compulsory registration of all practitioners (León Enrique 1975: 41). Until 1952, the Catholic *Diario de la Marina* coexisted in relative peace with the communist newspaper *Hoy*, and with many others of different political orientations. However, the system of public communication in pre-revolutionary Cuba was fatally flawed. The development of media throughout the country was uneven, and corruption widespread. Soon after the triumph of Castro's revolution, the new authorities divulged a list of publishers and journalists who had received monthly payments of up to 24,000 pesos from the presidential palace (Marrero 1999: 88). *Botellas*, jobs nobody work in but got paid for, were a common form of bribery. *Diario de la Marina* alone had 14 *botellas* in the Ministry of Economy, 14 in the Ministry of Communications, 19 in the Ministry of Agriculture, 21 in the Ministry of Public Services, and some others in several public institutions (Marrero 1999: 88). Unemployment was endemic. In 1953 the College of Journalists of the Province of Havana reported almost 200 journalists without a stable job (Marrero 1999: 88). But the fundamental problem for the Cuban media was the ideological complicity of the leading publishers and writers with the country's ruling classes, which had so tremendously failed in guaranteeing institutional continuity, political stability, economic development, social justice and national sovereignty.

That sealed their fate. But the only immediate transformation in Cuban media after the fall of Batista and the rise to power of Fidel Castro was the closure of five newspapers and three radio stations whose owners were closely linked to the disgraced dictator (Marrero 1999: 75). Their place was occupied by newspapers and magazines that had been closed under Batista, like the Popular Socialist (Communist) Party's newspaper *Hoy*, and the revolutionary underground press, such as the newspaper *Revolución*, of Castro's Movimiento 26 de Julio (The 26th of July Movement: the revolutionary organization planned and led by Castro that in 1959 overthrew the Fulgencio Batista government in Cuba. The 26th of July Movement fought Batista on both rural and urban fronts), and the rebels' legendary Radio Rebelde, which had announced the triumph of the revolution from the mountains of Sierra Maestra. There is no evidence that the ideologically plural first revolutionary government of January 1959, or even Fidel Castro himself, had plans to take over the press or make any significant transformation of the media industry. The Cuban press overwhelmingly saluted Batista's deposition and the arrival of an immensely popular, young and charismatic leader. However, before the new ministers had had time to get to business, the revolutionary government fought the first battle of what would become a long propaganda war with its internal and external enemies. The government launched the so-called 'Operation Truth' to contest the negative coverage by national and international media of the trials of the military responsible for the crimes of the Batista dictatorship. Around 380 journalists from all the Americas were invited to Havana to attend the trials (Marrero 1999: 79). As the government became more radical (particularly after the Agrarian Reform of May 1959), internal opposition, not least from conservative newspapers like *Diario de la Marina*, grew. The antagonism between the authorities and the press had been stirred by Fidel Castro during a lunch organized by the National College of Journalists for the Day of the Freedom of the Press, on 27 June 1959, which most owners boycotted:

Journalism does not mean enterprise but journalism, because enterprise means business and journalism means intellectual effort, means thinking, and if anyone must appreciate the freedom of the press, it is not the one who makes a business of the freedom of the press, but the one who thanks to the freedom of the press writes, orientates and works with thoughts, using a right the Revolution conquered for the country and the Revolution keeps for the country, even in the middle of all the campaigns trying to rise as much enemies as possible against the revolutionary work we are doing.

(Marrero 1999: 86)

One after the other, most of the publishers and editors, and a large number of the finest Cuban journalists, fled the country. Among them, the Rivero family, Goar Mestre, owner of radio and television empire CMQ, and Miguel Ángel Quevedo, director of *Bohemia*, Cuba's oldest general affairs magazine, founded in 1908, which somehow has survived to date. The media were nationalized, and by the end of 1960 the whole system was under state control. Commercial advertising practically disappeared and was replaced by state subsidies as the main income of the media. The commercial media had become not only ideologically anachronistic, but also economically unfeasible: all the external trade and most of the internal, the banks and most of transport and construction industries, and more than a third of agriculture, were already in the hands of the government: 'This quick shift of property eliminated the capitalist system and provoked the interruption of the automatic mechanisms of market; as a consequence, the production and distribution of goods and services was not any longer determined by the laws of supply and demand' (Mesa-Lago 1994: 20). In January 1961 the USA, which had dominated the island's politics and economy for half a century, and whose companies had been unceremoniously expropriated by Castro the previous year, broke diplomatic relations with the Cuban government. On 16 April, 24 hours before the landing of CIA-trained and armed Brigade 2506 in the Bay of Pigs, Castro declared socialism. Three days later, he claimed victory over the invaders and perpetuated himself in power.

Inside the revolution

Having gained monopolistic control of the media, and crushed the internal opposition, Fidel Castro and his comrades had to decide what degree of freedom of expression would be allowed in socialist Cuba. American hostility towards Castro's government had quickly escalated with President Kennedy's proclamation in January 1962 of a total embargo, the provision of support to groups of exiles that carried out attacks against Cuba and the CIA's plans to kill Castro and invade the island. Continuing aggression from the USA and the need to protect the revolution from the attacks of external enemies and their internal allies would become Castro's justification for gradually restricting civil and political freedoms, just as 'the bombs of Kaledin' had been Lenin's pretext to refuse restoring the freedom of the press in Bolshevik Russia (Lenin 1979: 246). Castro repeated *ad pedem litterae* Lenin's devastating judgement 50 years earlier: 'The bourgeois freedom of the press ... is the freedom of the rich to be the owners of most of the means of thinking, which they use to defend their interests as a class against the exploited' (Castro 1966: 260). In a 1961 speech to revolutionary journalists, the

Cuban leader declared: 'We must be aware that the interests of the Revolution come before the newspapers. The interests of the newspapers must be subordinated to the interests of the Revolution' (Castro 1961a: 36). The 1976 Socialist Constitution would consecrate the freedom of the press but added, 'in accordance with the goals of our socialist society'. In the absence of any further legislation regulating the press or the broadcasting media (a press law was apparently once drafted but never discussed in the National Assembly), the boundaries between what can be said and what cannot in Cuban newspapers, radio and television, would forever remain conveniently blurred.

In 1961, an otherwise anodyne dispute between the Institute of Cinematographic Arts and Industry (ICAIC in Spanish, founded in 1959) and a group of writers and artists grouped around the literary magazine of the newspaper *Revolución*, was the detonator of a major political debate that escalated to require the intervention of Castro himself. In a speech to the cream of Cuban artists and writers in the summer of that year, Castro proclaimed his dogma:

> Inside the Revolution, everything; against the Revolution, nothing. Against the Revolution nothing, because the Revolution has also its rights, and the first right of the Revolution is the right to exist, and nobody can go against that right of the Revolution to be and exist. Because the Revolution includes the interests of the people, the Revolution means the interests of the whole Nation, nobody can have rights against it.
>
> (Castro 1961b: 11)

The revolution, however, would prove to be an elusive, changeable concept, subject to frequent abuse by opportunistic party leaders and media bosses. Necessarily, the meaning and ideological contents of a process with the extraordinary historical longevity of the Cuban Revolution varied throughout the years, not least due to the frequent political u-turns of the country's leaders to survive in ever-changing circumstances. 'Inside the revolution' would come very often to mean simply 'with Castro'. The disbandment in 1961 of the ideologically heterogeneous group of writers of *Revolución*, and the creation that year of the Union of Writers and Artists of Cuba (UNEAC in Spanish) was the first sign of a dramatic reduction of the spaces of public debate and increasing restrictions to the freedom of expression. UNEAC, and other new cultural institutions, like ICAIC, or Casa de las Américas (an organization that was founded by the Cuban government in April 1959, four months after the Cuban Revolution, for the purpose of developing and extending sociocultural relations with the countries of Latin America, the Caribbean and the rest of the world), and a reduced number of intellectual publications like *Revolución y Cultura* (1961) or *El Caimán Barbudo* (1966), and academic journals like *Pensamiento Crítico* (1967), became cultural and political cloisters where some form of ideological plurality (never frontal opposition to Castro) was allowed, but with scarce visibility and impact within the wider public. These publications wandered through periods of relative tolerance (as, notably, in the late 1980s, parallel to the Soviet *glásnost*) and obscure orthodoxy. *Pensamiento Crítico* was closed in 1971 (and the group of intellectuals who published it disbanded), in the climax of a political witch-hunt, but other cultural publications managed to survive in a state of perennial lethargy. Years later, in the midst of the economic crisis of the 1990s, when a new generation of cultural magazines and journals, such as *Temas* (1995) and *Contracorriente* (1995), together with older ones like UNEAC's *La Gaceta de Cuba* (1961), dangerously crossed the political *non plus ultra* marked by the Cuban leaders, they suffered an immediate retaliation. The principal victim was *Cuadernos de Nuestra América* (1983), the journal of the Centre of Studies of America (CEA in Spanish), a Communist Party think-tank, which had brought together in the early 1990s some loud-speaking reformist academics. Once again, in the spring of 1996, the authorities intervened to disband the group and returned the journal to orthodoxy.

Two years later, Fidel Castro launched a ferocious attack against ICAIC, and accused it of producing counter-revolutionary movies. Castro alluded to a series of films (such as 1990's *Alicia in the Town of Wonders*, 1994 Oscar nominee *Strawberry and Chocolate* and 1996's *Guantanamera*) which criticized political intolerance, moral hypocrisy and social decline. But for the first time ever he faced the stubborn resistance of writers and artists who refused to apologize and the ICAIC escaped the crisis mostly untouched. The existence of these always threatened niches of relative plurality within an otherwise extremely monochord media system was and still is an absolute political necessity: it is how the Cuban authorities manage and control dissent and criticism within the intellectual groups and the urban middle classes of professionals, state and party officials and skilled workers. Castro seemingly acknowledged the existence of this secondary tier of public communication in a 1971 speech, pronounced in the middle of an international scandal prompted by the imprisonment of dissident poet Heberto Padilla. He attempted to explain why Cuban newspapers had said nothing about Padilla, a conspicuous silence that would be the typical reaction of the country's media to embarrassing news:

> These matters are too non transcendent, too rubbish, to occupy the attention of our workers and the pages of our newspapers. Our problems are different. And the stories will eventually appear, and the little problems will appear in some literary magazine: that is enough.
>
> (Castro 1971: 26–7)

Clearly, the Cuban media system is managed from the very top of the country's leadership, which decide what sort of information is available to the public, through which channels and in which style of presentation. It is, in the words of a commentator, 'a model of communication based in a scheme of lineal transmission, extremely vertical, and tied to some ingenuous socio functionalism, with a conception of media as mere ideological instruments' (Cancio 2005).

The authoritarian model adopted by the Cuban leaders in the early 1960s was a carbon copy of that of the power that substituted the USA as the country's main political and commercial ally. The Soviet Union and the USA clashed in Cuba in the Missile Crisis of October 1962, which ended with President Kennedy's muttered promise of not invading the island. Despite some occasional disagreements between the two countries' leaders, the Soviet influence in Cuba never ceased until the collapse of communism in Eastern Europe, and became particularly strong after the entry of the island in the COMECOM in 1972. Soviet and other socialist countries' publications flooded the country. In 1985, in the dawn of Gorbachev's *perestroika*, 13 million copies of foreign newspapers and magazines circulated in Cuba (Gil and Ricardo 2000: 41), and only a tiny fraction of them had western origin. The Soviet press circulating in Cuba covered all areas of social life, from the children's magazine *Misha* to *Sputnik*, the Soviet version of the *Reader's Digest*. They were all banned in 1989, when the ends of *perestroika* became clear to Cuban leaders. While the Soviet Communist Party surrendered its media monopoly, the Cuban leaders only strengthened their grip on theirs. The core of the system is formed by a relatively small number of party and state media with a capacity to reach a large audience or readership, which constitute instruments not only of information but most significantly of political propaganda, ideological education and popular mobilization, all under the watch of the Cuban Communist Party, founded in October 1965 after the merge of the revolutionary groups that had toppled Batista. The beating heart of the system is the newspaper *Granma*, named after the boat in which Fidel Castro had sailed from Mexico to Cuba to fight Batista. *Granma*'s first, half a million-copy issue circulated on 4 October 1965, and it was itself the result of the merger of Movimiento 26 de Julio's newspaper 'Revolución' and the communist newspaper *Hoy*. Being the official organ of the new ruling party, *Granma* acquired a semi-normative role within the Cuban press. It publishes the communiqués of party and government, and Castro's speeches, marking the political line other media have to follow. Only a few days after the inauguration of *Granma*, *Diario de la Tarde* merged with the magazine *Mella* to create *Juventud Rebelde*, organ of the Young Communist League. By 1968, when *El Mundo* (the first truly modern-styled Cuban newspaper, founded in 1901), burned to ashes, *Granma* and *Juventud Rebelde* were the only daily newspapers left in the country, and they were mere stylistic variations (*Juventud Rebelde* being more youthful and lively than the supremely austere *Granma*) of the same political stance.

Trabajadores, newspaper of the unions, was founded in 1970, forming with *Granma* and *Juventud Rebelde* a holy trinity of the Cuban press. A fourth national newspaper, *Bastión*, organ of the Revolutionary Army Forces (FAR in Spanish), founded in 1987, was short-lived and ceased its publication in October 1990. The system was completed with local newspapers, one in each of the 14 provinces of the country and one more in the special municipality of Isle of Youth. These newspapers run under the supervision of the local committees of the Communist Party, which appoint their directors and editors and watch every word that is published in them, very much in the same way the Ideological Department of the Central Committee (previously the Department of Revolutionary Orientation, the infamous DOR in Spanish) watches over the national press. These local newspapers replicate in each province the normative role *Granma* plays on a national scale. The Ideological Department of the party exerts the same degree of control over the rest of the country's publications, and radio and television, and to a lesser extent over the rest of the cultural institutions, such as publishing houses, record and theatre companies and the ICAIC, which are under the watch of the Ministry of Culture. There has never been official censorship in Castro's Cuba. Instead, the party imposes its authority mostly using the same three procedures Wilbur Schramm once described in the Soviet Union. 'Their first consideration', Schramm wrote, 'is, of course, to get a politically reliable appointee' in every decision-making position within media. In second place, the party issues 'a very large number of directives as to what material is to appear in the press and how it is to be handled'. Finally, Schramm said, the party 'reviews and criticises the press ... At each level of the party, there is a committee which samples and criticises the press of its corresponding level' (in Siebert *et al.* 1963: 132–3). Rarely does a story that might cause controversy slip past the guardians, as in the case of El Caso Sandra (The Sandra Case), a story written by Luis Manuel Garcia Mendez, concerning a young prostitute that shocked the country in 1987 and cost the director of the magazine *Somos Jóvenes* (founded 1977) his post. Party bosses and media directors seldom ban a story straightforwardly, instead suggesting keeping it for *el momento adecuado* – the right moment to publish – when it will not mean giving *armas al enemigo* – weapons to the enemy – the 'bombs of lies' both Lenin (1979: 246) and Castro have so much feared. *El momento adecuado* usually means never.

War of words

Radio and television are organized in the same way the press is: there is a television station and a radio station in each of the capitals of the fourteen provinces and in the Isle of Youth, although many other towns with a significant population or economic relevance have their own radio station, always supervised by the local party committee. These stations are all part of the Cuban Institute of Radio and Television (ICRT in Spanish) founded on 24 May 1962, an umbrella mechanism that administers resources and sets technical and aesthetical standards, but leaves matters of policy and ideology to the party. Radio is the one medium that experienced reletively few changes after 1959. Radio Rebelde, the station founded by Castro in Sierra Maestra in February 1958, kept its semi-official role after the triumph of the rebels, confirmed in the 1990s when it was assigned the production of the *National Radio News*, which most stations in the country broadcast simultaneously at 1 p.m. Monday to Saturday. Pre-revolutionary stations with national coverage such as Radio Progreso (founded 1929), news-only Radio Reloj (1947), and classical music-only CMBF (1948), managed to survive nationalization, as did many local stations such as Havana's COCO (1937), Santa Clara's CMHW (1929), Cienfuegos's CMHM Radio Ciudad del Mar (1936), Holguín's CMKO Radio Angulo (1936), Ciego de Avila's Radio Surco (1952) and Camagüey's Radio Cadena Agramonte (1957). Other stations were founded in many towns after 1959, but only two with national coverage, light music-only Radio Enciclopedia (1962) and the tourist-orientated Radio Taíno (1985). As today there are in Cuba six national radio stations, 18 covering entire provinces (four in the capital) and 57 more in other towns. Detached from international trends, Cuban radio conserved old-style formats, most notably the *radionovelas*, long-running dramatic series that still attract huge audiences with a winning combination of romantic clichés and sharp social commentary. The volatile, short-lived nature of radio broadcasts and the comparatively small size of their audiences gave local radio stations a higher degree of freedom than allowed to the press or television, and occasionally they have engaged in some sort of opinionated or investigative journalism that would be unthinkable in other media, as in the cases of Radio Ciudad de La Habana (founded 1978) and Santa Clara's CMHW. This latter's show *Alta Tensión* (*High Tension*) has dared for more than a decade, since the mid-1990s, to address controversial topics such as corruption, economic mismanagement, prostitution, drugs and alcoholism. But a programme like this, which depends entirely on the goodwill of the local party committee, and the tolerance of their national bosses, is *rara avis*.

A significant addition to the radio system was Radio Habana Cuba, whose creation was announced by Fidel Castro only 24 hours before the Bay of Pigs invasion. Denouncing the American involvement in the bombing of Havana's airports the day before, Castro asked: 'Do they believe they will be capable to hide the truth from the world? No. Cuba already has a radio plant broadcasting to the whole of Latin America, and countless friends in Latin America and the whole world are listening to us right now' (Radio Habana Cuba 2006). With broadcasts in nine languages (from English and French to Quechua, Creole and Guaraní), Radio Habana Cuba has played a crucial role in the half-century every-word-a-bullet propaganda war the Cuban government has fought against their real or imaginary external enemies, mainly *el imperialismo yanqui*, American imperialism. The Cuban leadership paid much attention to the country's international image and believed it to be of the uttermost importance to outmanoeuvre what they considered a world media's conspiracy against the revolution. Castro's regime has faced not only a mostly unsympathetic coverage in the world press, but also the intrusion of foreign radio and television in Cuba. In the 1960s CIA's Radio Swan, broadcasting from a tiny island in the Caribbean, supported anti-Castro opposition inside Cuba and encouraged armed resistance and sabotages.

In 1985, the Reagan administration launched Radio Martí, modelled after Radio Free Europe, a special service for Cuba of the 'Voice of America'. Radio Martí, based in Miami, has been accused by the Cuban government of inciting subversion and civil disobedience, and encouraging terrorism and illegal emigration. Castro could not prevent Radio Martí from being widely listened to in Cuba, but he moved fast to jam the signal of Tele Martí, a television broadcast inaugurated in 1990 and now generally regarded as a technological and political failure because of its scarce visibility on the island. For 2006 Radio and Tele Martí had a combined budget of $37 million (Unión de Periodistas de Cuba 2006). The Cuban government has declared that radio and television stations based in the USA produce every week over 2107 hours of anti-Castro programmes, reaching the Cuban public through 24 frequencies (Unión de Periodistas de Cuba 2006). In response, the Cuban government created an additional tier of communication, targeting foreign publics with a combination of news about Cuba and pro-Castro propaganda. The first piece in chronological order of this subsystem is Prensa Latina, a Latin American press agency with headquarters in Havana, founded in 1959. Prensa Latina dispatches could not be more different from those of AIN, the National Information Agency, founded in 1974. While Prensa Latina, in style and above all in facts, attempts to offer a more believable, seemingly balanced account of Cuban social and political life to foreign clients, AIN's monotonous, one-sided, politically-sanitized stories are intended for publication only in the national media. In 1966 *Granma* launched a weekly résumé in Spanish, English and French that in 1991 became *Granma Internacional*, now also available in German, Italian, Portuguese and, strangely, Turkish. Cubavisión Internacional, an international television channel available in cable and satellite, was added in 1986. The introduction of the internet ten years later offered the Cuban leaders a new platform to export a positive image of the country and fight back world media's reports about Cuba's fragile economy and crumbling society, and Castro's record on human rights. Fearful of the impact the internet might have among ordinary Cubans, but enthusiastic about its propagandistic possibilities, Castro once again adopted a two-tier solution: restricting and controlling access to the internet for ordinary citizens, and duplicating online the entire system of Cuban media. Cubans cannot buy the services of any internet provider, and only some special categories of individuals, such as journalists, scientists, artists and party officials are allowed a home connection. Meanwhile, most of the country's media, including some fairly small local radio stations, have launched their own websites, which in most cases only reproduce the stories, the style and the strongly propagandistic stance of the offline media. By 2005, according to official data, there were over 1500 Cuban websites in the internet, 136 of which were replicas of the island's media. But there were only 300,000 computers, at a dismal ratio of 2.7 per hundred persons. The number of internet users was estimated at 150,000, in a country of little more than 11 million inhabitants (Rosabal and Sanz 2005: 4–5). The most successful site of the Cuban press online (at least in terms of the reaction of friends and foes) is *La Jiribilla* (2001), a cultural publication that fights back, *Encuentro de la Cultura Cubana* (1996), a magazine founded in Spain by the late exiled writer Jesús Díaz that has attempted to bring a more meditative and intellectually rigorous (but clearly anti-Castro) approach to Cuban politics and culture.

Television is by far the most potent and influential media in Cuba. Very soon Castro discovered the importance of television and used it to exhaustion (three, four, six, seven-hour, two-day speeches) to talk to his people: 'One of the characteristics of the young Cuban Revolution was the intense and appropriate use of television as an instrument of communication and mobilization' (Díaz Castañón 2004: 116).

Until very recently, Cuba had only two national television channels, Channel 6, later rebranded Cubavisión, and Channel 2, renamed Tele Rebelde. Local television stations slowly appeared throughout the years, one in each of the 14 provinces and Isle of Youth, broadcasting only one or two hours a day. All are terrestrial channels; no cable or satellite television is yet available to ordinary citizens. The *National Television News* (the 1 p.m., 8 p.m. and late-night editions) is produced by the so-called Informative System of Cuban Television, a centralized structure under strict surveillance of the Ideological Department of the party, which seldom lets its reporters play the games of investigative or critical journalism (one rare case was, in the 1990s, Havana's former CHTV, now Canal Habana). It was only in 2001 that a third national channel, called Canal Educativo (Educative Channel) 1, was inaugurated, followed in 2005 by Canal Educativo 2, like its namesake dedicated to educational programmes, *teleclases*, and high quality films and documentaries. The epitome of the Communist Party's monopoly of information and opinion is the *Mesa Redonda* (*Round Table*), a panel discussing the widest imaginable array of topics, from globalization to anti-mosquito campaigns. Aired from 6.30 to 8.00 p.m. Monday to Saturday on Cubavisión (and a weekly résumé on Sundays), the *Mesa Redonda*, which features politically-reliable commentators and very often ministers, party officials and Castro himself, has come in recent years to challenge *Granma* as the preferred platform of communication of the Cuban leader. The *Mesa Redonda*'s never plural debates are daily reported in the rest of the Cuban media as news in their own right.

Cuban television is not only politically rigid, but also morally puritanical. Sex (not to mention homosexual or non-traditional sex) and nudity are rare and films are often mutilated before transmission. Even Tomás Gutiérrez Alea's 1994 *Strawberry and Chocolate*, the tragicomic story of love and friendship between a gay intellectual and a young communist student in 1970s' Havana, has not been given a television premiere. Musical genres like heavy metal or rap (and even, for a while, in the late 1960s and early 1970s, Silvio Rodríguez and Pablo Milanés's so-called *Nueva Trova;* a genre that is now officially accepted) have long struggled to gain legitimacy, as they have been associated with political alienation, cultural deviationism or drugs. Latin American *telenovelas* (mostly from Brazil, Mexico, Argentina and Colombia) are tolerated only because of their enormous popularity, but Castro has denounced them as damagingly frivolous and escapist. Not even the hugely popular salsa bands have escaped controversy, as they became unlikely commentators on social and moral transformations on the island. However, contrary to what happened in other socialist countries in Eastern Europe or Asia, western popular culture was never entirely banned in Cuba, although particular authors, bands and films were – most famously The Beatles in the late 1960s. Shortly after the triumph of the revolution, ICAIC's President Alfredo Guevara and newspaper Hoy's director Blas Roca bitterly disputed the merits of films like Pier Paolo Passolini's Accatone and Federico Fellini's La Dolce Vita, which the latter though unfit for the revolutionary education of the Cuban working class (see Guevara 1998: 201). Guevara, Castro's long-time friend and ally, won the day and ensured some degree of intellectual autonomy for ICAIC, which was reflected in the selection of foreign films shown in both cinemas and on television, and also in the outstanding quality of the early Cuban productions, such as Gutiérrez Alea's classics Death of a Bureaucrat (1966) and Memories of Underdevelopment (1968), Humberto Solás's Lucía (1968) or Santiago Alvarez's long series of landmark documentaries. With the exception of films that depict Cuba or its allies in a negative way, most of the mainstream Hollywood catalogue has been shown in either cinemas or on television, very often copies that Cuban producers have simply stolen, ironically protected by the US embargo provisions that prevent the country's media from buying the rights to American films or television shows. In the last few years, even series like Friends, The X Files, or CSI have been shown on Cuban television, just like documentaries from the Discovery or History channels. They have come recently to substitute the Soviet and other socialist countries' productions that filled Cuban television's schedules, including movies, documentaries, series and cartoons, and the infamous muñequitos rusos, Russian toons (although they also came from Poland, Czechoslovakia, Hungary and Rumania) which for a long time replaced Mickey Mouse and Donald Duck (considered vehicles of bourgeois ideology), until these latter were readmitted in the 1990s. The bulk of television time, however, has always been filled with Cuban productions, from telenovelas, sitcoms and talk shows to cartoons like Juan Padrón's emblematic Elpidio Valdés (1974).

Obviously, the works of authors or artists that have criticized Castro or his regime, although not officially banned, are not published or aired on either radio or television. In March 1959, only three months after Castro's triumphal entry into Havana, the new government inaugurated the National Publishing House of Cuba, with 400,000 25 cent copies edition of Don Quixote de la Mancha. Massive prints of Cuban and foreign classic and contemporary authors followed. At the same time, Castro was launching a national campaign to end illiteracy, the first step of his ambitious educational programme. By 2002 Cuba had an estimated adult literacy rate of 96.9 per cent (Human Development Report 2005), second in Latin America only to Argentina's and Uruguay's. The Cuban Institute of the Book, founded in 1967, grouped a relatively large number of publishing houses with the task of satisfying the demands of both a vast educational system and an ever-growing reading public. However, the catalogues of those houses show notable absences of authors whose works Cuban editors either cannot afford to buy, or do not want to. Needless to say, seminal works by Cuban exiled writers, such as Guillermo Cabrera Infante, Gastón Baquero, Lydia Cabrera, Severo Sarduy or Reynaldo Arenas have never been published on the island (or reprinted, if they had an early edition), until the death of their authors, and sometimes not even then, just as the records of exiled artists Celia Cruz, Arturo Sandoval or Albita Rodríguez are never played on Cuban radio. Some writers and artists that never left the country, such as José Lezama Lima or Virgilio Piñera (and many others suspicious of ideological or moral impurity) suffered a prolonged ostracism.

The episode that most clearly shows the reluctance (or chronic political incapability) of the Cuban media to transcend the myths of the official propaganda and accept dissent, took place in May 2002, when former US president James Carter visited Castro in Havana. A previous state visit, Pope John Paul II's in January 1998, had been a great propaganda success for the Cuban leadership, which allowed Havana's Archbishop Jaime Ortega to address the nation on television (the only time in almost half a century that a Cuban Catholic priest has been invited to the state media), and live broadcasts of the masses in which the pontiff and some Cuban prelates called for greater freedom on the island. Carter, however, during a speech at the University of Havana broadcast live on television, mentioned the Varela Project, an 11,000-signature petition to the National Assembly to call free elections. The ex-president asked the Cuban authorities to publish the Varela Project and allow the public to discuss it. The next day, *Granma* and *Juventud Rebelde*, neither of which had previously mentioned the Varela Project, managed to report Carter's speech omitting his request. The silence of the Cuban press became itself an international story (France Press 2002) and, after two days, *Granma* surrendered and published the entire speech. The Varela Project, whose organizers somehow collected an additional 14,000 signatures, has never been published or even mentioned since, in any of the three main Cuban newspapers. A few days after Carter returned home, the National Assembly rejected the petition and proclaimed socialism irrevocable.

Crisis and exodus

In the spring of 2003, Cuba's State Security service arrested 75 dissidents, among them 37 writers and journalists of some independent (although hardly visible and scarcely influential) papers and press agencies that had discreetly appeared in the early 1990s and until the crackdown had been grudgingly tolerated by the government. They were found guilty of conspiring with a foreign power against the Cuban state and condemned to long years in prison, where most of them still remain, prompting groups like Reporters Without Borders to call Cuba 'the world's second biggest (after China) prison for journalists' (Reporters Without Borders 2006). Foreign Minister Felipe Pérez Roque significantly made the point that only four of the detainees had studied journalism at the university or had ever worked in legal media. At the time of Pérez Roque's speech in April 2003, there were 2175 professional journalists working in Cuban media (Pérez Roque 2003). Almost all of them are members of the Union of Cuban Journalists (UPEC in Spanish), founded in 1963 and the only legal professional organization of journalists in the country. The National College of Journalists had been closed after Castro's triumph, just like the six professional schools of journalism running in the country in 1958. In 1962, the University of Havana inaugurated a degree in journalism, but it was not until 28 years later, in 1984, that a proper Faculty of Journalism was created in the same university. Only two Cuban universities (out of 54) – Havana and the University of Oriente in Santiago de Cuba – offered degrees in journalism until the inauguration of a third department in Santa Clara's Central University in 2002. Having a degree in journalism or equivalent qualifications is now compulsory for reporters. In addition to the three departments of journalism, the Faculty of Mass Communication Media of Havana's Arts Institute graduates personnel in other non-journalistic media occupations. The centralization of journalists' professional education in a few closely-watched schools has served well for many years the purpose of ensuring the loyalty of editors, writers and reporters to the party of which they were called 'ideological soldiers'. But studies like those by Segura et al. (1991) and Estrada (1994), confirmed by recent data (Pérez González 2005), now reveal a significant difference between those journalists' professional ideologies (particularly the youngest ones), increasingly leaning towards classical liberal values and ideals, and practices in Cuban media.

The economic crisis that hit Cuba in the early 1990s following the disintegration of the Soviet Union sparked an exodus of journalists out of the job or the country, or both. Between 1989 and 1993, the global social product of Cuba fell, according to different Cuban and foreign sources, by between 39 and 58 per cent (Mesa-Lago 1994: 161). When the crisis hit bottom, in August 1994, riots erupted in Havana and an estimated 35,000 people attempted to cross the Florida Stretch to reach the USA. Being entirely dependent on the subsidies of a near bankrupt state, and technologically outdated, the Cuban media were devastated by the crisis. By 1992, the Cuban print media had to reduce 58 per cent of its total print copies, with 78 per cent fewer copies printed than in 1989. Granma's daily print run was cut by 41.2 per cent and its Monday edition was cancelled. Juventud Rebelde, Trabajadores and the local newspapers became weeklies, leaving the country for the first time since the early nineteenth century with only one daily paper. Television time was cut by 34.9 per cent (Aldana 1992: 5). Only 265 out of 733 newspapers, magazines and journals published across the country survived. Of them, 212 were scientific journals with one or two issues a year (Cancio 1998). A slow recovery was noticeable in the late 1990s. In 1999, Juventud Rebelde was given a Tuesday to Sunday daily run, though Trabajadores and the local papers still have only one (Mondays, in the case of *Trabajadores*) or two prints every week. Special interest magazines that almost disappeared in the early 1990s, such as the children's publication *Pionero* (1961), university students' *Alma Mater* (1922) and women's *Mujeres* (1961) augmented their prints. *Granma* stabilized at over half a million copies a day. Computers replaced typewriters in the newsrooms and television and radio stations were refurbished. But this far from complete recovery has not stopped many professionals from moving out of their jobs to better-off positions in advertising and public relations (two fields that have timidly re-emerged, associated with the tourist industry and the joint ventures between state companies and foreign investors), or simply leaving the country, like tens of thousands of their fellow countrymen. To fill the vacancies, the Union of Cuban Journalists has heavily recruited graduates from other fields who are given short courses of basic writing and reporting and are dubbed 'emergency journalists' by their colleagues.

As he approaches the forty-eighth anniversary of his revolution, 80-year-old Castro seems obsessed with the so-called *Batalla de Ideas* (Battle of the Ideas), a vast campaign of old-styled agit-prop that had its most stunning, if unexpected, success with the return to Cuba of 6-year-old Elián González, a child who in November 1999 had been found floating in the sea of the Florida Stretch after the shipwrecking of the boat in which his mother and 13 other Cubans tried to reach the USA. Elián's triumphal return to Cuba (despite the desperate attempts of the Cuban exiles to keep him in Miami) strengthened the confidence of Castro in a model of intensive and highly-centralized use of media (particularly of television) for political propaganda and popular mobilization. New campaigns, although hardly as successful as Elián's, have been launched in the last five years, usurping the already diminished space and time for information and entertainment in Cuban media. But Cubans are seemingly looking for alternatives. In December 2005, the Havana police launched an operation to dismantle illegal satellite dishes (or any similar artefact) that ordinary Cubans had installed to catch the signal of foreign television channels. In Havana's black market, according to some sources, it is possible to buy a $10 card that activates a one-week subscription to satellite television (Cancio 2005). It was not the first time the police had launched an operation of this sort. After a while, the dishes always reappear.

9 THE MEDIA IN MEXICO: FROM AUTHORITARIAN INSTITUTION TO HYBRID SYSTEM[1]

Sallie Hughes

The Mexican national media system continues to change at a rapid pace compared to systems in longer-established democracies. In the last two decades, the media in Mexico has moved from an authoritarian institution of similarly behaving media organizations to a hybrid system exhibiting market-driven, oligarchic, propagandistic, ideological and civic elements.[2] However, while diversity rather than uniformity in journalistic norms is relatively new, the system's other central characteristics have been around for several decades: media access inequality, concentration of ownership, market share and advertising, and regulatory weakness. All of these traits are interrelated, of course, and improving media regulatory mechanisms, both government-directed and ethical self-regulation, has become a central focus of media reform struggles in the new era of democratic elections. Depending on how that plays out, access inequality and ownership concentration may moderate or strengthen.

Each of the four system traits can be traced to the incomplete transition from a 71-year period of one-party, civilian authoritarian rule to a participatory democracy. The political regime created under the Institutional Revolutionary Party, or PRI, gradually ceded to an electoral democracy in 2000. In the years since peaceful elections removed the PRI from presidential power, traditional liberal-conservative ideological differences have resurfaced and the corporatist structures created inside the former ruling party have weakened, but the media and economic power centres created during the PRI era continue to shape the political and economic development of the country.

Historical development

Mexico's political system and economic model enjoyed legitimacy for much of the twentieth century. Stability prevailed as compared with the rest of Latin America and economic advancement, if uneven, was relatively constant for a majority of urban dwellers until 1982. The Mexican media system grew out of this stability. Media owners and journalists considered themselves part of the system producing the Mexican 'miracle' – growth with stability in one of the least-coercive regimes in Latin America. In return, they received material benefits and prestige, but the system also became internalized rather than remaining a simple quid pro quo exchange. Mexico's authoritarian media system was intact for five decades, from roughly the mid-1940s to the mid-1990s, and its associated behaviours, values and ways of interpreting reality became so pervasive that it could be called an institution of similar organizations and individuals. The media were subordinate rather than autonomous, passive rather than assertive, and reproducers of regime voices and messages rather than a diversity of voices and perspectives.

By the time that newspapers and radio chains coalesced around elite families in the 1940s and 1950s, the media's role and structure had become oligarchic. A small number of elite families controlled most of Mexico's broadcast media and used it to further group interests by supporting the one-party state, with which they were allied and in a few cases connected by family ties (Fernández Christlieb 1985; Sinclair 1986; Bohmann 1989; Torres 1997). The country's current television giant, Televisa, is the direct descendant of these early state-granted concessions, as are some of the largest radio chains. Most of the major newspaper owners, however, are not. The publications owned by the oldest newspaper families could not make a successful shift to the more democratic, market-based media environment of the twenty-first century.

Mexican radio was developed in the 1920s and 1930s along a US-influenced, commercial model rather than a European, public-based system. Many of the broadcast media's founding families had US education and were backed by the US music industry and radio networks, which sought to extend their markets southward. When deciding how to develop television, President Miguel Alemán (1946–52) disregarded the recommendation of a public system from the technical experts and academics he convened, and established instead a commercial television model in Mexico.

Some of the early radio entrepreneurs moved seamlessly into television thanks to their new broadcasting know-how and political connections. Automobile, radio and newspaper entrepreneur Romulo O'Farrill received the first commercial television licence in 1949. Emilio Azcárraga Vidaurreta had built a network of 13 radio stations by the time he received one of the early television concessions, beginning operations in 1951. These families combined with Alemán's own son to form Telesistema Mexicano in 1954, dominating the central Mexican airwaves. Nineteen years later, in 1973, they combined with the only large competing network in the country, Monterrey-based Televisión Independiente de México, to form Televisa.

Televisa operated essentially without commercial competition in Mexico until a network of state-owned stations was privatized in 1993. The state network was sold to Ricardo Salinas Pliego, a retail store magnate and partner of the brother of the sitting president, Carlos Salinas de Gortari. The network became TV Azteca, today's no. 2 network behind Televisa. Televisa's majority shareholder and chief exectutive officer is Emilio Azcárraga Jean, grandson of the radio network founder (Sinclair 1986; Preston 1996; Barrera 1999).

The highest circulation newspapers in the country were not connected to the political class by family, but by material exchange and, to a greater or lesser degree, conviction. Instead of concentration, newspapers proliferated above market capacity. State support in advertising, subsidized inputs such as newsprint, tax breaks, and sometimes direct payments meant few newspapers actually had to survive in the market alone. This fragmentation remains evident in Mexico's overcrowded major newspaper market, despite the closure of O'Farrill's *Novedades* and Televisa's newspaper *Ovaciones* in Mexico City. For example, today there are 25 daily newspapers registered in Mexico City, which together reach only about 1.5 million readers (IPSO-BIMSA 2005).

Despite the large number of dailies, newspaper readership is concentrated in just a few of the major publications in each major city. In Mexico City, readership and advertising are dominated by two newspaper groups, *El Universal* and *Reforma*, which publish their flagship newspapers and the tabloids *El Gráfico* and *Metro*, respectively. Readership diversity is much greater than in most US cities, however. In addition to the big two dailies, another four daily newspapers have smaller, but well-defined readerships that group by ideological or business interest – *La Jornada*, *Milenio*, *El Financiero* and *El Economista*.

Table 9.1 lists Mexico City's newspaper market by readership share, including the racy tabloid *La Prensa* and the sports tabloid *Esto*. Guadalajara and Monterrey's newspaper markets are similarly fragmented, with many newspapers in circulation, but only a handful that reach a meaningful readership level. Thirteen of the country's 20 most expensive newspapers for advertisers are based in Mexico City (Zapata 2004). Many more survive on low budgets or cash injections from undisclosed sources. Political factions continue to support some newspapers (Lara Klahr 2005: 188–273), while major players such as *El Universal* and *Reforma* survive on the market with only about 5 per cent of advertising revenues from governments and political parties.

Table 9.1 Saturated Mexico City newspaper market

Newspaper	Readership share (%)
El Universal Gráfico	5.33
El Universal	3.81
La Prensa	3.38
Metro (Reforma Group)	2.87
Esto	2.07
La Jornada	1.69

Newspaper	Readership share (%)
Reforma	1.68
Récord Diario Deportivo	1.37
Milenio	0.65
Excélsior	0.53
Ovaciones la Segunda	0.45
Ovaciones Deportivo	0.43
El Financiero	0.39
El Sol de México	0.36
Diario Monitor	0.33
El M	0.26
Uno más Uno	0.20
Crónica de Hoy	0.19
El Economista	0.19
El Día	0.09

Source: IPSO-BIMSA (2005)

The mutually beneficial relationship between media owners and the PRI regime continued until societal diversification and a series of economic and political shocks overcame the capacity of a single-party state that had solved the problem of authoritarian succession with the naming of a powerful new president each six years. For journalists who had internalized the PRI media system's values, the repeated devaluations and loss of purchasing power, high-level corruption scandals, political assassinations, electoral fraud and the rise of an indigenous guerrilla movement in the impoverished south were paradigm-shaking. By the eve of the regime-changing 2000 presidential election, journalists in 13 of the leading newspapers across the country espoused values and norms in line with a more citizen-focused approach to journalism.

Variants of authoritarian journalism survive today as the dominant model within government-owned television, where newsroom personnel and direction are imposed by state governors in propagandist fashion and in pockets of the private media outside major cities. Subordination in those media outlets is based on quid pro quo exchanges of advertising or other financial incentives for news content rather than internalization of such norms because the authoritarian model has lost legitimacy. Based on author interviews conducted in four states and the Federal District since 2000, the majority of the journalists in Mexico will espouse values of autonomy, assertiveness and a diversity of viewpoints in interviews, even if they cannot or will not actually practise that style of journalism.

Public broadcasting, in the sense of editorially and financially independent state media, really does not exist in Mexico. The closest examples are Channel 11 of the state-run National Polytechnic Institute, Radio UNAM at the National Autonomous University of Mexico, and four radio stations that are part of the Mexican Radio Institute. All have small audiences. In some states, state governors have purposefully distanced themselves from editorial decisions of state-owned media, but the next governor in line could change that directive and again use state media for propagandist purposes. Content monitoring during the 2006 election suggest this continues to be a problem in many states.

The decline of the PRI media system in a society with an oligopolistic market economy and concentrated social power has produced a hybrid media system with the four general characteristics noted above: (1) inequality in access to media content; (2) concentration of broadcast media ownership and market share, as well as advertising; (3) diversity rather than uniformity in journalistic norms; and (4) regulatory weakness. The rest of this chapter describes these traits in greater detail.

Access inequality

The Mexican media system as a whole offers a wide number of perspectives for the attentive urban dweller, but it is more difficult for people with lower incomes and residence outside the major cities to obtain diverse viewpoints and verified information. Access to diverse perspectives in the media increases with the ability to purchase the elite press, cable and internet in all parts of the country (IPSO-BIMSA 2005; Consejo de Investigación de Medios 2006). While internet use has grown, its reach is still limited and new media development has been slower because of market concentration (Budde Communication Pty Ltd 2006).

Mexico has one of the highest income gaps in Latin America, and this influences the diversity of media that Mexicans can access. Table 9.2 reproduces household income data seen by media programmers and advertising executives. The wealthiest Mexican households, known in marketing parlance as the A and B sectors, comprise 4.5 per cent of the population and make a monthly income of $8200 and above. The 'C+' sector comprises 16.3 per cent of the population and makes a monthly income of $3300 to $8100. The 'C' sector makes $1100 to $3200 per month. After reaching that plateau, most advertisers' interest wanes. The remaining 46 per cent of households in the country live on $1000 or less per month. Figure 9.1 shows Mexico's income pyramid.

Table 9.2 Mexican household income structure, 2004

	%	Cum. %
A / B	4.5	4.5
C	16.3	20.8
C+	9.3	30.1
D	35.2	65.3
D+	20.5	85.8
E	14.3	100.1

Source: Mercamétrica, with minimum wage data from the National Statistics and Geography Institute (INEGI)

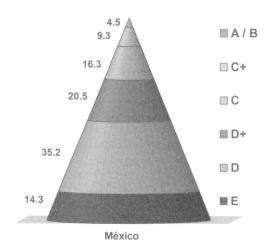

Figure 9.1 Mexico's income pyramid

Source: courtesy of Sergio Lara, *El Universal*

The strong relationship between household income and media access is apparent in Table 9.3, which shows media use patterns by income level in the three largest media markets of Greater Mexico City, Guadalajara and Monterrey (IPSO-BIMSA 2005). Broadcast television is by far the most accessible type of media. About 76 per cent of Mexicans in the three poorest market segments have access to broadcast television. Following that, 43 per cent of the poor have access to FM radio, which is listened to mostly in public transportation. Magazines (29 per cent) followed by newspapers (18 per cent) and AM radio (14 per cent) are next. AM radio reception is probably hampered by technological issues rather than radio receiver ownership, whereas newspaper readership among the poor has increased substantially because of the development of lower cost, tabloid versions of the main elite dailies in the three cities. The tabloids cost a third of the amount of the mainstream newspapers and focus on urban issues, with varying attention to gore and sex. Pay-television and internet, the media offering the widest range of content, perspectives and quality, are also the hardest for the poor to access. Only 4 per cent of the poor watch pay-television or have access to the internet.

Table 9.3 Access to media by type and income level

Type (%)	A/B/C+	C	D+	D/E
Open Air TV	66.41	71.50	74.98	**76.84**
FM Radio	**51.88**	44.46	42.02	44.27
Magazines	**53.18**	42.07	31.27	26.43
Daily Newspapers	**27.46**	23.10	18.23	15.77
AM Radio	12.76	12.41	**14.35**	14.21
Pay TV	**21.33**	12.05	6.28	4.50
Movie Theaters	**18.04**	10.40	5.39	3.18
Internet	**21.73**	11.08	4.91	2.18

Source: IPSO-BIMSA (2005)

Note: data are for Mexico City Metropolitan Area, Guadalajara and Monterrey

Question key: TV, radio, daily newspaper, internet: yesterday; magazine: last edition; movie theatre: last week

The gap in media access is probably larger than the figures from the major metropolitan areas show. Not only is rural poverty more pervasive than urban poverty, but the difficulty of access to radio and print media is greater simply because of distance from urban centres where those media are usually based. One indication of the rural-urban access gap is that while 83 per cent of respondents to a national survey said they watched television news, only 58 per cent of respondents in the survey's rural sample said they did so (MIT/Reforma 2005).

Advanced age may create a different kind of access barrier. Eighty-five per cent of Mexican internet users are between the ages of 13 and 35 (IPSO-BIMSA 2004).

Concentration of broadcast ownership, market share and advertising

Mexican broadcast television is the most-accessible of Mexico's mass media, but it is held by the fewest number of owners. As a result of what

Sinclair (1986) calls 'the Mexican formula' of broadcast media development under the PRI, Mexican broadcast television's ownership structure is
among the most highly concentrated private-sector systems in the world
(Hughes and Lawson 2005a).

More than 90 per cent of the national, open-air television market is
controlled by just two companies, Televisa and TV Azteca. Televisa is also
a major player in radio and the dominant magazine publisher in the
country. Commercial radio is slightly less concentrated. About 70 per cent
of stations are controlled by nine companies (IBOPE AGB 2005; Consejo
de Investigación de Medios 2006; Grupo Radio Centro S.A. de C.V.
2006).

Tables 9.4 to 9.6 display the market players for broadcast television,
television news and Mexico City radio, along with a commonly accepted
measure of market concentration for each media type, the Herfindahl-
Hershman Index, or HHI. The HHI is created by squaring the market
share of each firm competing in a particular market and then summing
the resulting numbers. In this way, the index takes into account the
number of firms and the degree of variation in the size of market share of
each firm. The HHI approaches zero when a market consists of a large
number of firms with roughly equal market shares. The higher the index
score, the more concentrated the market. According to the US Department
of Justice's guidelines for assessing possible mergers, a market with an
HHI of 1000 is moderately concentrated while an HHI score of 1800 is
considered highly concentrated.[3]

Table 9.4 Market concentration in broadcast television

	Market share (%)	Square of market shares
Televisa	64	4,096
TV Azteca	28	784
Local TV	9	81
HHI = 4,961		

Source: IBOPE AGB, 6–24 hours, 28 cities, 2005

Note: all local stations calculated as one entity

Table 9.5 Market concentration in broadcast TV news

Response to the question, in general do you watch a television news programme?

	National (%)	National sum of squares	DF sample (%)	DF sample sum of squares	Rural sample (%)	Rural sample sum of squares
Televisa Network	49	2,401	56	3,136	33	1,089
TV Azteca Network	25	625	25	625	17	289
Local News Outside Mexico City	3	9	0	0	7	49
Polytechnic Institute Channel 11	3	9	2	4	0	0
Others	5	25	6	36	1	1
None	11		7		32	
DK/NA	6		4		10	
		HHI = 3,069		HHI = 3,801		HHI = 1,428

Source: MIT/Reforma Study, Round One, October 2005

Note: none, DK/NA not calculated as part of HHI

Table 9.6 Market concentration in Mexico City radio

	Market share	Market share squared
Grupo Radio Centro	45	2,025
Grupo ACIR	17	289
Televisa Radio	11.4	129.96
NRM Comunicaciones	8	64
IMER	4.2	17.64
MVS Radio	3.9	15.21
Radio Formula	3.7	13.69
Imagen Telecomunicaciones	1	1
XHCME-FM	0.8	0.64
XEDA-AM	0.3	0.09

	Market share	Market share squared
XEABC-AM	0.2	0.04
UNAM	0.1	0.01
XEEST-AM	0.1	0.01
XENK-AM	0.1	0.01
XHVZ-FM	0.1	0.01
HHI = 2556.31		

Source: Arbitron, winter trimester 2006, 6 a.m. to 12 a.m., Greater Mexico City, age 12 and up

As the tables show, the Mexican broadcast television and television news markets are highly concentrated. The Televisa network controls 49 per cent of the national market, 56 per cent of the Mexico City market and 33 per cent of the rural market. TV Azteca controls 25 per cent of the national market, 25 per cent of the Mexico City market and 17 per cent of the rural market. The state university-administered Channel 11 garners 3 per cent of the national market and 7 per cent of the Mexico City market. The HHI calculation for each geographic area finds the highest market concentration in Mexico City (3801), followed by the national market (3069) and then the rural market (1428).

Radio property ownership in Mexico City is not concentrated. There are 15 separate stations or groups offering radio content in the city, according to Arbitron's 2006 winter quarter market survey (Arbitron 2006). However, radio market share is highly concentrated. Not all stations have many listeners. It is unclear whether this is the result of programming, marketing or signal power.

Cable and satellite television services around the world are thought to offer the greatest diversity in media content. Mexican pay-television is no exception, with hundreds of channels available. However, there is little domestic media content production on pay-television and only 4.9 per cent of the country can afford to receive it.

Cable ownership is more diverse than open-air broadcasting at the national level, but concentrated at the city level. Four companies control 50 per cent of the national cable subscriber market, mostly in the big cities, while the rest is fragmented. The largest cable operator in Mexico is Megacable, which controls 18 per cent of the market and operates in the cities of Guadalajara, Hermosillo and Veracruz. Megacable is not part of a conglomerate. Cablemás has 15 per cent of the market and brings together systems across Mexico. It is owned by the Alvarez family, with minority venture capital backing. Mexico City market leader Cablevisión is owned by Televisa and controls 13 per cent of the national market. The smaller Cablevisión Monterrey is owned by media conglomerate Multimedios Estrellas de Oro, which owns newspapers, magazines, radio stations and cinemas. While it dominates the Monterrey market, Cablevisión Monterrey controls only 4 per cent of the national cable market (Budde Communication Pty Ltd 2006).

The degree of market concentration means that broadcast media owners have tremendous power to determine the diversity and quality of content that Mexicans receive from their broadcast system. Moreover, the national television broadcasting companies have become political power-houses. Market concentration coupled with the rise of mediated political campaigning put Televisa in a powerful position months before the 2006 presidential campaigns, when each candidate needed equal access and fair-handed treatment on television to win the election. A radio and television law reform that critics say was tailor-made to give the current television companies control of developing the digital media markets passed the lower house of Congress in late 2005 without a single vote in dissent. The reform passed the Senate intact in early 2006 by a wide margin, even after objections from a coalition of lawmakers from the three main parties, academics, non-commercial radio operators and business owners who wanted to enter the broadcasting and digital markets. The law is currently being challenged in the Supreme Court.

The media advertising market is also concentrated. Like the mega-media companies, there are particular families and people behind the largest domestic advertisers. IBOPE broadcast television advertisers for 2002 are listed in Table 9.7 along with the wealthy families or individuals that own them in part or whole. According to the IBOPE study (IBOPE AGB México 2007), information from companies listed on the Mexican and New York stock exchanges, and the *Forbes* magazine billionaires list, the largest advertiser in Mexico is billionaire bottler and financier Eugenio Garza Laguero. Carlos Slim, the richest man in Latin America, controls companies that make up the second-largest advertising group. Other wealthy individuals and family companies control the remaining major media advertisers.

There are indications that advertisers' power influences Mexican media content beyond the tailoring of content to higher market segments seen in other countries. For example, some newspaper editors have argued that major banks threatened to pull advertisements over critical coverage of the $12.5 billion debtor relief fund Fobaproa in 2003 (Fárber 2003).

Some reporters also stated that they believed large companies pulled weight in their publications. A young reporter commented in 1999, after reporting the troubles of a major manufacturer: 'I realized that in newspapers, or at least where I worked, big business governs the reporting manual and one should be more cautious' (Consejo de Investigación de Medios 2006; Hughes 2006a: 94–100).

Table 9.7 Broadcast advertising giants[1]

Name of principle shareholder or family of shareholders	Wealth in billions of US dollars (latest year 1987–2000)	Year entered Forbes list	Economic sector of holdings	Advertiser controlled	Advertising rank – excluding MNCs – and expenditure (millions of dollars)
Eugenio Garza Laguero	$2.0 (2000)	1993	Soft drinks, beer, banking	Coca-Cola Femsa, Cervecería Cuauhté-moc, Grupo Financiero BBVA Ban-comer	1 $287
Carlos Slim Domit	$7.9 (2000)	1991	Telecommunica-tions, television, retail, other	Telmex, Radiomovil Dipsa/Telcel and 50% Phillip Morris de México	2 $258
Lorenzo Ser-vitje and family	$1.2 (1994)	1993	Baked goods	Grupo Bimbo	3 $194
Angel Losada Gómez	$1.4 (1994)	1993	Retail	Grupo Gigante	4 $117
Enrique Molina Sobrino and family	$1.4 (1994)	1993	Soft drinks	Pepsi-Gemex[2]	5 $115
Pablo Aram-buruzabala Ocaranza/ María Asun-ción Aram-buruzabala	$1.4 (1996) /$1 (2000)	1993 /2000	Beer, television	Grupo Modelo	6 $67
Ricardo Sali-nas Pliego	$3.2 (1998)	1994	Appliance store chain, TV net-work	Grupo Elektra	7 $55

Name of principle shareholder or family of shareholders	Wealth in billions of US dollars (latest year 1987–2000)	Year entered Forbes list	Economic sector of holdings	Advertiser controlled	Advertising rank – excluding MNCs – and expenditure (millions of dollars)
Roberto González Barrera	$1.7 (1997)	1994	Food, baking	Grupo Financiero Banorte	8 $50
Alberto Bailleres	$1.98 (1996)	1993	Mining, banking, ranching, depart-ment store	Palacio de Hierro department Store	11 $41
Bernardo Garza Sada, Eugenio Garza Laguero and Garza Sada family	$2 (1993)	1987	Insurance com-pany, beer, bever-ages, industrial conglomerate	Sigma Ali-mentos	13 $37
Jerónimo y Placido Arrango	$1 (1992)	1992	Retail	Wal-Mart	15 $35
Carlos Per-alta and family	$2.5 (1996)	1994	Telecommunica-tions, manufac-turing	Lusacell	16 $30

[1] Reprinted from Hughes 2006: 96. Constructed from IBOPE advertising data for 2002, public company information and magazine billionaire lists.
[2] Pepsi Bottling Company bought control of Molina's Pepsi-Gemex in 2002.

The federal government's decline as a major advertiser bound broadcast media content more closely to consumer preferences, increasing the importance of ratings in the late 1990s and stimulating the creation of a professional media market research industry. As in other countries, however, quality programming is not always the result. Mexican *telenovelas* win acclaim and are exported worldwide, but broadcast television is also full of cookie-cutter reality shows and mainstream newscasts have become very tabloidized. In the summer of 2003, the author documented a focus on individualized episodes of crime, deforming illnesses and politics depicted as candidate personalization and conflict. For mid-2006, when not covering the presidential election or post-election struggle, the networks filled their newscasts with the World Cup, crime, moderate flooding and weather reports before Israel launched the 'new war' against Hezbollah and provided market-driven television with the dramatic images it thrives upon.

Attack advertisements and negative campaigning by political parties and business interests were a contentious issue in the 2000 and 2006 presidential campaigns, as was the amount candidates spent on media purchases (Moreno 1999, 2002; Avila 2006: 2; Montes 2006: 6).

However, analysts considered the 2006 presidential race to be the dirtiest ever. Moreover, conservative business groups ran attack advertisements against the left that were not counted in the spending caps that electoral laws set for political parties. These advertisements buttressed the Conservative Party's projection of centre-leftist candidate Andrés Manuel López Obrador as dangerous and intolerant. Following are translated transcripts of two of the advertisements, one from the centre-left Democratic Revolution Party (PRD) criticizing the National Action Party (PAN) presidential candidate Felipe Calderón and another from the conservatives criticizing López Obrador.

PRD-sponsored ad: 'The uncomfortable brother-in-law'

Announcer: Calderón said …

Calderón's voice: During my term in the Energy Secretariat, not a single cent was granted either discretionally or in accordance with [contract] regulations to a relative of mine.

Announcer: They explain just one company, but there are 18 more that have millionaire contracts and they want to hide them. That's why the uncomfortable brother-in-law made the single contract public.

Brother-in-law's voice: In Petróleos Mexicanos [the state oil company] we had an income of 20 million pesos in 2004. Of that, 8.5 million would correspond to the period in which Felipe was there.

PAN-sponsored ad: 'A danger for Mexico'

Announcer: López Obrador accepts barbarism that breaks the law. This is what he said after a lynching.

López Obrador's voice: The lesson is with the people's feelings, their beliefs, it's better not to get involved. [Ad repeats track of 'not get involved' in a loop]

Announcer: López Obrador is a danger for Mexico.

Diversity rather than agreement on journalism norms

Cultural and behavioural change among Mexican journalists over the last two decades has been enormous. Where once subordinate, passive and non-diverse, signature traits of an authoritarian news model, two alternative models of thought and action arose to challenge the traditional Mexican media institution. Neither of the two newer journalism models are practised in pure form, but are orientations from which to assess the beliefs and behaviours of journalists, media owners and media organizations. They developed in response to changes in the political economy of news production, such as the retreat of the state from the media advertising market and the rise of public campaign financing for all political parties, but also because of changes in newsroom leaders' mental models of journalism and society.

A civic model, which fosters a participatory form of citizenship and is linked to the awakening of Mexican civil society in the 1980s and 90s, is practised by a cadre of independent and assertive publications across the country that provide their readers with a number of perspectives on politics and social issues. Most are the opinion leaders in their communities, and often the market leaders. They have moved other publications in their areas to practise journalism more akin to their style, either to counteract their circulation gain, because of rising prestige, or because they are the reference points of new generations of journalists. Market-driven journalism, on the other hand, subordinates autonomy, assertiveness and the presentation of diverse viewpoints to ratings and other corporate interests. This is most apparent on network television. Its effects have included more balanced electoral coverage, but also tabloidization of the agenda of mainstream newscasts to focus on crime, image-based dramas and political conflict. Radio journalism, which is more talk-orientated and interview-based, tends to reflect a mix of the two models.

Once the electoral transition occurred, some of the civic trends noted during the transition seem to have slowed. While the largest newspapers have more financial autonomy from the state and criticism of the president and other political figures is now commonplace, deep investigation of political or economic issues and actors is not. Economic and religious figures are seldom criticized.

Importantly, in many publications, partisan or ideological identities seemed to strengthen during the divisive 2006 presidential elections. In other Latin American countries where innovative, civic-orientated newspapers altered the dominant values and behaviours of journalism during or soon after transitions from authoritarian rule, the strengthening of ideological identities foreshadowed the decline of assertive and autonomous journalism. Once governments with similar ideological outlooks took office, the critical edge of journalism dulled. This may be the fate of Mexico's civic press (see Hughes 2006a: Chapter 10).

Coverage of the post-electoral dispute between presidential candidates hints at strengthening ideological identities in top newspaper editors. The conservative, Felipe Calderón, won the preliminary count by less than 1 per cent. The left candidate, Andrés Manuel López Obrador, or AMLO, questioned both the veracity of the preliminary vote count and the Federal Elections Institute, or IFE, which ran the election and conducted the count. He eventually petitioned the Federal Elections Tribune for a vote-by-vote recount. On the day after the preliminary vote count, the main headlines in the country's leading newspapers suggested the conservative leaning of *Reforma*, the leftward leaning of *La Jornada*, and a centrist or balanced intent on the part of *El Universal*. Roberto Madrazo was the PRI candidate, and lost by a wide margin. Roberto Campa was a small party candidate who had no chance of winning. Translation of the headlines follows. The text in bold was the dominant headline that striped across the top of the front page.

Reforma — **Calderón takes the lead ...** and AMLO rejects the result. The IFE closes the preliminary count; a little more than 2000 polling places are left to be counted. Roberto Madrazo supports the IFE. The PRI loses almost everything.

La Jornada — **López Obrador: 3 million votes were lost.** The IFE justifies the number with a 'file of polling place inconsistencies'. The PRD candidate doesn't recognize the preliminary count. The count program was manipulated and has an infinity of anomalies, he accuses. Of the total votes, 827,617 were annulled.

El Universal – PRI leaders negotiate with Calderón behind the scenes. **Governors force Madrazo to give up.** The PRI candidate admits his defeat. Calderón appreciates the Prísta's gesture. Campa asks for the panista to be backed. AMLO questions the preliminary count's figures. The winner will be named by computing the tally sheets.

Television journalism has moved from a style supportive of the state to a mixture of market-driven journalism and the protection of corporate interests. This has produced more-balanced television election coverage and vibrant political discussion shows, but also tabloidization of the mainstream news agenda to focus on crime and individualized maladies. IFE monitoring of political coverage on the national networks over the course of the 2006 campaign found little of the skew in time and value judgments so palpable during political coverage in the PRI era.

While the news was balanced, the television networks were criticized during the 2006 presidential race for providing advertising airtime at a discount to a favoured nominee for the conservative PAN's nomination (Montes 2006). A popular political parody show, *El Privilegio de Mandar*, ended its season of light jokes poked at all political figures with a two-minute speech lambasting López Obrador's demand for a recount of the votes. 'What Mexico needs is to work in peace, united,' said the normally goofy character who ended the season by chastising López Obrador.

The ideological orientations and business interests of the major media outlets mean citizens have to turn to several outlets for full information. Focus group discussions held with college students and blue-collar workers of a similar age at the beginning, middle and end of the 2006 campaigns suggest that much of the public understands the political and commercial agendas of the news media and interprets media content in a sophisticated but cynical manner. The problem, of course, is what may happen because of that cynicism.

Aside from the concentrated advertising market and media owners' ability to push personal agendas, there are other important limits to journalistic autonomy. One is journalists' working conditions. Many of the country's reporters make less than US $500 a month, opening them up to payments or after-hours work that conflicts with their journalistic duties. Probably the biggest challenge to journalistic autonomy is the growth of drug violence along the US border and in a few interior states, which has created a pervasive climate of self-censorship amid increasing attacks and threats against the press (SIP 2006).

Not only do the threats seem to have grown, but the Vicente Fox administration has done little to negate feelings that they go uninvestigated and unpunished. Nineteen Mexican journalists died and two disappeared between the beginning of President Fox's term in 2000 and mid-2006, in attacks thought to be related to coverage of drug trafficking. Newspaper association efforts to investigate the threats and attacks have made little headway in an atmosphere of overwhelming fear. Border newspapers and journalists are just too afraid to fully participate. A new federal prosecutor's office for crimes against journalists lacked resources and other support in the months after it was formed in May 2006, and little headway has been made on the cases since.

Another problem is that state-level politicians occasionally use weak judiciaries and holdover authoritarian laws to punish journalists whose work they dislike. The most infamous recent case is that of freelance journalist and human rights activist Lydia Cacho. Cacho published a book alleging the involvement of important businessmen in a child prostitution ring in 2006 (Cacho 2006).

Cacho was detained in Cancun on criminal defamation charges and driven incommunicado 1500 kilometres to Puebla to face charges. She was held in custody for 30 hours before being brought before a judge. She faces up to four years in prison. Recordings of conversations between a Puebla businessman and that state's governor suggest they plotted to harass the journalist. In one conversation, the businessman suggests to an associate that the journalist be sexually assaulted while in prison.

Regulatory weakness

Reform of PRI era media regulations under the first democratically elected government (2000 to 2006) made advances in terms of institutionalizing access to government information. The 2002 Law for Transparency and Access to Government Information is perhaps the best-designed law in the hemisphere (Doyle 2002; Gill and Hughes 2005). A coalition of independent media, academics, non-governmental organizations and opposition lawmakers pushed through the creation of an independent institute that oversees the process, including final word on appeals regarding petitions for information that were rejected in other federal offices. Laws governing other federal branches and states are weaker, but in general the opening-up of the Mexican government has been remarkable for the short amount of time the country has been an electoral democracy. Another protection for journalists was passed in 2006, allowing reporters to protect their sources from disclosure. This occurred in response to a spate of federal police subpoenas demanding that reporters reveal sources.

However, legal reform has come up short when dealing with ownership concentration. The new Radio and Television Law, passed in 2006 over opposition from non-commercial media, most academics, business owners and even the executive's Communication and Transportation Secretariat, may have created a system for media digitalization that will extend concentrated broadcast ownership patterns into digital and new media for several decades. This could inhibit media content diversity and drag development of new media generally. Internet service providers have complained that internet development was slowed until liberalization in 1997 because telephone giant Telmex, owned by the same financial group that owns internet service leader Prodigy, slowed installation of new lines and service capacity (Budde Communication Pty Ltd 2006). The new law may do the same thing for digital services and new media development, but in a more systematic and legally defensible way. It is no coincidence that the two largest cell phone providers, Telcel and Lusacel, are owned by Telmex, which shares several key investors with Televisa and TV Azteca. Congressional action on the law and the naming of members to the new Federal Telecommunications Commission (Cofetel) who supported the criticized reform suggest that the main television networks have effectively captured sections of the state regulatory capacity.

Conclusion: The Mexican public sphere

Mexico's media reform agenda is dealing with issues such as how to increase diversity in the commercial and non-commercial media; in which way broadcasting in the digital spectrum is going to be developed; as well as how to protect journalists who report on drug trafficking and its dangerous spread into other spheres of society. For journalists, better salaries and working conditions, as well as more in-depth reporting and critical analyses of a wider range of issues and actors, is on the table. A number of non-governmental organizations in Mexico City are working on journalism training, but their reach is very small. An interesting question is whether the return of the left-right ideological axis in the press will overwhelm civic trends toward autonomy, assertiveness and diversity of viewpoints in the news. Should *La Jornada* continue its movement toward pro-PRD coverage and *Reforma* toward the PAN, that will leave *El Universal* with the need to increase its investigative capacity and present explanatory journalism in a non-skewed fashion rather than only presenting balanced information as it is forwarded by political actors. Trends in national television news suggest that tabloidization will continue, interspersed with messages in support of varying company initiatives. On the positive side, the vibrant political talk shows – featuring diverse viewpoints – may also continue. On the table is how to create vibrant local commercial television, which is growing but still rare, and how to reorientate state-owned local media so that they act with editorial autonomy and for the public interest. Unfortunately, many of these initiatives will directly confront powerful economic actors, so their fate is likely to be the status quo. Media reform – greater diversity, autonomy and assertiveness – is linked to the activism of professional journalists, new business actors who want to enter the field, opposition lawmakers who see an opportunity to level the playing field in their favour, and whether organized civil society will be reinvigorated after the close and contentious 2006 presidential election.

Notes

1   The author would like to thank Sergio Alejandro Lara Esperón of *El Universal* for research assistance, Clara Carneiro and Aleida Varela of Arbitrón de México for sharing of Mexico City radio data and Abel Vicencio for access to part of the archives of Medialog: Lógica en Medios, S.A. de C.V. Interpretations of the data are, of course, the author's.
2   Unless otherwise cited, information in this chapter is based upon Hughes (2006a).
3   See the following for an explanation of the Department of Justice's criteria. US Department of Justice and the Federal Trade Commission 1997, horizontal merger guidelines. Available at www.usdoj.gov/atr/public/guidelines/horiz_book/hmg1.html.

10 THE MEDIA IN NICARAGUA: AN ESCAPE VALVE FOR A DYSFUNCTIONAL DEMOCRACY

Arturo Wallace-Salinas

It has been a while since Nicaragua was the regular subject of interest of the international news media and therefore a fairly well known reference for informed citizens around the world. Leiken (2003: 13) noted that in the 1980s Nicaragua was placed among the top ten countries mentioned in US media news stories, just behind Great Britain. The country then fell from grace among media gatekeepers and scholars alike, at the beginning of the 1990s, to the point of practically vanishing. Thus, a little bit of context might be necessary for the younger generation to adequately understand the particularities of Nicaragua's current mediascape. I will try to do this in just a few paragraphs, although I acknowledge this will necessarily entail important omissions and blatant oversimplifications.

The first thing to take into account is poverty. Nicaragua is, in World Bank parlance, a highly indebted poor country, the second poorest of the western hemisphere after Haiti. The latest socioeconomic indicators are an internet search away so here I focus on but in a few. The breakdown of income distribution shows that 45 per cent of all income goes to the richest 10 per cent of the population, while only 14 per cent goes to the poorest, which are the vast majority. More conservative estimates suggest that from a 5.1 million total population, poverty affects 2.3 million people, 831,000 of whom live in extreme poverty, mainly in the Central and Atlantic regions (UNICEF 2006).

For 2003, the UNDP (2005a) estimated the illiteracy rate at 23.3 per cent of the adult population – but functional literacy skills might be even rarer. Radio is the preferred – and sometimes the only – medium available to most Nicaraguans. Radio penetration for 2001 was 80.1 per cent of all urban and rural households. That same year, television sets were available in 59.1 per cent of all households, but only in 30.6 per cent of rural households. Meanwhile, personal computers existed in only 2.2 per cent of all households, almost exclusively in urban areas and more specifically in the capital city of Managua (INEC 2002). This speaks of a country with highly differentiated access to basic resources, because of geographical constraints but mostly because of economic inequality.

To deal with Nicaragua's particular history in a few lines is a much more difficult task, since it still is a subject that stirs passions and sharply divides both Nicaraguans and outsiders' opinions. The question is whether one is willing to summarize this small Central American country's recent political history simply as the story of a transition from dictatorship to democracy, or as a complex and painful evolution from a dictatorship, to a popular democratic project that had to be aborted because of war and American interventionism, and finally to a free-market liberal democracy. Given that there seems to be little discussion about the dictatorial nature of the Somoza regime (1932–79), the subject of controversy is naturally the Sandinista Popular Revolution (1979–89). Both regimes, however, behaved similarly, severely limiting press freedom and other civil liberties. Some argue that authoritarianism was inherent to the Somoza regime whereas in the Sandinistas case it was somehow forced upon them by the circumstances, most noticeably a civil war (the Contra war), waged with the staunch support of the Reagan administration. That might be true to a certain extent, but it actually took very little time for the revolutionary government to start closing down critical media outlets, including some at the left of the political spectrum. That was the case for the small daily *El Pueblo*, shut down in January 1980 for not moving quicker toward socialism (Kodrich 2002). A Sandinista officer reportedly explained: 'Journalism has a right to be free, but it does not have the right to attack this process, even indirectly' (Kagen 1996 quoted in Kodrich 2002: 19). Instead, perhaps the main difference between the Somoza and the Sandinista regimes was that the Sandinista state had direct ownership of important segments of the media system, instead of only colluding with the dominant players of an eminently commercial market or resorting to censorship and other forms of intimidation in order to keep criticism on a leash, being common practice in other Latin American authoritarian regimes (see Fox 1997; Waisbord 2000; Fox and Waisbord 2002).

Things greatly changed after the 1990 electoral defeat of the Sandinista Party. The radio-electric spectrum was liberalized and many new players entered the field. Most press restrictions, notably the possibility of prior censorship, were also lifted (to be replaced by the use of advertising as a pressure mechanism). The whole world could now recognize Nicaragua as a democracy. Nicaragua's current democracy, however, does not differ much from the rest of Latin America's. It is, to a large extent, an 'incomplete' democracy that struggles to deliver its promises in a context of poverty and inequality. Most Latin Americans profoundly distrust their political institutions and a region-wide survey carried out in 2002 found that 54.7 per cent of them were willing to support an authoritarian regime if this would solve their economic problems (UNDP 2004: 131). It is in this context that one has to understand the Nicaraguan media and identify its main virtues, shortcomings and challenges.

A good starting point is to acknowledge the fact that, during the last 16 years, the media have featured prominently in the list of institutions Nicaraguans trust the most. The situation contrasts sharply with the low levels of trust the media and journalists enjoy in countries such as the USA and the UK (see O'Neil 2002), but it is also part of a wider trend, observable throughout the whole of Latin America. According to

Latinobarometro (2005), in 2004, Latin Americans placed only the firemen and the Church above radio, newspapers and television in a list of more trusted institutions. For years in Nicaragua, it was the Catholic Church that usually topped the tables until the media started to take the lead at the beginning of the millennium. By 2001, more Nicaraguans said they trusted the media than they trusted the church (Chamorro 2001). And the situation does not seem to have changed much in the last five years (see *La Prensa* 2005).

However, it would be naive to assume than the Nicaraguan media are outperforming their Latin American, American or British peers. As Chamorro rightly points out 'more than an indicator of the quality of the press – which carries clear ethical and structural deficiencies – this perception indicates that the media are seen by the citizenry as an "escape valve" which allows them to express their discontent with the lack of functionality of other institutions' (Chamorro 2001). Indeed, the high level of trust Nicaraguans seem to have in the media has to be assessed against the performance of a set of political institutions generally perceived as weak, corrupt and failing to deliver on the twin promises of peace and democracy. In this sense, one should not lose sight of the fact that the very same polls that elevate the media also tell a story of profound mistrust and disappointment with the political parties and all the branches of government, which routinely come at the bottom in the ranking of public opinion.

With all of this in mind, I propose we use the next few pages to explore the state of the traditional mass media in contemporary Nicaragua and that we do so both trying to understand the role of the country's particular recent history in shaping the media system, and focusing on the potential the various media have and the challenges they face as Nicaraguans set to building or consolidate a democracy that serves all. To do this, I invite readers to follow me through three different journeys: the written press, radio and television. These three tales will by no means result in a comprehensive portrait of Nicaragua's media system and its history, but they may serve as a beginner's guide for those interested in further exploring the intricacies of mass mediated communication in an emerging democracy. Following Morris and Waisbord (2001), these three accounts share a fundamental concern for the relationship between the media and the state.

Written press: the impeached state

Newspapers have come and gone in Nicaragua during the last 80 years, with only the conservative *La Prensa* (founded in 1926) staying as a constant reference point of the Nicaraguan mediascape. During all this time, with the notable exception of the Sandinista period, the country's newspaper market has basically been a highly polarized one, with a strong second paper usually disputing *La Prensa*'s leadership, and very few other options struggling to compete in a very small market, both in terms of readership and advertising. Since 1990 the main alternative to *La Prensa* has been the left-leaning *El Nuevo Diario* (founded in 1980), which in some periods has even managed to surpass the former in circulation figures. For the last few years, the role of the outsider has been played by *Hoy* (founded in 2003), the sole tabloid format daily that exists in Nicaragua, which is published by the La Prensa group.

Taken together, these three dailies sell a daily average of some 107,000 copies, if one is to believe the latest and highest circulation figures as reported by the papers themselves. (Approached for this chapter, *La Prensa* reported daily sales of 40,017 copies, *El Nuevo Diario* 40,000 and *Hoy* 27,000.) This would mean that, in 2006, there were approximately 21 newspapers for every 1000 inhabitants; a sharp decrease from the 50 per 1000 figure reported for 1990 (UNESCO 2006) and the 83 per 1000 that would constitute the Latin America and the Caribbean average (Kodrich 2002: 56). The rest of the current printed press market is basically limited to a few newsletters that circulate almost exclusively among Nicaragua's small political and business elite (the high-quality *Confidencial*, the gossipy *Bolsa de Noticias* and the political pamphlet *Trinchera de la Noticia*, which after being closed down temporally in June 2005 because of accusations of tax evasion has being focusing on its internet edition); a few glossy magazines, with an even more restricted circulation; and one weekly tabloid, *El Mercurio*, which caters almost exclusively for Managua's huge sprawling market – 'el Mercado Oriental' – with a staple diet of blood and sex. Overall, the written offering is limited (even for a country of 5 million people); but so is, for many reasons, demand.

Still, for such a marginal medium, written press commands a huge influence on Nicaragua's public affairs. This is particularly true for *La Prensa* and *El Nuevo Diario*, which for the last 16 years have practically monopolized the newspaper market. According to Chamorro (2002) this bipolarity is comparable in Central America only to El Salvador, where two editorial groups account for 86 per cent of circulation. He found that in the rest of the region – with perhaps the sole exception of Costa Rica, where the La Nación group has a quasi-monopolistic control over circulation and advertising – the competition tended to be stiffer. The small size of the Nicaraguan market partly explains this. In 2002, Nicaraguan newspapers received only 22 per cent of a paltry US$30 million advertising market. Newspapers' share tends to be much larger in the rest of sub-region, and so is the advertising cake.[1] Another possible explanation, however, involves politics. Even though neither of the two leading newspapers can be considered partisan, they are both fundamentally political. The newspaper offering thus basically mirrors the bi-partisan political tradition that has existed in Nicaragua' for a long time.

Thus, not surprisingly, political actors have played an important role both in trying to broaden, but also in limiting, the offering through direct and indirect censorship and other forms of pressure. The case of *El Pueblo*, mentioned in the introduction, is a drastic example of the latter.

The story of *Barricada*, *La Tribuna* and *La Noticia*, all defunct journalistic projects that once responded to political interests, are good examples of the former.[2] By the same token, the role and success of *La Prensa* and *El Nuevo Diario* can only be understood in the broader context of Nicaragua's politics. To say that *La Prensa* has played a truly important role in Nicaragua's political life would be a gross understatement. For once, the daily is owned by one of the most prominent families in the political history of Nicaragua: the Chamorro family.[3] Its truly defining character, Pedro Joaquín Chamorro Cardenal, left an enormous imprint on Nicaragua's journalistic and political life. Under Chamorro Cardenal, the paper became the main civilian opposition force to the Somoza regime. Chamorro Cardenal's assassination on 10 January 1978, allegedly on the dictator's orders, was instrumental in the establishment of a broad opposition alliance that paved the way for the Sandinista triumph in July 1979. Eleven years later his legacy would also prove instrumental in the electoral defeat of the Sandinistas, at the hands of his widow, Violeta B. de Chamorro. Throughout all this time, *La Prensa* managed to maintain high levels of readership by boldly confronting state power in very difficult circumstances. These actions against *La Prensa* included the destruction of its facilities by members of the Somoza-controlled National Guard in June 1979. The daily, which faced regular censorship under Somoza, also suffered from censorship under the Sandinista government, which accused it of being a tool for American aggression. According to Kunzle (1984: 151) *La Prensa*'s trade was to 'twist facts, slant stories, and peddle lies and half truths in order to undermine the government and make it look bad home and abroad'. Thus, by 26 June 1986, the Sandinista government had prevented the paper from publishing 41 times because of excessive censorship (Kodrich 2002: 20). *La Prensa* was also to be closed on at least nine different occasions during the 1980s, but would come back every time to great acclaim, averaging a circulation of 80,000 during the decade (Kodrich 2002: 56). It was only once Violeta B. de Chamorro took office, in 1990, that the daily started to lose ground and was eventually surpassed in sales by *El Nuevo Diario*, for being considered 'too close' to the sitting government. Eventually, this would force *La Prensa* to undergo a profound renovation (see Kodrich 2002). The paper started to aggressively prosecute Violeta B. de Chamorro's successor, Arnoldo Aleman, and uncovered evidence that later proved key for his eventual imprisonment because of corruption. The opposition daily had found its voice again.

 El Nuevo Diario's story is, at the same time, also part of *La Prensa*'s. It is the story of a split within the Chamorro family, as it had to decide which way to go after the Sandinista triumph of 1979. Suspicious of the Sandinistas' democratic credentials, an important part of the family wanted the paper to back its traditional constituencies, the Catholic Church and the country's conservative business elite, which were shaping up as the main opposition groups (Rockwell and Janus 2003: 74–5). To do this also meant remaining truthful to the daily's traditional hypercritical stance, seen by many as the key to its success. But others, including

Xavier Chamorro, one of Pedro Joaquin's brothers and the daily's main editor after his death, begged to differ. They believed the revolutionary project deserved the daily's support and thus entered into a battle for its control. The split resulted in Xavier Chamorro receiving 25 per cent of *La Prensa*'s capital and the newsprint necessary to start an independent journalistic project (Rockwell and Janus 2003: 74–5). Seventy per cent of *La Prensa*'s staff, including the managing editor, Danilo Aguirre, also walked away with him (Kodrich 2002: 18). *El Nuevo Diario* was born.

The new daily quickly found a space in the media market, happily mixing pro-Sandinista rhetoric with a fair share of what can be generously defined as human interest stories, mostly related to crimes and bizarre events. But for most of the 1980s the paper lagged behind *La Prensa* and *Barricada* in terms of circulation. This would begin to change towards the end of the decade, and would only be fully reversed as *El Nuevo Diario* replaced *La Prensa* as the main opposition newspaper and increased its coverage of politics. Thus, although the relative success of *Hoy* – which carries very little political content – and *El Mercurio* – which claims to have a weekly circulation of 50,000 thanks to its offering of sex and blood (Rockwell and Janus 2003: 80) – suggests that there is demand for something other than politics, the Nicaraguan written press has made its mark (and apparently, also found its place) fundamentally acting as watchdogs of the state. Both *La Prensa* and *El Nuevo Diario* often lead the critique of the political class and political institutions. The aggressive brand of investigative journalism they favour tends to assume an adversarial tone and to focus on high profile corruption cases. Both outlets seem to have concluded that in democratic Nicaragua there is no space for partisan newspapers. A large part of their success lies behind this. Theirs has not been a small contribution to Nicaraguan democracy.

However, their aggressive prosecution of political power seems to leave little time for anything else. And the independence both newspapers exhibit in their often crude assessment of the traditional political class, including the government and other state branches, hides more subtle patterns of broader ideological alignment (*La Prensa* is clearly conservative and aligns with the business elite, whereas *El Nuevo Diario* represents a left-of-centre populist alternative). Moreover, this supposed independence and objectivity does not always apply when they cover key economic and political elites. The almost exclusive focus on political affairs, and both newspapers' dependence on advertising revenues, has also limited their interest and capacity to investigate and denounce private sector abuse and adequately defend consumers' rights in an increasingly deregulated market. Moreover, Nicaraguan papers are not providing their readers with the in-depth information and analysis they need to adequately assume their role as citizens. Recent studies (e.g. Wallace 2007) show that newspaper articles very seldom try to put daily events in their broader context or to identify patterns, structural causes and possible solutions, even when following a story for several days. None seem interested in articulating an informed dialogue with the state, busy as they are in impeaching it. One has to ask what consequences this might have for the future of democracy.

Radio: the absent state

Radio arrived to Nicaragua between 1921 and 1929, from the hands of the US Marine Corps, during one of the many US military interventions that marked Nicaraguan history during the first half of the twentieth century. As Crabtree (1996) puts it: 'Radio began in Nicaragua as it did in most Latin American countries: the United States provided the technology and training in order to create markets for American goods, services and ideas'; and radio in Nicaragua has indeed been essentially a commercial activity, with the notable impasse of the Sandinista period.

This does not mean its development was not affected by the dictatorial nature of the Somoza regime. The Somoza family owned several radio stations and through the infamous 1960 Radio and Television Code the dictator also tried to suffocate dissident voices. Article 47 of the 'Black Code', as it became known, prohibited any transmission that would go against peace, the state's safety, public order, private property and Nicaragua's good name; as well as any kind of Marxist or atheist propaganda. Limits were also established as to who could be involved in media operations (O'Donnell 1995). What the regime could not get through the strict interpretation of the Code was obtained through physical repression, bribery and the selective allocation of the government's and the Somozas' business empire advertising. To avoid possible sources of conflict, most radio stations did not carry institutional news broadcasts. Instead, radio owners leased space to independent journalists, who had to make a living out of the advertising they sold. Even though by 1973 the total number of radio stations did not exceed 52 (Lapple-Wagenshals quoted in Crabtree 1996), the number of registered news programmes throughout the 1960s was 134 (O'Donnell 1995).

Still, news was only one of the features, and perhaps not the main one, that made radio the most important communication media in Nicaragua until 1990. It was with the start of medium-wave transmissions, in 1948, that radio became the driving force behind the creation of some sort of shared national identity, mostly through the broadcasting of *radionovelas* (soap operas) and professional league baseball (Rothschuh 1990; O'Donnell 1995). The voices of Radio Mundial's cast were familiar to pretty much all Nicaraguans, who laughed and cried with the station's soap operas. Owned by a prominent conservative family (Arana Valle), Radio Mundial was the dominant force during the 'golden age' of radio broadcasting in Nicaragua, producing up to 12 different *radionovelas* a day and exporting them to the rest of Central America (O'Donnell 1995).

The arrival of the Sandinistas to power changed many things. According to O'Donnell, the Frente Sandinista de Liberación Nacional (F.S.L.N.) agenda in the field of media and communications focused on two main objectives. Firstly, it wanted to eradicate American cultural domination by building a new national culture based on popular class-cultural practices that had been forbidden or neglected by the ruling elite. More importantly, though, it also wanted to strengthen 'the revolutionary political practice' by educating and providing people with the tools needed to better understand their own reality, analyse it and transform it (O'Donnell 1995: 149). This was to set the basis for an ambitious community or popular radio project, perhaps the only one to have been pursued at a national scale (Crabtree 1996). This demanded the state's involvement, and the state did get involved. Only four non-commercial radio stations existed before 19 July 1979 (Crabtree 1996). By 1988, from a grand total of 44 radio stations, 19 were state-owned (most of them confiscated from the Somoza family and from those deemed too close to the regime) and the state also had partial control of another three (Rothschuh 1988: iv). The Sandinista government also made an effort to ensure radio coverage of the whole of the national territory, including those areas traditionally neglected by the commercial operators that focused in Managua and the wealthier Pacific coast. Most state-owned radio stations were part of the the Corporacion de Radiodifusion del Pueblo (the People's Radio Broadcasting Corporation, CORADEP), formed in 1981 to create a participatory model of alternative community-orientated radio broadcasting. According to Crabtree (1996) CORADEP stations were pioneers in implementing regionally specific radio programming that addressed the most urgent needs of the population, as identified by themselves, thanks to a great deal of interaction between radio station personnel and the communities they served. The project, however, would be conditioned by the importance of the medium for the ideological and psychological war waged between the Sandinista government and its opposition. As Rothschuh (1988: 17) puts it, 'In war times, the use of mass media has to be redefined ... Both internally as externally its use has to be conditioned to military strategy and tactics. This is the main feature of the American propaganda apparatus in the war it has waged against Nicaragua since 1981'. But, the same also applied to Sandinista-controlled radio, which became recognized as 'the main defence in the "radio wars" implemented as part of Reagan administration efforts to avert Sandinista success' (Frederick quoted in Crabtree 1996). Thus, in practice, the model empowered people who had not formerly been taken into account in the conduct of public affairs. However, the debate and discussion was limited to administrative issues or diverging views on how to attain the Revolution's goals. These goals, and the basic principles underlying the options under discussion, as 'orientated' by the 'revolutionary vanguard' that was the FSLN, were never to be discussed, nor questioned. Whether people in practice accepted this because of conviction – because in a context of war they were ready to accept that to criticize was to 'provide ammunition to the counter-revolution' – or because of fear, is something that deserves to be discussed; but the fact cannot be denied. Critique was clearly divided between 'constructive popular critique', as expressed through CORADEP radio, and 'irresponsible critique', that was not to be tolerated (see

O'Donnell 1995: 160). Non-Sandinista commercial radio stations had to submit to the censorship of the General Directorate of Media at the Ministry of the Interior, charged with making sure that no 'wrongful information' on economic and military matters was broadcast or published. In March 1982, after a state of emergency was declared to respond to the Contra war, 24 independent news programmes in seven independent radio stations were closed down (Kodrich 2002: 19).

The situation eased up a little towards the end of the decade and as the Central American peace process progressed. As the 1990 elections approached, many restrictions were lifted. However, the end of the armed conflict and the consolidation of democracy would bring about important changes not only in terms of less restrictive media laws: it also signalled the end of a national project of alternative community-orientated radio broadcasting. The Sandinista government had already stopped supporting economically most of the CORADEP stations in 1989 (the exception being those operating on the Caribbean coast) and electoral defeat meant the property regime would also have to change. Most of the state-owned stations were privatized in favour of Sandinista sympathizers that had been operating them, as part of what has been called *La Piñata*. They would have to survive in a completely new context and try to accommodate either their community-service orientation or their role as ideological apparatuses (or both), with the demands of increasing commercial competition.

The new democratic regime involved itself heavily with radio only between 1990 and 1995 in order to lift most press and ownership restrictions, authorizing 54 new frequencies in AM and 68 in FM and thus basically exhausting the available spectrum in favour of mostly commercial operators (Rothschuh 1995). The liberalization process proceeded indiscriminately, ensuring political plurality but without making sure the system acknowledged its public service obligations. In the new Nicaragua, the market alone was left to guarantee content variety. However, radio's advertising share started to shrink significantly as a result of the boom in television and as the number of radio stations increased exponentially, mostly thanks to numerous small FM stations operating at the municipal or departmental level. By the end of 1995, Rothschuh estimated the number of stations operating in Nicaragua at a grand total of 117, 68 of which were operating from the capital city of Managua (Rothschuh 1995: 31). In 2002, Chamorro estimated the total number at a mesmerizing 250, which had to make do with a paltry 13 per cent of a US$30 million advertising market (Chamorro 2002).

This has of course had significant effects on the radio network. Very few stations can call themselves national broadcasters or claim to be able to systematically attract a significant share of the audience. The best placed ones to do so are generally stations with clear political leanings, which Rockwell claims are mostly interested in rallying their supporters and disseminating their political agenda: 'The ethical ideal of serving the public by providing information seems to have been lost in this equation, ranking somewhere below making profits' (Rockwell and Janus 2003:

89). This critique also applies to the only state-owned radio, Radio Nicaragua, which acts as a mouthpiece for government. Those radio stations that try to make a profit, or at least to guarantee their sustainability, tend to cater for the same reduced type of audience and focus on the cheap recipe of popular music plus phone-ins, especially on FM. Meanwhile, the practice of leasing space to independent journalists, which still continues, has not helped to improve the quality of radio journalism. In a weird twist of the participatory radio model that characterized Nicaragua's radio during the 1980s, several stations happily open their microphones to bystanders to report, through their mobile phones, on any kind of incident they might happen to have seen. These 'news hunters' reports, as a popular Managua radio station calls them, are usually based on hearsay, and are rich in speculation and unnecessary gory details. This has affected the medium's prestige to the point that the country's main Media and Communications School was forced to close down its radio degree, because of minimal demand.

There are, of course, notable examples of exciting radio, some of which builds upon the participatory school of the 1980s. However, most of these stay at the periphery (both literally and figuratively speaking) and thus have a very limited impact on the system. A case in point is 'Radio Cumiche', an Estelí-based radio station produced entirely by and for children ('*cumiche*' meaning 'the little one' in Nahuatl). More recently, UNESCO also recognized Radio Stereo Yes, a Matagalpa-based radio station that has run a literacy campaign for five years. However, without an adequate regulatory framework that makes public service values an obligation for the richest and better-equipped commercial stations, these sorts of practices will remain the exception and not the rule. And large parts of the Nicaraguan population will continue to rely on the radio, without being adequately served.

Television: the missing state

Television is perhaps the medium less conditioned by Nicaragua's recent history. Television's story is basically a contemporary one, more influenced by relatively fresh trends such as the internationalization of media markets and the commercial nature of the system than by Nicaragua's political history (although one could argue than the apparent aversion to public service broadcasting is largely informed by the latter). It was Somoza who first introduced television to Nicaragua in 1955, more as a private commercial venture than a political tool. Televisión de Nicaragua, S.A, which broadcast on Channel 6, would stay as Nicaragua's sole television station until 1965, when Somoza opened the market to a second player, Televicentro de Nicaragua, S.A. Canal 2. By then, the infamous 'Black Code' (see previous section) was already operating, but in television's case this was not as relevant as in radio's. Canal 2 was operated by Somoza's fellow liberal, Octavio Sacasa, and the audience was very limited.[4] Thus, for most of the 1960s and 70s, the Nicaraguan television system was basically a two-channel one which catered for a growing but still small audience. Programming did not differ much, consisting of mostly imports, including Mexican *telenovelas*, which attracted the bigger audiences.

At the 1979 Sandinista triumph, the revolutionary government seized both television stations and created the Sandinista Television System, SSTV. Things were to change quickly and dramatically in the next few years, although not always in the direction the Sandinista authorities predicted. The elimination of the 'ideologically reactionary' soap operas, for instance, posed two important problems: first, audiences, including Sandinista militants, really liked them. Second, there was nothing else to replace them. The same applied to American cartoons, filled with violence and 'capitalist ideology' but readily available in the broadcasters' warehouses. Efforts to replace this sort of programming with more high-brow content from the socialist bloc failed because of a cold reception from the audience.

For the Sandinista political project, the acceptance of the masses was something truly important. It was a project fundamentally based, according to Mattelart, not on the *imposition of*, but the fight *for* cultural hegemony (Mattelart 1986). This required some sort of 'normality' and at least the impression of plurality. And it was certainly safer to guarantee that plurality at the more abstract symbolic level, rather than at the level of political debate. Thus, to watch television in Nicaragua's 1980s was sometimes a surreal experience. Old and new American series (such as *Columbo, The Six Million Dollar Man, Alf, Punky Brewster* and *The Knight Rider*) and Hannah Barbera and Warner Bros cartoons shared air space with Mexican (and later Brazilian) soap operas, outdated Spanish nature documentaries, Cuban-made series picturing Cuban revolutionary success in fighting American aggression, and a fair share of national programming. This plurality, however, never translated into the journalistic sphere. The one-sided approach to television news during the 1980s was evident from the name of the SSTV main newscast, aptly called *Noticiero Sandinista* (the *Sandinista Newscast*).

National programming was an important feature of Sandinista television. According to O'Donnell (1995: 171), national television programming made up 37 per cent of all programming in 1985. A big part of the local production focused on news and current affairs shows, including a few attempts to adapt popular radio practices, but national programming also included children's programmes and other cultural and educative programming as well as sports broadcasts. Local-made fiction was less common, and when it made it to the screen it was clear that the message mattered more than the aesthetics. Several state institutions such as the Ministries of Defence, the Interior or Agriculture were equipped and trained so they could produce their own material, which sometimes fed the television schedule (O'Donnell 1995). Some would have called their products 'educational', others 'propagandistic'. It is accurate to say that never in the history of Nicaragua did the state support cultural initiatives, including video and film production, as during the 1980s. However, it also would be accurate to claim that this support was mostly limited to forms of expression and content deemed functional for the revolutionary project.

Things began to change when the Central American peace process resulted in the 1990s elections and Canal 6 allowed the opposition to broadcast an independent newscast. And as was the case for radio and the written press, the electoral defeat of the Sandinistas greatly changed television in Nicaragua. Canal 6 stayed as a state-owned broadcaster but the new government did not assign to the medium the importance its predecessor had. Without adequate funding, the channel abandoned any pretension of responding to some of the basic obligations of a public service broadcaster, and quickly started to lag behind in the newly liberalized market. News-wise, the channel also continued to act in essence as a mouthpiece of the government, which did not help in the fight for ratings. When president Arnoldo Alemán started to pay more serious attention to Canal 6 towards the end of his term of office, he seemed to do so mostly out of personal economic interest. It was Alemán's indictment for embezzling US $1.3 million from the state-owned broadcaster in March 2002 (a year after he had left office) that started the judicial process that resulted in his being sentenced to 20 years imprisonment. Canal 6 was shut down that very same month and has stayed off air ever since.

The second half of the SSTV, Televicentro de Nicaragua, Canal 2, was returned to its previous owner, Octavio Sacasa, who had fled to Miami after the Sandinista revolution. Canal 2 quickly became the dominant force in Nicaragua's television network, mostly thanks to an offering of soap operas and UNIVISION programming, but also thanks to its American-styled news that set the station apart from the state-owned broadcaster. Thanks to the staunch support of both the Chamorro administration and the Nicaraguan business elite, which favoured the station with the biggest chunk of the advertising market, Canal 2 was soon able to cover most of the national territory and keep investing in the newest technology and programming. Thus, when other commercial television stations were authorized to broadcast, Canal 2 was already miles ahead of the competition. For most of the 1990s the broadcaster would command up to 75 per cent of the country's total audience. However, local programming was and remains rare (it currently accounts for only 22 per cent of the station output) and it is almost exclusively composed of news and current affairs programmes, light-hearted talk shows and variety magazines. In September 2006, US programmes took up 38 per cent of Canal 2's airtime, whereas Latin American and Hispanic programming took up 47 per cent (the rest coming from more 'exotic' sources such as Japan, Canada and Europe).

Although perceived as a conservative station, with strong links with the government and influential economic groups, Canal 2's news operation tended to be recognized as the country's most professional (Rockwell and Janus 2003: 83). However, as the consolidation of media groups connected with trans-national players started to threaten Canal 2's dominance of the market, the station started to remove some of its more sober nationally produced programmes in favour of more imports, while also embracing the trend towards the tabloidization of news that currently afflicts most of Nicaragua's television. In the Nicaraguan case tabloidization does not refer only to a shift towards more entertainment-orientated content and the prioritization of visual elements over rational ones but, more worryingly, it expresses itself as an almost complete abandonment of the political agenda in favour of news coverage almost exclusively limited to violence and crime, and rich in gory imagery. Nicaragua's television screens are thus filled with graphic representations of both violence and the results of violence, showing close-ups of injuries, people in pain and even corpses (Wallace 2007). No channel embodies this trend more than TeleNica, Canal 8, one of the first commercial television stations to air after the Sandinista defeat. Violeta B. de Chamorro's administration assigned the Channel 8 frequency to Carlos Briceño, who had handled part of the communications operations of the then president's campaign. With a much smaller purse than Canal 2, Briceño set up a station that at first covered only Managua and would mix second-rate American programming with pro-government news and heated political debates. Struggling economically and unable to compete with the popular Brazilian and Colombian soap operas broadcast by Canal 2, Briceño started to experiment with a less political approach to news and a keen eye for bloody events. The formula proved a success. Not only was it cheaper to produce (especially if one was willing to broadcast raw material without editing out the grossest bits), it also seemed to interest audiences much more than the continuous political feuding that characterizes Nicaragua's politics. At the beginning of the millennium, Noticiero Independiente quickly started to catch up with Canal 2's flagship newscast, *TV Noticias* (UCA 2003) and eventually became the nation's preferred news show. These developments took all television operators by surprise and most of them, including Canal 2, decided to try to beat Briceño at his own game, launching their own versions of tabloid television news. In the meantime, Canal 8 became the main broadcaster of national programmes, mostly news and current affairs, which account for almost half of the station's programming and represents 76 per cent of all of its output. American shows account for 10 per cent, and Hispanic or Latin American shows for 11 per cent.

Over the other half of Nicaragua's television spectrum looms large the figure of Angel Gonzalez, a Miami-based media baron with large interests in Central America (see Rockwell and Janus 2003). Although Nicaraguan legislation states that no foreigner can exert majority control of electronic media outlets, Gonzalez is the controlling force behind Radio Televisión de Nicaragua, S.A. RATENSA, which operates Channels 4 and 10, as well as four FM radio stations. Gonzalez's involvement in Nicaraguan television forced a change in the whole system. His flagship station is Canal 10, which has challenged Canal 2 as the dominant player in terms of audience. Fundamental for this reshuffle was Gonzalez's capacity to take away from Canal 2 its more popular programmes (coveted soap operas,

UNIVISION favourites such as *Sabado Gigante*, and the latest American films), thanks to a large extent to his dominant position in the sub-regional market. Imports take up 87 per cent of the station's air time (US, 42 per cent, Hispanic or Latin American, 45 per cent). Of all of the Nicaraguan television stations, Canal 10 is the one that broadcasts the least locally produced output (only 13 per cent of weekly airtime), and all of it is local news. The commercial imperative of maximizing audience figures clearly informs the station's approach to news (in 2003, the well respected *Noticias 10* was cancelled and replaced by a tabloid television newscast, *Acción 10*). However, this approach has also allowed the station to distance itself from potential sources of conflict with Nicaragua's political classes. In another controversial decision, in August 2006 Canal 10 chose not to broadcast a particular edition of an UNIVISION show that carried an interview with Zoilamerica Narvaez, stepdaughter of the Sandinista leader and presidential candidate Daniel Ortega, who had accused him of sexual abuse. Off the record, the station explained it had taken the decision 'because they did not want to get involved in politics' (*La Prensa* 2006).

RATENSA's ownership of Canal 4 may also the deference shown to the Sandinista leader, especially from a man reported to align with the Central American far right (see Rockwell and Janus 2003). Shortly before abandoning power, the Sandinista party obtained the Channel 4 frequency, hoping to use the station to consolidate its position as the main opposition force in Nicaraguan politics. For a while, Canal 4 acted as the mouthpiece of the FSLN, although without being able to reciprocate the sophisticated approach to partisan television they favoured in the 1980s. Without state support, and facing the boycott of Nicaragua's business elite, the station struggled to stay on air and maintain an already limited audience, composed mostly of the Sandinista faithful. Gonzalez offered to provide fresh programming to the ailing channel on credit, and then offered to exchange the resulting debt for partial ownership of the station. The populist party and the conservative media baron thus become business partners. Even though Canal 4 is now officially part of RATENSA, the Sandinista's have retained editorial independence over all the station's news programmes, which account for 74 per cent of all locally-produced content broadcast by the station. However, as with Canal 10, most of Canal 4's output is composed of imports coming from the USA (32 per cent) and the big Latin American and US-based Hispanic networks (43 per cent). Only 25 per cent of the content is made in Nicaragua. So much for fighting what Sklair (2201) calls 'the culture-ideology of consumerism'.

The latest actor in Nicaragua's television system is Nicavisión, Canal 12, also licensed to a prominent conservative family shortly after the 1990s' elections – the Arana Valle family, of Radio Mundial fame. With limited reach and limited resources, Canal 12 competes with Canal 4 both for the title of the most partisan broadcaster of the contemporary Nicaraguan television system (Canal 12 is closely aligned to former president Arnoldo Alemán) and for the last place in ratings. Interestingly, these two are the only channels that have clearly rejected the trend towards tabloidization (although the quality of their news content suffers from their partisanship). This is particularly noticeable since Canal 12 is the second channel in terms of airtime devoted to national production (31 per cent of the total, 88 per cent of which is news and current affairs).

As it is the case in radio, political plurality seems to be somehow ensured by the whole of the television system, although the fact that the outlets paying more attention to political issues generally assume fierce partisan positions suggests that established political forces may struggle for adequate representation. More worryingly, however, is the fact that the importance assigned to public affairs has been rapidly shrinking to leave space for more human-interest stories, as commercial interests push television to focus more and more on entertainment and commercial gain.

To a certain extent, the tabloidization of television news has contributed to making visible problems traditionally neglected by an elite-focused media, exposing urban violence and criminality that especially afflict the poorest segment of Nicaragua's population. Wallace (2007) found that a sizeable part of the audience of the sensationalist Nicaraguan newscasts identified themselves with the people and the difficulties they face. The news was useful to them because they could use the stories as cautionary tales, and make practical decisions, such as avoiding a particular neighbourhood or taking a different route to work. The same study, however, also found that these news stories are seldom placed in the wider context and that the aggressive way the cameras and reporters approach people in pain or suffering from the consequences of violence very often also borders on the abuse of basic human rights. Negative stereotypes are being reinforced, and poverty is being criminalized. In a context were possibilities for content regulation can easily degenerate into political censorship and where commercial operators have little incentive to change a cheap winning formula, a public broadcaster able to offer itself as an example of different and successful practices, engaging with the audience in a different way, appears to be needed. Thus, in the case of television, the state is not simply absent, it is badly missing, and Nicaragua's current political situation makes its return extremely difficult.

Conclusions

By having played a decisive role in exposing corruption and denouncing the wrongdoings and limitations of the political system, the media in Nicaragua can claim to be one of the few functional democratic institutions in this small Central American country. However, by focusing almost exclusively on their role as watchdog in relation to the state and by neglecting other important public service roles, the various media have limited their potential contribution to the consolidation of Nicaragua's still incipient democracy. These limits are related to the fundamentally commercial nature of the current Nicaraguan media system, but also greatly conditioned by the country's political history. Decades of governmental abuse, control and censorship have generated a resistance to the idea of any sort of public intervention. The result is a concept of public service broadcasting that is problematic even for those placed on the left of the political spectrum, and fears of undue outsider intervention greatly limit the prospects for truly accountable media.

The profound suspicion that characterizes Nicaraguans' relationship with the political system frames the debate. The debate, on the other hand, concentrates and limits itself to the issue of press freedom, making it difficult to engage in a discussion about other issues such as communicative rights and citizenship, key themes in current debates in other parts of the world (Murdock 1999). Nicaraguans should engage therefore in this alternative debate. The possibility of finding the 'proper distance' (Silverstone 2003) between the media and the state will be fundamental for the future of the Nicaraguan democracy.

Notes

1   According to Chamorro's estimations, in 2002 Guatemala had six newspapers, which shared 30 per cent of a US$126 million advertising market. Costa Rica also had six different dailies, which received 38 per cent from US$125 million. In the case of Panama, five newspapers took 28 per cent from US$120 million. El Salvador also had five dailies whose share amounts to 41 per cent from US$110 million, whereas Honduras has four dailies sharing 36 per cent of US$84 million advertising market (Chamorro 2002).

2   *Barricada*'s is perhaps the most dramatic story, and one that actually illustrates well both the constructive and destructive instincts of Nicaragua's political class in its relations with the press. Born as 'the official organ of the Sandinista party' on 25 July 1979, a few days after the Sandinistas took power, *Barricada* enjoyed broad circulation during the 1980s, under the direction of Carlos Fernando Chamorro, son of the *La Prensa* director, Pedro Joaquín Chamorro. Once the Sandinistas were voted out of office in 1990, *Barricada* tried to reinvent itself as an independent and professional media outlet, able to articulate a constructive and informed opposition. However, without the support of the state, and lacking advertising from the mainly Conservative business community, the paper started to suffer economically as the party leadership also started to grow more and more uneasy with this new type of journalism. In 1994, Chamorro was forced to resign and 80 per cent of his staff were either fired or resigned (Rockwell and Janus 2003: 79). *Barricada* returned to act as a mouthpiece of the FSLN and eventually closed down in January 1998, averaging sales of less than 8000 copies (see Kodrich 2002). *La Tribuna* (1993–9) and *La Noticia* (1999–2001) were both journalistic projects associated with members of the incumbent Liberal Party (in *La Noticia*'s case, the then president Arnoldo Alemán), both of which only managed to survive for less than 10 years. For more details, see Kodrich (2002).

3   Five members of the Chamorro family have occupied Nicaragua's presidency: Frutos Chamorro (1853–5); Pedro Joaquín Chamorro (1875–9), Emiliano Chamorro (1917–21 and 1926), Diego Manuel Chamorro (1921–3) and Violeta B. de Chamorro (1990–6).

4   Only 60,000 television sets existed in the country in 1975, most of them in Managua (O'Donnell 1995: 145), whereas by 1979 radio ownership amounted to some 650,000 sets (Crabtree 1996).

11 THE MEDIA IN PARAGUAY: FROM THE COVERAGE OF POLITICAL DEMOCRACY TO THE OBSESSION WITH VIOLENCE

Susana Aldana-Amabile

Paraguay borders Bolivia, Brazil and Argentina and covers 406,752 square kilometres with a population of less than 6 million.[1] Forty per cent of this population lives in poverty.[2] Of this number, 38.4 per cent live in urban areas, while 40.1 per cent are in the countryside. It was not until the 1990s that the urban population overtook that of the countryside, with the highest concentration of people living in the capital and surrounding cities (Greater Asunción). This chapter discusses the changing role of the media and the shifting thematic agendas during a period of dramatic political transition from the end of Stroessner's dictatorship in 1989 to the present. In the period immediately following the transition to democracy, the media reflected a rise in public political engagement and enjoyed a high degree of credibility. Towards the end of 1999, however, there was a downturn in public confidence as large sections of the mass media took an increasingly partisan stance.

The Red Party (Colorado Party) has been in power since 1947[3] and has exhibited a range of political tendencies and leadership styles by means of powerful groups that occupy the administration of the state 'from within'. This party remains in power due to agreements made between economic and factional groups. Paraguay suffered one of the longest dictatorships in South America with the same leader for almost 35 years: General Alfredo Stroessner (1954–89). Since the establishment of democracy in February 1989, there have been four presidential periods, with a new written constitution in 1992 and new state institutions.[4] However, these have not effected major changes in the country's poverty, inequalities and concentration of power. Nevertheless, the influences, credibility and themes of the mass media have changed alongside people's attitudes to it. Television offers mainstream audiences news that is generally perceived as credible, but the elite audience prefers newspapers and cable channels (mostly foreign programmes, especially from Argentina).

Another important factor in understanding the influence and consumption of the media in public life is that Paraguay has two official languages, Spanish and Guarani, with 59 per cent of households usually speaking

Guarani and 35.8 per cent predominantly speaking Spanish.[5] There are two 'types' of audience-consumers: the poor, unemployed population in suburban or rural zones who only have access to free (terrestrial) television,[6] and another group, small in number but with a great deal of political and purchase power. The latter group has access to the internet, cable channels and so on. Their consumer habits differ greatly from those of their poorer counterparts in ways that further widen the experiential gap between the two. These strikingly different patterns of consumption extend to media outlets in ways that account for the influence of the mass media on the country's democratic processes. The 1990s saw the rise of popular newspapers,[7] which were consumed by vast numbers of people at a time when advertising investment plunged and there was an economic recession, bringing high levels of poverty and unemployment.[8]

Paraguayans now have greater access to information than during the long period of Stroessner's dictatorship, which was accompanied by high levels of censorship and self-censorship. However, media ownership is concentrated in the hands of national economic groups that seek to influence public opinion and obtain political power. The idea that the media sets the public agenda for discussion is not widely understood either by Paraguayan citizens or by its republican institutions, nor is it the instrument of further democratization. The country's media outlets are 'private businesses' that have failed to hold the government to account for its corruption or to interrogate the position of media moguls. Although the 'ordinary Paraguayan' is present in the media, he is increasingly less of a 'counter-power' and more a dupe of those who already have power.

After having endured one of the longest and most oppressive dictatorships in the Southern Cone of South America, Paraguay has been opened up to a series of innovations related to the production, circulation and consumption of cultural industry. Three specific periods can be identified in relation to media ownership (groups to which they belong), the media's credibility and the type of public agenda that they pursue (themes and actors).

The final years of the dictatorship

Newspapers appeared at a later stage in Paraguay than in the rest of South America's Southern Cone, having emerged around the mid-nineteenth century.[9] Radios appeared around the beginning of the twentieth century and television during the 1960s.[10] However, it is only possible to talk about competition and diversity from the 1970s onwards, with Paraguay's entry into the international market. This was achieved thanks to the construction of Itaipú, the largest electricity generation dam in the region, together with the implementation of an agro-exportation economic policy that brought money to the rural areas, increased employment and supplied electricity to the country, both urban and rural.[11] With only a few exceptions, the media supported Stroessner's 'democracy without communism', which saw a long period of printing the 'official story'. To remain in circulation, they only needed to inform the public about matters relating to the dictator or to 'official' political and social actors.

At the beginning of the 1980s, which also saw the beginning of the economic downfall,[12] the radio, television and press were owned by the private sector and had few explicit ties to any political party. For this reason, some of the emerging private media started to show some independence. However, this provoked an immediate reaction from the government. In some cases, such as *Ultima Hora*, media outlets were closed for a month in 1979, while in other cases they were closed for a number of years – for example, the newspaper *ABC Color* (1984–9) and Radio Ñandutí (1987–9). This group does not include alternative publications belonging to political parties, popular organizations or the Catholic Church. These were persecuted and their journalists harassed and/or their families placed under immense pressure. There remains a need for a more exhaustive study of the contribution of alternative media to the dissemination of ideas opposing the regime, since Paraguayan citizens sought refuge in the alternative media in order to inform themselves of events held by political opposition parties and informal groups linked to peasant, union and university opposition movements during the dictatorship.[13]

During this period there were four national newspapers: *Diario Noticias* (1984),[14] *ABC Color*, *Hoy* (1976) and *Ultima Hora*. There were two terrestrial television channels. One of these was Channel 9, a public limited company created in 1965 and which was the sole leader of the television market. Its main owner was Gustavo Stroessner, the dictator's son. After the coup, President Rodriguez's 'entourage' took over this channel and his son-in-law Gustavo Saba[15] became the owner. Channel 13, which was created in 1981, joined other media outlets to become one of the strongest communication networks. These channels had their heyday in the beginning of the 1990s and thereafter began to decline until they finally closed. The owner of the media conglomerate was a commercial and industrial group[16] headed by Nicolás Bo. At this time, the newspaper *Diario Noticias*[17] was also part of RPC (Private Communication Network).

Rise in consumption and fall of trust

When the *coup d'état* took place on 2 and 3 February 1989, new public spaces were constructed in a climate of institutional vulnerability. This vulnerability resulted from regime crisis and weak standing of those political parties[18] that provided the media with what Landi has described as 'a strategic new relationship with politics' (1993: 6). Landi believes that, during this period, the various media began to 'absorb' the political conflict in the way that they formatted their news programmes and formulated their language.[19] Moreover, news media outlets embarked on a phase of more open competition for larger audiences, a change driven both by political liberalization and the existence of a 'free market'. The changes in Paraguay's political and economic situation intensified the competition for audiences. News programmes thus opened up new spaces to consider the power struggles of the transition leaders, focusing (within the limitations of the coverage itself) on those actions that were affecting key political and social actors. Since Paraguayan audiences were interested in these power struggles, the media consolidated their audience base during this period. As a result, the media gained legitimacy, thereby increasing their influence on public debate as well as on the day-to-day agenda of the new transition to power.

Television underwent drastic changes during this period. Presenters, formats, backdrops, music and the news agenda were literally changed from one day to the next. The change was therefore highly 'visible'. The media began to find its preferred mode of news coverage, to define that which might be considered as newsworthy and to develop techniques for covering non-official events. Journalists had to learn to talk without using a script, to put questions to the authorities, to conquer the fear they had experienced for so many years and – perhaps most importantly – to resist self-censorship. Radio stations, particularly those broadcasting on AM, started to produce 'open mike' programmes, allowing audience participation and phone-in programmes about a given topic of debate or some theme of interest.[20] Newspapers, especially those that had openly supported Stroessner's regime, also underwent a great deal of change in order to adapt to the 'new times'. The newspapers became the first to denounce any human rights violations, and this radical change of direction affected their themes, their points of view and the kind of protagonists that featured in their news stories.

This was evident within days of the coup, and information 'flourished' during the following years alongside state reorganization and widening political participation among Paraguay's citizens.[21] This was followed by a series of civil claims and the establishment or reorganization of social groups into 'independent' movements, resulting in wider public participation between 1989 and 1993.[22] This level of participation began to subside after the national elections of 1993 (which installed a government that ruled from 1993–8). During this period, the peasant leadership was co-opted into complicity with the dominant political power and there was a financial crisis between 1995 and 1997, which led to rising public disenchantment with national politics.

My own study found that there were 66 radio stations broadcasting in 1992 with 86 radio transmissions, 42 of which were transmitted on AM, 7 on OC (short wave – SW) and 37 on FM. Of these stations, 3 were state owned, 61 privately were owned and 2 were owned by religious organizations.[23] Of these stations, 33 were located in Greater Asunción (12 on AM, four on SW and 17 on FM). Channel 9 and Channel 13 were also on the air. During this period, political themes were firmly in the public arena for discussion, as reflected in the media monitoring studies we conducted. Our 1992 monitoring study provided the following data on the media's prioritization of themes (see Table 11.1).[24] Channel 13 had a predominance of political themes, which accounted for 56 per cent of its coverage, followed by socioeconomic themes (22 per cent), with 22 per cent taken up with other themes (and only 20 per cent of this last thematic category taken up with crime). Channel 9, the other television channel with a larger audience at the time, divided its time according to the following themes: politics (64 per cent), socioeconomic themes (20 per cent) and various other themes (16 per cent), of which 29 per cent was dedicated to discussion of crime.

Table 11.1 Media news monitoring (%) in 1992

	Television		Newspapers		Radios	
	Channel 13	Channel 9	ABC Color	Hoy	Cardinal	Ñandutí
Politics	56	64	44	39	71	60
Social	22	20	36	46	16	23
Various	22	16	20	15	13	17

The AM radio stations with the greatest share of the audience had the following percentages: Radio Ñandutí gave priority to politics in 60 per cent of its news, followed by 23 per cent given to socioeconomic themes and 17 per cent to various other themes (again, the topic of crime occupied 39 per cent of 'other themes'). Cardinal, the other station with large audiences, followed the same criteria, giving over 71 per cent of their airtime to politics, followed by socioeconomic themes (16 per cent), with various other themes taking up 13 per cent of airtime (with crime occupying 65 per cent of this last category).

Newspapers prioritized their themes rather differently to television and radio stations since they allocated similar amounts of space to political and socioeconomic themes. In this way, the newspaper *Hoy* dedicated a total of 46 per cent to socioeconomic themes, followed by 39 per cent dedicated to politics and only 15 per cent to various other themes (with crime occupying only 13 per cent). In the newspaper *ABC Color*, priority was given to political themes (44 per cent), followed by socioeconomic themes (36 per cent) and 20 per cent for various other themes (with the topic of crime occupying only 10 per cent of that).

Television monitoring studies carried out in 1997[25] (see Table 11.2) show that there was a major shift in the way that themes have been prioritized by the media and, correspondingly, that occupy people's day-to-day agendas for discussion. Channel 9 prioritized social themes (30 per cent), followed closely by crime (24 per cent) and politics (13 per cent). However, Channel 13 still prioritizes politics (35 per cent), followed closely by social themes (32 per cent) and crime, with an even lower percentage than the other channel with only 11 per cent (the rest of the news time being dedicated to sports and international news).

Table 11.2 Television news monitoring, 1997 (%)

| | Television channels | |
	Channel 9	Channel 13
Politics	24	35
Social	30	32
Police	13	11

This predominance of political and social themes continued until 1999 because the activities of people in social movements and/or political parties were still considered as newsworthy. But between 1992 and 1997 a shift in political themes became increasingly evident and socio-political themes began to decline alongside a loss of public confidence in the media's treatment of politics, especially in the press. Around this time, Paraguayans increasingly preferred the 'veracity' of television news images (even though the themes were changing at the time) to newspapers' coverage.

The turning point of the period of transition of power from one regime to another occurred in 1999, which saw the resolution of the military-political crisis that began in 1996 during Wasmosy's government (1993–8). In 1998, the political coalition Cubas-Argaña took office. Both came from different and opposing factions of the Colorado Party. Vice-president Argaña was assassinated in May 1999 by order of ex-General Lino Cesar Oviedo, who was the 'power behind the power', when he was about to obtain sufficient votes to carry out a political trial to remove president Cubas from office. At this point, the 'Paraguayan March' took place. This was a week of political crisis, a struggle between the three state powers, which led to the resignation of the president, Raùl Cubas. Following dramatic public protests in front of the National Congress,[26] Luís Angel González Macchi, then president of the Congress, took over the presidency of the executive power until 2003. During his time in office there was widespread disillusionment with the new government and a sharp decline in public political engagement. This period of government ended with the suspension of pension payments and of civil servants' salaries. Moreover, there was a high fiscal deficit and a large number of corruption allegations pertaining to the actions of president González himself, as well to members of his family and many of his ministers.[27] It was one of the most corrupt and weak governments of Paraguay's recent political history, and one that was in perpetual crisis. This period of governance accelerated the loss of public interest in national politics, which was reflected in the media's shifting priorities and themes. This was particularly apparent in television coverage, which dedicated increasing amounts of attention to crime, violence and details of ordinary people's lives. Around this time, the media took an increasingly political stand, one which often negated the facts at hand. From this time onwards, two types of media can be identified: those wielding a great deal of political influence but for whom the mass media was one of many business concerns, on the one hand, and, on the other, those that ascribed to a political project beyond business concerns and advertising revenue.

The decline of newspapers and the rise of broadcasting

Access to information and communication technologies has been growing, not only due to sales promotions and low-cost instalment methods, but also because of the availability of technologies to assist faster person to person communication at local, national and global levels. According to the latest data from the Permanent Homes Survey 2003, 65.3 per cent of Paraguayan homes have a television, 13.2 per cent have a landline, 19.1 per cent have mobiles, 7.8 per cent have video/DVD players, 3.7 per cent have cable television, 3.9 per cent have computers and 0.4 per cent have computers with internet access.[28]

Currently there are five national newspapers[29] (whose sales do not exceed 50,000 copies per publication on Sundays), one local newspaper,[30] four national terrestrial television channels,[31] 115 FM channels and more than 100 radio stations known as 'community radio'.[32] There is a large concentration of media consumption in the metropolitan area (13 of the AM radio stations and 30 of the FM stations are in Asunción and Greater Asunción), where the advertising revenue in 2005 was US $47,500,000, rising to an estimated US $50,650,000[33] in 2006. In general, all the newspapers are linked to other mass media organizations and to economic groups with ties to political groups that dispute the hegemony of the national political scene.

The public agenda is still set by radio stations and newspapers even though a national survey suggested that television has retained its public credibility.[34] For the purposes of this part of the discussion, the radio stations concerned are some six AM stations[35] based in Asunción that prioritize on a daily basis the most relevant civic and political events according to their own calculations. These radio stations are not wholly related to newspaper and television owners, being relatively small groups, apart from Cardinal radio, which belongs to the same multimedia group as Channel 13.

According to a 2002 survey into the consumption and credibility of the mass media (See Table 11.3), 66 per cent of Paraguayans said that they trusted 'quite a lot' of television, yet 52 per cent of the people interviewed could not say the same of newspapers and 44 per cent had no opinion regarding their ability to trust radio. This could be interpreted in two ways: either they do not have access to these media or they do not consider these media as a main source of information. According to the same survey, given a choice of the three media for dependability, 66.4 per cent of the people interviewed believed in television, 21.6 per cent believed what is said on the radio and only 7.4 per cent in what the newspapers say.

Table 11.3 Credibility in the media, 2002 (%)

Variable	TV	Newspapers	Radio
Very credible	28	7	18
Credible	38	22	30
Quite credible	4	9	5
Less credible	1	3	1
Neutral	27	52	44
NS/NC	2	7	2

Studies comparing television news content in January 2005[36] clearly show the radical change in the media's news agenda. In the past decade, most of the media coverage has concentrated on crime. Channel 9's national coverage gave over 64 per cent of its main newscast to this subject and Channel 4 (which has a larger audience) dedicated 43 per cent of space to crime. This was to the detriment of social and political themes (see Table 11.4).

Table 11.4 Monitoring of TV newscasts, 2005 (%)

	Television channels	
	Channel 9	Channel 4
Politics	11	36
Social	25	21
Police	64	43

Violence and unlawful behaviour (traffic accidents, killings, street fights, sexual assaults etc.) are what make the news and are what Paraguayans 'want to see' when daily life remains insecure, with the perpetual persistence of 'violent incidents'. Meanwhile, what has ceased to be news is the democratic process, the role of political and social protagonists in the institutionalization of the republic and the civic role in the process of democratization. The importance of public accountability in aid of sustaining democracy had once made the news, yet what Paraguayans as a society had wanted has now disappeared from the agenda. In its place is a preoccupation with violence, insecurity and the defencelessness of Paraguayan citizens.

Furthermore, this study reveals the main protagonists of the media. For Channel 9, 43 per cent of interviewees are non-official actors, or 'ordinary people', 39 per cent of these are civil servants and 16 per cent of interviewees are politicians, while 2 per cent are specialists and intellectuals. Channel 4 has a similar ratio of non-official to official actors (48 per cent 'ordinary people', 26 per cent civil servants, 16 per cent politicians and 10 per cent specialists and intellectuals).

Overall we can say that since the millennium, the Paraguayan media in general, and its television stations in particular, has preyed on the most atavistic fears that humans have: violence, death and uncertainty about the future. This has become a new form of social control resulting in widespread public disengagement in the democratic process. Meanwhile, politicians and the powerful elite continue to decide the fate of their citizens by determining their economic and employment situations irrespective of their earlier desires and dreams of fairness and respect for diversity.

Notes

1 The entire population totals 5,701,675 (57 per cent in urban and 43 per cent in rural locations). From the total population, 32 per cent is concentrated around the capital Asunción and the outlying urban areas known as Greater Asunción (1,840,360 people) (DGEEC 2004).
2 17 per cent of these live in 'extreme poverty' (DGEEC 2004).
3 Paraguay's president is called Nicanor Duarte Frutos, elected for five years, period 2003–8.
4 The Judiciary Council, The Public Prosecutor, the State's Controller, the Citizen's Defense Bureau, and so on.
5 The language spoken by the majority of Paraguayans is Guarani (3,946,904 people), followed by Spanish (3,170,812) (DGEEC 2002).
6 65.3 per cent of homes have a television, 7.8 per cent have a video/DVD player and only 3.7 per cent have cable, according to data from the Permanent Homes Survey from 2003 (DGEEC 2004).
7 *Diario Popular* (1994) and *Crónica* (1999).
8 According to the inequality index from the Report on Human Development 2005, Paraguay comes fourth in the list of most unequal countries in the world in terms of income per capita. The same document points out that it is the most unequal country in Latin America (UNDP 2005).
9 The first newspaper in the country was published during the government of C.A. Lopez, on 26 April 1845, called *El Paraguayo Independiente*.
10 Channel 9 (1965) and Channel 13 (1981).
11 According to the data supplied by the Population Census, the acquisition of televisions went from 28,480 to 241,987, in the period 1997–82. This means that it ranged from 6.7 per cent of homes with a television to 41.8 per cent in a decade. The biggest increase was in rural areas, which went from 771 televisions in 1972 to 68,548 at the end of the 1990s; in other words it went from a penetration of 0.3 to 21.9 per cent in less than 20 years. In Asunción the number of homes with television went from 31 to 82.7 per cent.

12   During the 1970s there was a 'boom' with the construction of the binational (with Brazil) dam of Itaipu, which generated high revenues and investments, making Paraguay, for a few years, one of the countries with the highest gross domestic product per capita of the region. However, in the 1980s this situation changed, especially in 1981 when the government had to acknowledge its economic difficulties. At the same time, international pressure for political liberalization intensified.

13   Their role as channels dedicated to criticism and analysis of the capitalist crisis, the Cold War, the role of the national states, the power taken by the masses, the 'avant-guard' and many other debates of the 1960s, 70s and 80s in this part of the continent should also be studied.

14   The group acquired the newspaper *La Tribuna*, changing its name, and in the year 2005 it closed. RPC group (Private Communications Net) remained composed of Channel 13 and two radio stations (one AM and one FM).

15   The group carried out the coup and took over a series of companies and businesses belonging to Stroessner and his associates, including this channel. Currently it is part of a Mexican group linked to Univisión.

16   A cigarette factory that expanded afterwards to hotels and shopping centres.

17   After the coup, Radio Cardinal AM and FM also joined, more powerful and with national coverage.

18   The coup that overthrew Stroessner was led by General Rodriguez, the father-in-law of one of his offspring. He was elected president of Paraguay in the general elections of May of the same year. It was a change made from above and from within, as it was organized by part of the army and a section of the Red Party, institutions that, together with the government, made a civic-military pact with those with whom Stroessner governed. It was only during the transition that party activities commenced again, such as electoral competition, campaigns, programme elaboration, etc. During the dictatorship, the Red Party simulated an electoral campaign but in reality there were no genuine elections; they took place only in formal terms.

19   Oscar Landi, 'Misfortunes and comforts of the educated democracy', paper presented in the seminar 'The press in the transition to democracy: Spain, Portugal and the countries of South America'. Organized by FLACSO/Chile Institute of Political Sciences and the University of Heilderberg, Santiago, December, 1991, mimeo, p. 6.

20   The use of this style decreased later, surviving only in some radio programmes. The radio stations themselves put in place control methods because these spaces were used by the so-called 'callers', who were linked to political groups. These people's objective was to call a variety of 'live' radio programmes to introduce the themes they wanted to bring into the daily agenda. In this way, such people began to influence the content of these radio programmes.

21 From 1991 the mayors and local authorities were elected for the first time by the residents of local communities. In 1992 the process of debate and approval of a new constitution took place (June 1992) and in 1993 the first national elections with new electoral registers and new electoral justice were carried out.

22 In 1991 we noticed the presence of 'independent movements' in local elections, giving new force to the political scene characterized by two centennial parties, the Red Party, ANR and the Authentic Radical Liberal Party, PLRA. Thus a third political force emerged. Also, in the 1993 national elections there was a new party-forming alliance with the PLRA.

23 The confessional radios are: Radio Caritas, Roman Catholic from Asunción, and radio La Voz del Chaco Paraguayo, from the Mennonite Mission of Paraguay, broadcasting from the western region of Chaco, which occupies 61 per cent of the territory and has just 2 per cent of the population of the country.

24 These data was gathered during three weeks in June 1992: 'News programmes during the Democratic Transition in Paraguay. Time of Mirrors and Masks'. Sao Paulo's Methodist Institute, Brazil. Sao Paulo, mimeo, 1993.

25 Menchaca, Rossana. El Paraguay a través de sus noticieros televisivos. Memoria de Licenciatura de Ciencias de la Comunicación. Asunción: Universidad Católica. Mimeo, 1998.

26 Vice-president Argaña was killed on a Tuesday, and the population demonstrated in front of the Congress demanding justice and the resignation of President Cubas. The population resisted the efforts of the police and Oviedo loyalists to break up the demonstration. On Friday night seven young demonstrators were killed and, on Sunday, Cubas finally resigned. On Sunday night the new president Gonzalez Macchi took over.

27 Initially, the government was formed by a coalition of the opposition parties that were in the Congress. Later, however, many sectors started to withdraw, and the designation of the social leaders was made taking into account the loans and donations to their organizations (peasants, unions, homeless, etc).

28 STP/DGEEC. Main Results EPH/2003. Fernando de la Mora, June 2004.

29 *ABC Color* (1967), *Ultima Hora* (1977), *La Nación* (1994), *Popular*, *Crónica*. The two last ones are called 'popular'.

30 Diario Vanguardia (2003), from Ciudad del Este, commercial capital, located in the border with Brazil and Argentina.

31 Channel 9, Channel 13, Channel 4 (1997) and Channel 2 (1997).

32 CIRD/USAID. Media and Communication Agencies Directory 2005. Support Programme for Citizen Initiatives. Asunción, mimeo, March 2006.

33 *Diario ABC Color*, 'ABC Color has been the leader in the market for the 6th year in a row, according to advertisers', Friday 26/05/06. p.13. Asunción.

34 Gabinete de Estudios de Opinión (GEO). WHERE IS THE PRESS GOING. Asunción. November, 2002. Mimeo.
35 Radio Ñandutí, Radio 1º de Marzo (1976), Radio Cardinal (1991), Radio Mil (2001), Radio Uno (1997) y Radio 970 (1999).
36 Franco, Rocío. 'News Merchants'. Memoria de Licenciatura de Ciencias de la Comunicación. Asunción: Universidad Católica. April, 2005. Mimeo.

12 THE MEDIA IN PERU: THE CHALLENGE OF CONSTRUCTING A MEANINGFUL DEMOCRACY

Celia Aldana-Durán

Democracy has had a chequered history in Peru. Since the creation of the Peruvian Republic, in 1821, military and democratic governments have followed each other. The last 50 years present a clear example, with a succession of democratic and military regimes, plus the government of Alberto Fujimori (1990–2001) which was democratically elected but soon became as authoritarian as any formal dictatorship. Democracy in Peru is still fragile and vulnerable, implying in many ways for both citizens and the authorities a process of continual learning and a transformation of the political culture. The challenges faced are several: the strengthening of institutions, more transparency in the way decisions are taken and the transformation of political culture. However, the report developed by the United Nations Development Programme on democracy in Latin America suggests a further challenge. It proposes that one of the problems with democracies in the region is that they are mainly constructed as electoral processes, meaning that the citizens' participation in public life basically takes place during elections. The alternative proposed is to transform them into citizens' democracies, where the population has a deeper involvement in public decisions (UNDP 2004). To do so, recommends the report, it is necessary to make democracies meaningful in terms of everyday life, allowing people to participate in the issues that are central for the control of their lives and their contexts. This is particularly important in a country that faces poverty as one of its main challenges.

It is in the task of fulfilling this aim that the various media have a role. They have been crucial actors in the recent political history of our country, as part of a sector that has actively worked for the consolidation of democracy. They have also played controversial roles, being involved in cases of corruption and support for non-democratic regimes. Furthermore, the media are also crucial in the challenge of linking together democracy and development: if democracy needs to incorporate the development agenda in order to become more meaningful, the media also need to do so. This is the central thesis of this chapter. It presents (1) an overview of Peru's media history, (2) a description of the features of the media, and (3) an analysis of the relationship between the media and development.

Peru's media history

The history of the Peruvian media, according to Juan Gargurevich (1987), goes back to the time of the colony, when the first newspaper (*La Gaceta de Lima*) appeared in 1715. It was controlled by the colonial government and the Catholic Church, and was mainly focused on the news that came from Europe, giving very little coverage to the local scene. In 1790 Bausate y Mesa founded the first daily newspaper, but without much success. *El Mercurio Peruano* was founded in 1791, and was the first paper run by the *criollos* (white descendants of Spanish people). Some of the most outstanding intellectuals of those days wrote for this paper. Despite this, it didn't last long and closed due to economic problems. In 1814 the colonial government allowed the freedom of print, and 27 different newspapers were founded. But, shortly after, this disposition was suspended and the newspapers were obliged to close (Gargurevich 1987).

In 1821 Peru declared independence from Spain and by 1828 several laws had been both allowing (and forbidding) the freedom of print. Several publications appeared, some of them supporting the emancipation from Spain, some denouncing it. Between 1829 and 1844 Peru went through a period of convulsion and continual internal wars. During these years of military *caudillismo* the media did not play a significant role, and continued to focus on commercial issues and switching support to the different leaders. It was during these years that *El Comercio* was founded (1839), which is not only the oldest mainstream media in Peru but also still one of the main and most influential newspapers.

In 1879 the war with Chile took place, and two years later different areas of the country were invaded. It was at this point – when the need for local news became more clear and urgent – that the media assumed a role of leadership, their readership increased and a true 'public' was finally formed. It is important to note that these media had audiences that were mainly urban and educated, hence excluding the vast indigenous majority. This exclusion was not a characteristic exclusive to newspapers, but represented a definition of the republic itself. Colonial and racist attitudes prevailed way into the next century. The indigenous population was perceived as a 'problem', as can be illustrated by this quotation from one of the most prominent intellectuals at the beginning of the twentieth century:

> Peru owes its disgrace to that indigenous race that has arrived, in its psychic dissolution, to obtain the biological rigidness of the beings that have definitively closed their evolutionary cycle ... It is fine to use the mechanical skills of the indigenous, even better to protect and defend him against his exploiters of every kind and to introduce among his habits the hygienic habits that he lacks. But no further efforts should be taken, sacrificing resources that will be sterile in

that superior deed and that would be more fruitful in the urgent satisfaction of more urgent social needs. The indigenous is not and cannot be other than a machine.

(Deustua 1937 in Manrique Galvez 2006: 27)

The raise of mass media

According to Gargurevich (1987), the mass media appeared in 1903, with the foundation of *La Prensa*, which unlike to *El Comercio* was aimed at the wider public. During these years, several newspapers and magazines that represented the interests of different sectors were created. The press freedom laws had suffered changes, but in 1932 President Luis Miguel Sánchez Cerro (1931–3), decreed a law that penalized as a felony 'the diffusion of news that may damage the credibility of the country or disturb the peace and the internal order' (Gargurevich 1987: 20). During the first half of the twentieth century the different governments closed, penalized and put pressure on the media. During the 1950s the print media was modernized, following the principles of objectivity, increasing the number of news and improving their design. At the same time, the newspapers become more complex enterprises and required higher investment, establishing closer links with the groups in power. The industrialization of the media made more difficult the appearance of alternative and small media (Roncagliolo and Macassi 1989: 1).

The radio appeared in Peru in 1925. Radio stations did not suffer as much persecution as the newspapers because they were mainly focused on entertainment, and their participation in political issues was almost nonexistent. Between the decades of the 1930s and 40s, nine radio stations were founded, and in the 1950s and 60s 19 new licences were awarded (Gargurevich 1987: 27). They mainly produced music programmes and *radionovelas*, which were soon incorporated into television.

Television appeared in the 1950s, the first broadcasts aimed at promoting the purchase of television sets. Almost at the same time, during the late 1950s and early 1960s, five television channels were established. They showed programmes produced in other countries, especially other Latin American countries such as Mexico, Argentina and Cuba, but they also showed local productions. In 1961 the production of Peruvian *telenovelas*[1] (soap operas) began, with great success. Some scripts were written in Peru, while others were purchased from other countries and rewritten in Peru. The success of the *telenovelas* became greater and greater, *Simplemente Maria* the biggest success of all. Peru saw a flourishing enterprise that was stopped when in 1971 the revolutionary regime of General Velasco nationalized the television companies (Vivas 2001). Although most radio and television companies were private, some were owned by the state, and remain so to this day. In the case of television, the state owns Television Nacional del Peru, and in the case of radio it owns Radio Nacional. The state also owns the newspaper *El Peruano*, and the news agency Andina (Gargurevich 2005).

The military government of Velasco and the media

In 1968 the armed forces performed a *coup d'état*. As part of their first actions they nationalized the mining companies and the oil industries. Furthermore, they implemented an agrarian reform that was intended to give ownership of the land to those who worked it. An education reform was also introduced that was intended to broaden access to education, and to decentralize it, incorporating elements of local culture. In sum, the military regime strengthened and amplified the role of the state, undertaking a protectionist-progressive approach, closing national markets to foreign investors and products while attempting to resolve some of the inequalities that existed (and still exist) in the country. The media were also affected by this approach, and were also subject to repression (Gargurevich 1987). For example, the regime enforced a law that protected journalists, giving them different status to the owners. *Expreso* and *Extra*, two newspapers that were part of the same group, were nationalized. The idea was that these papers would be run by a cooperative formed by the journalists. Nevertheless, the project was short lived and those journalists that worked in these media outlets had to face the military regime's censorship.

In 1971 a telecommunications law was passed establishing the participation of the state in the ownership of the media. According to this law, the state expropriated 25 per cent of the shares in all broadcast media. In the case of the radio it established that 60 per cent of the programmes should be nationally produced. Nonetheless, in practice this law had little or no effect on radio or television programmes, because these media still depended heavily on advertising. The government's intention was merely political, trying to impose control (Gargurevich 1987: 223).

Following the corporatist ideas of the regime, the main newspapers were expropriated in 1974, and were assigned to different social sectors such as *campesinos* (peasants), workers, teachers etc. Therefore, the newspaper workers had little possibility of gaining any control over the media (Gargurevich 1987; Roncagliolo and Macassi 1989). The idea was to democratize communication, giving a voice to social sectors that had been historically excluded. According to this strategy, the organizations of peasants were supposed to run *El Comercio*; the unions would run *La Prensa*; the professional and cultural associations would be in charge of *Correo*; while *Expreso* and *Extra* would be managed by the educational organizations, among others. This was supposed to be a progressive process, in which the journalists would have initial control and the social organizations would gradually assume it, but this was not implemented and the media remained highly regulated with the military regime designating the directors and managers of the newspapers (Roncagliolo and Macassi 1989: 5). This process was interrupted when in 1975 another military group, with General Francisco Morales Bermúdez Cerruti (1975–80) as its leader, took control of the government. This new regime tried to reverse some of the reforms created by Velasco, including the expropriation of the media. In 1976 the transfer of the media to social organizations was suspended and a decree suspending fixed labour was passed. As a consequence a great number of journalists were fired (Roncagliolo and Macassi 1989: 6). Morales Bermúdez intended to devolve the media to their original owners, but incorporating the media workers, which was an aspiration of the journalists. Since this did not work, a process of reversal was assumed by the next government.

The last years of the 1970s were highly chaotic and the military regime convoked elections for a new Congress, which would have the task of writing a new constitution. By 1979 Peru had a new constitution, and in 1980 new elections were called. In that year former President Fernando Belaúnde Terry, who had been removed from power by the military regime of Velasco in 1968, won the elections with 45 per cent of the vote. He returned all the media to their original owners, without incorporating any change or regulation. At the beginning of the 1980s several new media appeared, as part of a return to democracy. This included the first publication of a left-wing newspaper (*El Diario de Marka*).

The 1980s was marked by political violence and economic crisis. The same day of the elections when Belaunde became the new president, the guerilla movement Shinning Path made its first major attack, and shortly afterwards the Tupac Amaru revolutionary movement also came onto scene. Belaunde was succeeded by Alan García (1985–90) and during his first government Peru went through one of its most serious economic crises that had as its worse indicator a 7000 per cent annual rate of inflation in 1989. It was at this point that the media returned to democracy and consolidated themselves as part of a market model.

The Fujimori decade

In 1990 Alberto Fujimori (1990–2000) was elected as the new president of Peru. During the first year his government focused on the fight against inflation and terrorism. In 1992, President Fujimori announced via a television speech that the Congress was closed due to its inefficacy. Shortly after this a new congress was elected and his party won the majority. A new constitution was approved, which allowed Fujimori to be re-elected. Fujimori's regime applied the Washington Consensus, stabilizing the economy and implementing a privatization process that drastically reduced the participation of the state in the economic field. It also imposed important restrictions on the media.

According to Acevedo (2002) the media faced difficulties in adequately representing the violence that the country suffered during the 1980s and the first half of the 1990s. Some of the media's focus was exclusively centred on a repressionistic perspective, lacking a deeper understanding of the reasons for the violence. In other cases the sensationalism that guided the news approach helped to create an atmosphere of fear, which assisted terrorist groups in their aim of creating a terror regime. Most of the media reproduced in their coverage the exclusion that characterizes the country: if there were difficulties in rural areas and the affected were the *campesinos*, members of terrorist groups or working-class people, little coverage was given in the news, compared to what happened when the military, entrepreneurs, official authorities or the area around Lima were affected (Acevedo 2002).

Some official estimates reveal that in Peru some 25,000 to 35,000 persons died during those years. Nevertheless, the *Truth Commission Report* (*Comisión de la Verdad*) established that it was actually twice that number. More than 60,000 people died as a consequence of the so-called 'dirty war' (Lerner 2003). However, even now the correct number seems to be in dispute, but the fact remains that the country's civil population suffered heavily during this period. It is impossible to accurately calculate how many persons died in part due to the fact that many of them were not even legally registered and had no documentation. A further issue denounced by the Truth Commission was the indifference of Peruvian society, and the exclusion that became so concrete: 70 per cent of the victims had *quechua* as their mother tongue, were peasants and lived in rural areas – the same persons who are excluded on a daily basis. The mass media were part of this indifference.

It was only in the early 1990s that the various media incorporated human rights in their discourse and raised awareness around this issue among the population. Previously, the media were relatively tolerant of the crimes committed by the army and the police. The written media and some television programmes now took the lead and developed some serious research around emblematic cases such as the massacre of La Cantuta (in which a university professor and nine students from Lima's La Cantuta University were abducted and 'disappeared' by a military death squad in 1992 during the presidency of Alberto Fujimori), and the killings in Barrios Altos, a working-class neighbourhood in Lima where 15 people were killed by members of the army (Acevedo 2000, 2002; Comisión de la Verdad y Reconciliación 2003).

It was during this decade that a network of corruption managed by the chief of intelligence Vladimiro Montesinos was organized. The pressure that the state exercised over the media followed different paths: in the past it had taken the form of expropriation, or the incarceration of journalists. During the Fujimori decade other tools were used, such as the tax system or the placement of state advertising as a way of favouring some media over others. The ultimate method was the payment of bribes. The country found out about this in 2000, when several videos that documented the payment of these bribes to the owners or managers of the media were shown (Acevedo 2005). The media that were linked to the Montesinos network of corruption included five of the six privately owned television channels (Palomino 2001).

Corruption also affected the print media, especially the *chicha* press. A type of media is defined as *chicha* according to its level of sensationalism. The *chicha* press was developed in the 1980s and they were, and still are, the most widely read papers in the country. Their readership is mostly located among working-class people. During the regime of Fujimori, the *chicha* press expressed open support for the political regime. Later on, when the bribe videos were shown it became clear that these newspapers had been part of the network of corruption (Cappellini 2004). As a result of all this, the levels of trust in the media declined, though radio was less affected than newspapers and television.

The current profile

Nowadays Peru has a vast media landscape. According to a report by the Organización de Estados Iberoamericanos (OEI 2005), Peru has 72 newspapers, and 31 of them are based in Lima. The other cities with the highest number of newspapers are Cusco, Chiclayo and Tacna, each of which has four. The OEI report also states that Peru has 1452 radio stations, 175 of which are in Lima and Callao. There are 52 television stations, 22 of which are in Lima. According to a report by the Ministerio de Transporte y Comunicaciones, Peru has a total of 913 television and radio stations (Ministerio de Transportes y Comunicaciones 2006). Due to the fact that many of the radio and local television stations are not registered, it is very difficult to get a concrete idea of how many media the country really has. Nevertheless, it is fair to say that the media cover most of the country, and that most people have access to some media. The radio is the media most consumed, followed by television. The rural nature of Peruvian society, where a great number of its people still work in the land, is perhaps the main explanation for this.

Most media outlets are owned by private companies, but few of them are owned by the state, as has been mentioned before. Peruvian media face several challenges and problems, but two of them are crucial in terms of democracy and development: one is related to their capability to represent the country where they are located, and the other is related to their loss of legitimacy and the need to regain it. Indeed, the representation of such a diverse country is a complex task. Peru is a country where 44 languages are spoken in the Amazon area (Instituto Nacional de Estadística 2006), while others say that a total of 93 living languages are spoken in the country (SIL International 2006). The people who speak Quechua are calculated to number 3 to 4 million, making it the second commonest language in the country. But being a Quechan-speaking person implies a stigma and results in discrimination, with the result that people abandon the language when they move to the cities (Ardito 2004). Therefore, Quechua is scarcely used by the media. All the print media are written in Spanish and almost all the television programmes are broadcast in that language. Other languages than Spanish are used in radio programmes, especially by small radio stations whose main audiences are in the rural areas. However, it cannot be said that the media only represent the middle and upper classes. The country has changed since the 1950s, when the immigration process began and later transformed the configuration of the country from one that was mainly rural to one that is eminently urban. The country became one that was more *mestiza,* mixed. The city that showed the most radical signs of change was Lima, which grew very quickly, incorporating vast groups of Andean immigrants. The media changed together with the city. Although they gave little space to native languages and to the representation of rural areas, marginal urban areas did become more visible. During the last decades, the media have incorporated languages, music and topics that are more diverse, including a better representation of the diversity in the country, and especially in Lima. From the 1980s, radio and newspapers began to feature languages that were in daily use by working-class people. Some music radio stations were also launched to broadcast a new style of music called *chicha*, a mixture of latin rythms and *huaynos*, traditional Andean music. However, it is necessary to point out that these media are marginal to the decision-making process, have no influence in terms of political representation and in many cases have been used as vehicles of manipulation, such as during the Fujimori regime previously mentioned.

Media face, then, struggle to successfully represent a very mixed population. A clear distinction between sectors represented and narrative genres is obvious: native people appear more frequently in the comedies, while in the romantic or melodramatic narratives white people are more common (Aldana 1997). Anti-racist groups in the country point out that the media tend to reproduce stereotypes that are profoundly racist (Ardito Vega 1999: 16). Some advertisers recognize that they use the image of *mestizos* when they want to signify that a product is cheap and affordable for everybody, while a notion of 'high quality' is associated with white representation. Even worse, this is not only the logic of the advertisers, but also that applied by consumers.

However, the biggest challenge the media face is to improve the representation of indigenous people. According to studies done by Calandria, indigenous people have a very low representation (in Macassi 2006). Indigenous people are featured in the mainstream media basically when a major catastrophe happens in their area (such as a gas leak due to problems in a pipeline, or an oil spill in a river). Even then, the media quickly forget what has happened and move on. This explains what the Comisión de la Verdad exposed: thousands of members of indigenous or rural communities can disappear and the other society, the one that is integrated to modernity, hardly notices it (Lerner 2003). Ardito Vega goes futher, stating that these people have never existed for the rest of society: they don't speak Spanish, they are not officially registered (many of them have no birth certificate or any other official documentation that legally proves their existence) and they have no participation in the national economy. He also says that in many cases crimes perpetrated against indigenous people are essentially ethnic ones, since they happen because those who commit them know that they will not be punished because of the exclusion of the victims (Ardito Vega 2004). The media exacerbated impunity with their lack of, or weak, reporting of these crimes, with their quick abandonment of these issues, and with their superficial indignation.

The loss of legitimacy

It has been previously mentioned that the media in Peru became part of the network of corruption that was organized by the Fujimori regime. Some media showed open support for this regime, sacrificing neutrality and objectivity. An example of this is mentioned by the Comisión de la Verdad, which reports that during those years a sector of the media surrendered to diverse forms of pressure and sacrificed its independence, serving instead the interests of a corrupt regime that censored all attempts to denounce the violation of human rights (Comisión de la Verdad y Reconciliación, 2003: 489). The Comisión report also indicated that even though some of the media outlets developed in-depth journalistic research, this did not cover the most relevant issues since it was mostly ideologically orientated in selecting topics and setting the agenda; therefore, giving unequal treatment to the problems of different sectors of the population. Furthermore, other media emphasized sensationalist crime reporting to increase their sales. As a result of this, or at least partially due to the lack of a better media approach, Peruvian society lacked a proper understanding of this phenomenon and, even worse, was indifferent to the suffering of the most poor and excluded sectors of the country, namely the *campesinos* and indigenous populations who were the main victims of the violence. Hence, the legitimacy of the media was weakened not only by corruption, but also by bias.

Protzel (2001) points out that the media, especially television, lost legitimacy in Peru due to their continual transgressions of democratic rules and the evident manipulation that media owners imposed on their news and entertainment programmes. The dependence of the media on advertising paid for by the government made them even weaker, and the corollary of that was the bribes received by owners and managers, acts that were tape-recorded and eventually shown to the whole country.

One of the consequences of this loss of legitimacy and trust in the media was the development of proposals and debates around the possibility of introducing some kind of media regulation. As a result of this, the Veeduria Ciudadana collected 80,000 signatures from citizens and presented a regulation proposal. As a result, a new law governing radio and television was approved and the *Consejo Consultivo de Radio y Televisión* in 2006. One of the conditions established by the law is the design and implementation of a code of ethics for every radio and television station.

Development and the media agenda

In terms of the role of the media as an agent of socioeconomic and political development, it is important to start by enquiring about the different ways of understanding what development is. Amartya Sen says that freedom is the ultimate goal of development; that is, the *concrete enjoyment* of freedom, not just the abstract possibilities given to it by laws but denied by realities. In other words, freedom to decide the kind of life we want to live (Sen 1999).

The United Nations (UN) refers to *human development*, emphasizing that people are the ultimate goal of the development processes, not just the improvement of macroeconomic indicators. The development of our capacities, access to opportunities, equality, sustainability and a responsibility for future generations are some of the elements that the UN emphasizes (UNDP 2005). Summing up, we can say that development processes and policies aim to improve the living standards of the population. But development, as Denis Merklen points out, also seeks to achieve social integration: a community of persons where everybody has a place, is recognized and listened to (Merklen 2001). Hence, development and democracy are closely linked. Democracy is means and ends: 'means' because it is by means of it that people can be heard, policies adjusted and needs targeted (Sen 1999) and 'ends' because it constitutes an essential part of the quality of life, because it is linked with our desire to be able to decide, to be heard and to play a part. Democracy requires development, because otherwise it is not relevant to people's lives.

In 2004 the UN Development Programme published a report on Latin American democracy. It states that the democracies in Latin America are basically formal, and more focused on the electoral processes, without being necessarily significant to people's lives. This implies that issues that are central to the quality of life of the population, such as access to education, health, employment and security are not being fulfilled despite the fact that political freedoms are guaranteed and elections happen regularly (UNDP 2004). Democracy, then, is not meaningful to people's lives because it is not addressing the basic issues that affect them on a daily basis. There are whole aspects, such as the definition of economic policies, which have been taken away from the public domain and citizens can no longer influence the decisions made in these areas. As Rosa María Alfaro points out, the population perceives an unfair social situation and considers that democracy is legitimate only if it addresses social conflicts and effectively helps to overcome them: 'The political cannot be separated from the social' (Alfaro 2006: 62).

In order to achieve this, it is necessary to intertwine democracy and development: if democracy is about participation, public debate, freedom of information and freedom to express opinions, then it is important to make these issues relevant to people's daily lives. We need the media, the authorities, leaders and citizens to discuss the issues that are relevant in terms of quality of life. But this is not, unfortunately, the case. As some authors have pointed out (Pedraglio 2006), the social agenda is rarely included in the media agenda. Furthermore, the media devoted most of their time and space to stories regarding conflicts among the candidates, while social issues were mostly absent. Pedraglio points out that the media showed no interest in developing a social and economic agenda (2006: 36), while Macassi states that issues such as poverty, health or the environment are notoriously absent, constituting only the 8.2 per cent of the news that was analysed over a three-year period (2006: 46–50). Indeed, one of the most relevant characteristics of the Peruvian media is that when it presents information regarding politics and elections, it tends to do so in terms of conflict, emphasizing the difference in electoral polling, rather than constructing a space for dialogue, deliberation and – eventually – agreement about the issues that are of real interest to voters.

If development is about social integration, the representation that the media construct of the members of a local or national community is crucial. Nevertheless, as already mentioned, the media in Peru tends to exclude important sectors of the population. The news agenda imposed by the mainstream media does not include the cultural and geographical diversity of Peruvian society. Indeed, according to the non-governmental organization Calandria (Macassi 2006), the news that the media presents is primarily focused on the capital city, Lima, and gives scant attention to other cities and even less to rural areas. This is also confirmed by the Comisión de la Verdad (2003). Macassi also found that groups such as women, young people and indigenous people are misrepresented by the media (2006: 48). Furthermore, social activists working against racism continuously point out that the various media focus mainly on white people (Ardito 1999, 2004), with the result that the non-white audiences feel excluded from public debate (Aldana 1997).

Can anything be done to improve this situation, and if so, what? Very often, the media in Peru rarely considers development issues as important in its agenda, and focuses on crime and entertainment. At a basic level, the information processed and disseminated by the media needs to respond to the basic principles of journalism: plurality, equality and truth. The media in Peru therefore needs to ask itself if it is providing sufficient space for those voices that represent not a few but *all* members of the community. If it is not doing so, then it is failing to construct a space for equality and truth. In addition, the news agenda should be profoundly reviewed, so that democracy becomes meaningful people's lices, and hence valuable and worthy.

Even within mainstream outlets, some positive examples of the media in Peru show that they can promote debate and exercise pressure regarding issues that are important to the public and key in the development strategy. *El Comercio*, for example, claims to be 'representing the voice of the citizens who are being affected' (*El Comercio* 2006). Some of this paper's campaigns have enables it to make important contributions and push for change in national environmental policy. Furthermore, *El Comercio* has been promoting discussion forums where different citizens gather and present their opinion concerning the issues proposed by the newspaper. Peru also has examples of education-entertainment proposals – for example, Manuela Ramos and Calandria have addressed issues such as HIV/AIDS, domestic violence and family planning – among others – via the production of *radionovelas* (radio soap operas), carefully crafted so that the story incorporates a proposal for change. The problem in this case is that such programs only reach rural areas, and are therefore almost invisible to the majority of the population living in the cities.

The media, then, are crucial both for development and democracy. They are needed to enforce democracy, and to do so they need to play an active role in terms of addressing the needs of the whole population. They need to provide spaces for public debate, and emphasize social inclusion as pivotal by reflecting and fairly representing cultural and geographical diversity. Sadly, to this date, they have privileged some sectors to the detriment of others, particularly the rural and indigenous populations. This is certainly not only a challenge for the media, but for the excluded sectors themselves, as they need to be empowered and develop a capacity to speak with their own voices and in their own terms (Calderón 2004). The challenges are in fact not only for the Peruvian media but the whole country itself.

Notes

1   The *telenovelas* belong to the melodramatic genre of soap operas. They are characterized by strong emotions, but can be distinguished from their counterparts in the USA, Europe and Australia by the fact that they have a clear beginning and end, and most have a duration of less than six months.

13 THE MEDIA IN VENEZUELA: THE REVOLUTION WAS TELEVISED, BUT NO ONE WAS REALLY WATCHING

Andrés Cañizález and Jairo Lugo-Ocando

Venezuela's media system has undergone profound changes, mostly in the face of the political and economic transformations of the last ten years. The rise to power of Hugo Chávez and his Bolivarian Revolution translated into an open confrontation with the commercial media. At no time was this more evident than during the military coup on 11 April 2002, when President Chávez was ousted from power for 48 hours. Indeed, as Hugo Chávez himself pointed out, it was a 'mediated coup' (Cordova-Claure 2002: 26); a view shared by the managing editor of *Ultimas Noticias* (owned by the media group Cadena Capriles), Eleazar Díaz Rangel, one of the few pro-Chávez editors for whom 'the most powerful force in the attempt of coup was the media' (Díaz Rangel 2003). In any case, it is possible to say that the media has been a key element in structuring and amplifying opposition against the government in Venezuela (Ansidey and Díaz 2007: 57).

However, as discussed in this chapter, the confrontation between the commercial media and Chávez occurred in the realm of the current climate of anti-politics. A situation that precedes the rise of Chávez to power and that is characterized – at times – by a symbiotic co-dependence on the part of those in political power and the media. As will be argued here, because of the nature of both ownership and structure, this relationship was defined by a tacit agreement among political and economic elites which recognized the media's influence on Venezuelan public opinion (Villasmil 1980), while making use of hidden and explicit controls that determined the news agenda (Lugo-Ocando 1998: 32). What we aim to do in this chapter is to offer not only a descriptive account of the media's structure, influence and ownership in Venezuela, but also an analysis of its relationship with political power.

The media system in Venezuela

In terms of media access and reach, Venezuela has, since the 1970s, been among the four top countries in Latin America (Cañizales 1990: 4).

Indeed, compared with other countries in the region, there are more users and subscribers for television and radio per capita than in either Brazil or Mexico (see Figure 13.1).

- ❏   300 radio receptors (2006)
- ❏   190 television sets (2003)
- ❏   19 cable and satellite television subscribers
- ❏   161 newspaper copies
- ❏   32 cinema seats
- ❏   150 landline phones
- ❏   321 mobile phones (2004)

Figure 13.1 Number of media devices for every 1000 people

Source: Data based in data from IUT, CONATEL, INE, UNESCO

Media consumption in Venezuela is highly sophisticated and media-related skills are widely spread among the population. Even those living in very poor areas, such as urban shantytowns, are avid consumers of the media, especially free terrestrial television and radio. Depending on the nature of the media, consumption occurs in private or public spaces. While television is mainly consumed at home, the internet is often used in cyber-cafés, public internet centres (public libraries, etc.) and in offices. Although only 1.3 per cent of the population had installed broadband at home by 2004, for example, there were over 4 million users of the internet that same year (CONATEL 2007).

However, Venezuela has a poor track record in terms of producing content. As Antonio Pascuali, one of the leading media studies academics in Venezuela, points out, 'the country is very developed in terms of media consumption, but highly underdeveloped in content production' (1991: 91). Venezuela's main media outlets depend heavily on global networks for their content (Cañizales 1990: 6). Almost 90 per cent of all newspaper articles on international news in Venezuela's leading newspapers come from Associated Press (US), Reuters (UK) and EFE (Spain). Only two newspapers have stringers abroad, but none of them works on a permanent basis for the newspapers. In fact, as some authors have pointed out, Venezuela is an 'under-informed' country (Díaz Rangel 1976), to rephrase the term 'underdeveloped'. The problem is therefore not in terms of consumption but in terms of the lack of production of content.

In terms of property, most of the media in Venezuela are owned by national entrepreneurs and international groups (Cañizales 1990: 26). However, the private media coexists with large media systems owned either by the state or by religious groups such as the Catholic Church. In many ways, the mainstream media in Venezuela reflects the diversity of political players together with those particular historical developments whereby each particular economic group came into power during the twentieth century. Nevertheless, in recent years, those same groups have become increasingly divided and polarized into camps: pro- and anti-Chávez. In terms of structure, in contrast to other countries in the region, Venezuela's media system is not vertically integrated. Only a handful of broadcasters also own radio networks or newspapers. This is despite the fact that there has been no law prohibiting media owners from acquiring other types of media outlet. The reasons are multiple and complex, but it can be suggested that it has had to do mainly with the profitability of each media platform. With a few notable exceptions, the media system in Venezuela is characterized by different groups controlling different media platforms. Therefore, analysis of the media system in Venezuela needs to consider the distinctive nature of each type of media according to its economics and particular relation to political power.

In terms of ownership, both the national and regional media are characterized by their diversity in Venezuela. Indeed, in the Venezuelan media system, national and regional (local) media coexist for both broadcast and print media. The regional media has a distinctive pattern of ownership since it is mostly concentrated in the hands of industrialists and business entrepreneurs (e.g. in banking, construction or insurance). It has been the case that media owners have run media businesses at a loss in order to retain their influence over local governors and city mayors so as to accrue lucrative business contracts. Some of the particularly influential regional media include *Panorama* in Maracaibo city, *El Impulso* in Barquisimeto, *El Carabobeño* in Valencia and *El Correo del Caroni* in Bolivar, among others. However, none of these newspapers exerts any national influence.

In summary, one could say that the structure of media ownership in Venezuela remains diverse and is not concentrated in the hands of only a few. There are numerous reasons for this state of affairs. An important cultural element is that, contrary to common perception, there has always been a sort of distrust between the political and economic elites. Both in dictatorship and in democracy, Venezuelan governments have been reluctant, with only one exception, to award broadcast licences to traditional economic groups or support their attempt to develop print media. They have preferred instead to allocate the licence or support the efforts of 'newcomers', preferably groups associated with incoming political elites, mainly to guarantee a symbiotic relationship.

The print media

The two largest truly national newspapers in Venezuela are *El Nacional* and *El Universal*, which have combined bulk sales of over 350,000 copies per day. However, these numbers are estimates by the National Association of Advertisers (or ANDA in Spanish), since both newspapers pulled out from the ABC measuring system after the financial crisis of 1983 when it became clear that all print media had to make drastic cuts in the number of printed copies in order to deal with problems of lack of paper supplies or access to hard currency. According to the Federation of Advertisement Agencies (FEVAP), the strongest selling quality national newspaper is *El Nacional*, which is closely followed by *El Universal*. Nevertheless, *El Universal* captures almost a third more advertising revenue (Instituto Venezolano de Publicidad 2001) due to a variety of factors. *El Universal* attracts a more loyal and concentrated metropolitan audience. There is also a stronger and more complete business section – a very important source of advertisement revenue – and a very traditional job search section, which guarantees a stable readership regardless of the rest of its content. Moreover, the newspaper's daily agenda is widely held to have a more business friendly approach (Pellegrino 1999). In the past few years *El Nacional* has tried to gain ground in this respect – one of the many reasons it turned against Chávez – but the strong belief remains that it is a 'liberal' media, too intellectual with too 'in-depth' to suit the tastes of the vast majority. Other important players on the national scene are the Cadena Capriles group, which owns more than a dozen publications, and the Bloque de Armas group, which represents the Hearst Group publication interests in Venezuela. The Cadena Capriles publishes *Ultimas Noticias*, which has the highest circulation of all newspapers in Venezuela even though it is mainly read in the capital, Caracas. There are over 100 titles published on a daily basis in Venezuela, but most are constrained to local communities and cities. The main publishers are all located in Caracas as can be seen in Table 13.1.

Table 13.1

Group	Daily and weekly publications	Origin
Otero-Calvo	*El Nacional* Several magazines	Created by the award-winning left-wing writer Miguel Otero Silva in 1943
Mata-Nuñez	*El Universal* Several magazines	Created by the poet and writer Andres Mata in 1909
Cadena Capriles	*Ultimas Noticias* *El Mundo* Several magazines	Created in 1958 by Miguel Angel Capriles, a Cuban in exile living in Venezuela
Bloque de Armas	*Diario 2001* *Meridiano* Several magazines	Created in 1968 by Armando de Armas, a Cuban in exile living in Venezuela

There are some specialized papers such as *Reporte de la Economia* in Caracas, which focuses on business and finance and *Merdiano* (owned by the Bloque de Armas), which is the largest sports newspaper in the country. Nonetheless, it is the regional press that tends to set the agenda in the regions themselves. Data from ANDA-FEVAP (2001) reveals that most populations in the provinces rely on their own local daily newspapers for news. The same study points out that the middle-range economic segments of these populations buy their local newspapers on an almost daily basis and only acquire one national newspaper twice a week. Yet there is a catch to this apparently decentralized media scenario, since most provincial media cannot afford correspondents or news desks outside their own locations, which limits the scope of their content. They therefore rely on freelance services to obtain news from the capital. Several of these services are offered by people who work in the mainstream media in Caracas, who merely recycle their own articles. It is also very common for these local newspapers to rely on information supplied by the official news agency ABN.

Broadcast media

Until very recently, there were three main private television networks with open terrestrial signals: RCTV (Channel 2), Venevisión (Channel 4) and Televén (Channel 10). Two of them, RCTV and Venevisión, captured over 75 per cent of the audience share and almost 80 per cent of all of the broadcast advertisement revenue in 2005. Meanwhile, the state owns two television channels; VTV (Channel 8) and Vive (Channel 5), managed by the Catholic Church since 1998 but now back in state hands. There are currently more than 20 television stations, although until recently 70 per cent of the audience share was controlled by the three main commercial broadcasters: Venevisión, Radio Caracas Television (RCTV) and Televén. Another important channel is Globovision (Channel 41), which is broadcast by UHF signal, cable and satellite. Globovision is a 24-hour news channel and, while its audience is relatively small, it is very influential in setting the news agenda.

Television and radio stations operate under licence agreements allocated by the authorities (Cañizales 1990). In most cases, and in all cases for television, licences are awarded because of close links with the government of the time and in none of the cases did the awarded groups represent any of the traditional political or economic players. Table 13.2 gives details of the national television broadcasters.

Table 13.2

Broadcast Media	Licence was awarded	Ownership	Origins
Radio Caracas Television (RCTV)/ Originally Corporación Radiofónica Venezolana (CORAVEN).	1935 – Radio 1957 – TV	Groupo 1BC Phelps-Bottom	William H. Phelps was an AP correspondent during J.V. Gomez's dictatorship
Venevisión	1960	Grupo Cisneros	Diego Cisneros was a Cuban exile that came to Venezuela after the revolution. He bought the TV station that year
Televén	1988	Grupo Camero	Omar Camero was a former adviser to president Jaime Lusinchi (1985–8)
Venezolana de Television (VTV)	Nationalized	State owned	Originally owned by Time Warner. Later was nationalized by the government
Vale TV	1996 since 1952. Originally Televisora Nacional YVKA-TV, Canal 5	Catholic Church	For many years this was considered the public service broadcaster in Venezuela. During the second government (1993–8) of the Christian democrat Rafael Caldera it was given to the Church to administrate
Globovisión	1988	Jose Federico Ravell	Ravell was vice-minister of information during the first government of Carlos Andres Pérez (1973–8) and later a close adviser for Jaime Lusinchi

However, on 27 May 2007, RCTV's broadcast licence for terrestrial broadcasting expired and the government decided not to renew it. At the moment of the closure, RCTV was Venezuela's most popular television station with an average audience of 5.6 million. Now RCTV continues to broadcast by cable and satellite and remains popular with viewers, to the point that cable subscriptions jumped 20 per cent after RCTV stopped broadcasting its terrestrial signal. The government confiscated the transmission equipment of RCTV to use them for its own new channel (TeVES) to ensure national reach, but the latest ratings show that the new channel is watched by less than 1 million people at a time. This is not the first time that a Venezuelan government has 'nationalized' a television network. In 1974 the government bought Venezolana de Television (VTV) from the Time-Warner group and transformed it into a government station (Pellegrino 1999). However, far from adopting a public service broadcasting model, VTV operated for many years as a traditional commercial channel. It is only recently that it has become more political and news-related. It is worth mentioning that VTV barely reaches 5 per cent of the population (Salas 2003). Furthermore, most studies point out that its main audience share falls with the economic levels AB of age 25+, which is paradoxically the sector that is typically most antagonistic towards Chávez (AGB Panamericana de Venezuela Medición 2001).

There are also over 80 local cable channels that broadcast by open terrestrial signal, cable or satellite. These include Niños Cantores Televisión (NCTV Channel 11), owned by the Catholic Church and which can only be watched in the west of the country, together with several channels owned by public and private universities. Regional (local) television has become increasingly important in Venezuela's media landscape; however it is still the main national networks that dominate the market share.

Television certainly dominates the mainstream media in terms of public opinion. It is true that the print media, especially the national newspapers, are extremely influential in terms of agenda-setting (Bisbal *et al.* 2002), but it is television that is the most powerful media, able as it is to influence public opinion both cognitively and behaviourally, since newspaper circulation is very low in relation to the overall population. This is directly related to the way modern politics in Venezuela is driven by a mercantile and commercial logic, which is basically the result of the impact of television on the electoral process, where personal leadership has become a commercial commodity.

In this commercialized environment, political broadcasting was until recently very lightly regulated and there is no set time limit for candidates or political parties during electoral campaigns. Officially, electoral campaigns begin three months before the election and so should the television advertisements, which must cease to broadcast 48 hours before the election itself. This does not happen in practice, however; past electoral campaigns have started six or seven months before the actual election. Since 1961, all political parties have been given free but limited time on

VTV during elections, while the presidency can call for national and simultaneous broadcasts via all channels with limitations neither on time nor the itinerary.

Radio is not so very different in this respect, since it also operates under licence. As with television, some radio station licences have been awarded because of close links with the government in power at the time or simply thanks to bribes. Radio has a particularly good reach in rural areas, and in urban workplaces. The most popular content is music, followed by non-political talk shows (AGB Panamericana de Venezuela Medición 2001). There are currently 412 radio stations operating on FM and over 209 operating on AM. They are locally owned in many cases, but most are affiliated or syndicated to national networks. The main radio network is Circuito Nacional Belfort, which incorporates some 40 radio stations all over the country; the second largest is Unión Radio, with three main national affiliated networks: Unión Radio Noticias, Mega, Éxitos and Onda and over 30 affiliated stations. Unión Radio rebroadcasts in Venezuela the Latin American news services of the BBC and CNN. The third radio network is Circuito Radial Continente (CRC), which incorporates 11 radio stations all over the country.

Beside privately owned commercial radio stations, there are other types of radio station. The government, for example, has a very powerful presence on the radio, especially after the Venezuelan banking crisis of 1994. The political and economic instability at the time hit the already fragile bank sector, and after the first bank collapsed, a 'domino effect' of collapsing banks took place that eventually cost the government $11 billion and inflicted damage on the Venezuelan economy, the effect of which would be felt for years. Since some banks were owners or shareholders of some of the biggest radio networks at the time, many passed to the hands of the government as collateral. Indeed, until 1994 the government owned only two radio stations, Radio Nacional in AM and La Voz de Venezuela in SW, which target internal and external audiences (Pascuali 1991). These stations were under-funded and most of their directors and managers were appointed because of political links and had little or no experience in radio. Needless to say, the governments of the time did not give importance to these stations in terms of communication policy (Lugo-Ocando 1998: 31). This situation changed abruptly in 1994, when the financial collapse of several banks left more than a 100 radio stations in the hands of the government, which seized all bank assets after injecting several billions of dollars into them, although some were sold the following years. Even though Rafael Calderas' administration (1993–8) tried to sell most of these radio networks, the state still owns three of the most important radio networks with 35 stations across the country. The state is presently one of the biggest direct administrators of radio licences in the country. This was the case with YVKE Mundial, one of the main radio news networks, formerly owned by the insurance and banking Grupo Latinoamericana. The network now reports directly to the Ministry of Information, which appoints its director and oversees its content (Jiménez 2007). None of these government-administered radio networks can be considered public service broadcasters, nor are they independent from government interference. In addition, since commercial radio is often managed as a low budget production media, it relies heavily on information received from the official news agency ABN or news services, allowing the government to have a strong presence in radio broadcasting. Meanwhile, most radio stations are financially dependent on central and local government, which provide official advertising and a range of subsidies – soft loans, exchange of basic services for advertisements, and so on.

Equally important in radio is the presence of alternative actors such as the Catholic Church, other religious groups, universities and, increasingly, communities and non-governmental organizations. Besides a newspaper, *La Religion* (recently re-named) and two television networks (NCTV and TAM), the Catholic Church has by far the most extensive radio network in the country outside commercial networks. This is mainly constituted by the network Fe & Alegría which operates on AM and a dozen other stations broadcasting on AM, FM and SW. The radio network managed by Fe & Alegría, a Jesuit organization that delivers education to poor areas all over Latin America, can be considered to be a public service radio broadcaster. Besides daily news and talk shows, its content offers literacy and numeracy classes, health advice and special programmes for peasants. The Instituto Radiofónico Fe y Alegría (IRFA) has been running since 1975 and today incorporates ten radio stations all over the country. Other religious groups also have a strong presence on the radio, especially the evangelical sector, which owns over a dozen radio stations in the country, mostly operating on AM. The Evangelical Church also buys time from commercial broadcasters, mostly off-peak slots. Some of these stations are linked to international evangelical and Protestant networks such as the PTL Club. Contrary to the Catholic Church network, the evangelical and Protestant radio stations devote all their content to matters of religion and evangelization, although like those stations operated by the Instituto Radiofónico Fe y Alegría, they are subsidized by donations.

Another important sector is that which incorporates community radio and other radio stations managed by universities and non-governmental organizations, which since 2000 have received significant resources and investment from the public sector. There are now over ten universities that own or manage radio stations in the country. The university-owned stations operate with subsidies, but in most cases run commercial advertisements. They do not officially have a public service broadcast role, but in some cases they perform part of this function. Another important group is community radio stations. These are managed by local groups and in some cases only broadcast within the immediate vicinity and cannot be heard beyond the community which they serve. Since 2002, the government has approved over 50 new radio licences on both AM and FM for this sector in order to encourage the democratization of the radio sphere.

Cultural and creative industries

For more than three decades, Venezuela has been an important centre for the creative industries. This can be accounted for by a combination of internal and external circumstances. On the one hand, Venezuela is one of the top three countries in Latin America in terms of advertisement investment per capita, with over 1.3 per cent of its gross domestic product generated by advertising. On the other, Venezuela has established itself as a leading exporter of soap operas and music. This, together with a professional and modern television infrastructure, the low cost of personnel and a long tradition in the area, means that Venezuela is a base for many producers and advertising companies. Contrary to other countries in the region, which are dominated by a single television network that often outspends and outdoes its competitors, in Venezuela there were (until recently) two powerful soap opera producers/exporters (Coral Pictures and Venevisión). The export market for Venezuelan soap operas is estimated to be worth more than the national exports of automobiles, textiles or pulp/paper products (Mato 1999). However, the market share of this sector has declined in the past few years.

Other areas of the creative industries present a far more complex picture. Despite low readership, book publishing is relatively profitable, mainly because of schoolbook editions. However, the main editorial house, Monte Avila Editores is subsidized and owned by the government. Other publishing companies are linked to newspapers (Editorial El Nacional, Editorial Ambos Mundos, Bloque de Armas, etc.) or to international publishing companies (Planeta, Salvat, etc.). The software industry is small but incipient, especially administrative software and, increasingly, open-source software based on Linux. This operative system is being adopted by all government offices and government-related institutions.

Venezuela's theatre and film sectors are relatively small and rarely commercially viable. Theatre is almost entirely subsidized by the state and only in a few cases has it been able to become a commercial enterprise (mainly by means of low cost monologues and minor plays). Film production has also traditionally depended on government subsidies. Recently the government opened Villa del Cine, a full equipped studio that is allowing local producers to make Venezuelan movies in the country. However, film consumption is profitable despite widespread piracy. As in other parts of the world, multiplex cinemas now predominate in urban cities, but they mostly show US-Hollywood productions. According to Luis Girón, president of the film institute Centro Nacional Autónomo de Cinematografía (CNAC), up to 98 per cent of the movies screened in Venezuela are from the USA (Márquez 2007). Girón points out that in 2006 there were 11 Venezuelan films premiered in commercial cinemas and at one point there were as many as four nationally-produced films showing in local theatres. One of these, *Francisco de Miranda* by Diego Rísquez, based on the biography of one of Venezuela's national heroes, opened in August 2006 in 35 of the country's almost 400 movie theatres, surpassing Hollywood blockbuster *Superman Returns* as the biggest box office hit. The government has created Amazonia Films, a distribution company, which has acquired films from Latin America, Europe and Asia. A new law to be implemented from 2008 will oblige all cinemas to show Venezuelan movies as part of their regular schedule.

Overall, it can be said that Venezuela's creative industries are diverse and, in most cases, dependent on government subsidies. Fine arts and classical music are in this category. However, popular music record companies and television production companies are healthy and sustainable industries in general. This situation is nevertheless threatened by a volatile political climate and widespread piracy, which has created an unpredictable and difficult environment.

Raising leviathan's voice

Today, the relationship between politicians and the media in Venezuela is characterized by the deterioration of institutional agreements. Until 1998, the relationship between the media and the government could be defined as one of 'symbiotic dependence'. It involved a complex system of joint interests based on a series of balances and counterbalances of power. This delicate equation between the media and political actors, even though it was created long before the system of consensus, in many ways reflects the same spirit of the political consensus system often known as the *Pacto de Punto Fijo* of 1961. As Méndez and Morales (2001: 17–18) argue, this was a non-democratic agreement between the political and economic elites to create a context in which a harmonic coexistence of economic and political agents was possible thanks to the political demobilization of the country. This agreement was complemented by two others: one with the armed forces and another with the Catholic Church (*Concordato* of 1964). There is however a fourth agreement, which has been in place since the 1930s, which was revisited in democratic times. This agreement was not as explicit as the *Pacto de Punto Fijo* or the *Concordato,* but had instead similar characteristics to the one between the political elites and the armed forces. This agreement gave preference to foreign investment and non-traditional players. Never formalized, it was the result of an implicit understanding that developed over the years in which every new regime restructured media ownership to reflect its own interests (Lugo and Romero 2002).

Thanks to the renewal of this agreement in 1961, both agents of power would recognize their influence and their limitations in a symbiotic relationship that established undeclared but very tangible rules and boundaries and that would reflect the relationship of political parties with the economic elites. In other words, this was an agreement that portrayed the same consensual system that enabled the nation to neutralize – and later absorb – guerrilla groups, coup attempts and even social unrest. However, the system of consensus of 1961 that framed most relationships between the agents of power was built upon the fiscal resources provided by oil revenue and therefore, by 1998, was already under considerable strain. As the historian and former president of Venezuela, Ramon J. Velasquez correctly predicted in 1990, 'until now the immense oil revenues had allowed the political parties to subsidise their excesses, but from now on either they become more politically creative or they will end up burying the system' (Lugo-Ocando 1990).

Overall we could say that Venezuela's media, as in the case of many other societies, became a space in which modern politics was played out. It became an area for consensus and political negotiation among different elites. Obviously this is not to say that the nature of this political space was simply a dichotomy between open 'consensus' and 'confrontation'. On the contrary, depending on particular political, social and cultural circumstances, the media and the different social/political actors engaged in a complex process of negotiation and struggle to participate in the hegemony of power. But until Hugo Chávez's arrival in the seat of government, they were committed to institutional stability in order to preserve their own hegemony. Until then, the media, by means of its symbolic content, was able to promote agreement, framing the political debate according to the existing institutional realm. Therefore, while some debate and confrontation happened in public, the political and economic actors were always able to reach agreement and consensus in private. In this sense, apparent contradictions in the past were solved or at least re-framed within the media during crises that threatened to jeopardize the stability of the system. Even in those cases where the political actors became total antagonists, the media would take the role of consensual actor, playing down the confrontation and promoting instead elements of common interest. This happened for example in 1962 during the coup attempts known as the *Porteñazo* and the *Carupanazo*, where radio and television limited the coverage and reinforced the idea of compromise between all political actors as harmonious with the ideal of democracy and peace. It occurred again with the guerrilla period known as *Foquismo* (1961–73), when on very few occasions the government had to use explicit censorship against broadcast media. Years later, the media did not cover the attempted coup of 1986, called the *Viñeta*, with the exception of two articles published several weeks later by *El Nacional* and *El Diario de Caracas*. Another example is the case of media orchestration during the riots of 1989 known as *El Caracazo* when television channels banned all images of the riots and started calling for peace and order by means of their artists, news presenters and personalities, while later suppressing the image of the army killing people in the streets (Febres 1991). During the two attempted coups of 1992 against Carlos Andres Pérez, the media became a crucial agent in restoring stability. The links between some of the key mainstream media and Chávez were also very close at the time of the 1998 elections, as was to be expected. As Teodoro Petkoff, director of the daily *Tal Cual* wrote during the campaign, 'Chávez received a generous treatment from some of the print and broadcast media. When it was clear he was going to win, his performance received more coverage (Petkoff 2002: 89). The media consensus pact even operated at the start

of Chávez's administration when Globovisión not only refused to broadcast a live message from an officer of the National Guard calling for the
overthrow of the government, but handed in the videotape to the
government itself. It was clear that at least the media still played by the
rules of consensus and avoided calling for the subversion of the constitutional order.

It has only been in the past few years that the media has adopted a
more subversive position. During the events of 11 April 2002, there was
extensive but uncritical coverage of the brief overthrow of Chávez, while
hours later there was almost absolute self-censorship when people came to
the city centre to defend President Chávez. Later on, the media started to
broadcast live messages from insubordinate members of the military and
openly support actions that subverted the constitutional order. Some
observers such as the International Federation of Journalists (2002) have
denounced some segments of the media as instigators of the 2002
attempted coup.

There are several explanations for the deterioration of relations
between the media and Chávez's government. The argument frequently
tendered by the opposition takes a positivistic approach, whereby the
media has a commitment to democracy and freedom of expression; its
confrontational attitude towards the current administration is therefore a
moral and ethical crusade against a quasi-dictatorship that threatens to
undermine basic civil liberties. On the other hand, the government claims
that the media is not a neutral player – and neither is the state – since it
colludes with the dominant class to suppress a process that has undermined dominant hegemony. According to this view, the media has played
a conspiratorial role from the beginning and it asserts that it did not react
sooner because Chávez still had popular support. In other words, while
one point of view sees this confrontation as a subjective issue, the other
perceives it as an objective process. However, as an attempt to develop a
more comprehensive theory, both approaches are too general and their
conclusions too relative, since they fall short of a real understanding of
events leading to the current situation. There is an urgent need to
structure an analysis that is adequate to the task of assessing the
microcosms surrounding the media's behaviour while incorporating a
critical understanding of the macro-political process in order to appreciate
the dynamics that have provoked the transition.

On villains and heroes

In a way, the election of Hugo Rafael Chávez Frías was a process of social
catharsis. The accumulated frustration and resentment of most of the
population towards the political and economic elites erupted as a
powerful volcano that had been suppressed for too many years. His
predecessor, Rafael Caldera, who also came to power by means of
adopting an 'anti-politics' formula, tried in vain to contain this volcano
by means he knew and trusted. He tried to incorporate the emerging

leadership into the pact system using the methods of traditional populism (offering them jobs, scholarships, diplomatic placements and even political participation through local elections). He offered to relaunch the two-party system, attempting to strengthen his new recently-created party, Convergencia, while establishing an alliance with the social democratic Acción Democrática. As the journalist and former UPI editor in Venezuela, Pablo Bassim, puts it: 'His failure was that he tried to make of his second presidency a legacy of stability, which was what everyone was expecting, but he tried to do it through the mummification of dynamic and powerful forces that were much alive'.[1]

The contrast between an almost silent Rafael Caldera, who would only speak on very special occasions, and Chávez, whose presence pervades every corner of Venezuela's public life, reveals not only the personal characters of both presidents, but overall the gap between a political generation that acted through consensus and an emerging political agent that had resorted to public confrontation as a means of holding onto power. This is the tangible manifestation of the emerging regime, which is yet to consolidate its power and which is defined and legitimized by a public confrontational character. Since the electoral triumph of Chávez in 1998, Venezuela has suffered a process of transition within the democratic system. No longer is consensus of political and economic groups the main determining element of politics. Instead, the political debate tends to be expressed mostly in the public sphere in terms of confrontation (Romero and Lares 2002). This political question is of course defined by its public confrontational nature and successive events have only reinforced the perception of the new political elites that this is the only way in which they can hold power.

Indeed, as has been well documented, the arrival of Chávez marked the formal end of the consensus system. This system was substituted by a state of permanent confrontation in every sphere of public life (Romero *et al.* 1999; Méndez and Morales 2001; Rivas 2002) – a new order, which would also come to dominate relations between the government and the media. As a result, Venezuela witnessed a state of permanent confrontation between a media that had the ability to control access to the public and the new government, which attempted to 'oblige' the media to follow and obey the new norms and procedures associated with the newly-elected president. The initial and logical reaction of the media was to distance itself from government policies, orchestrating a permanent critique through their media spaces. The government reacted as expected: it tried to put pressure on the media through available legal and political mechanisms. The brief honeymoon between newspapers such as *El Nacional* and broadcasters such as Venevisón and Televén ended abruptly. They aligned themselves with *El Universal* newspaper and the television networks Globovisión and RCTV, which had opposed Chávez from the start.[2] The scenario became extremely polarized. Only a handful of private media outlets such as newspapers owned by Cadena Capriles and some regional media, such as the influential *Panorama* in the state of Zulia – were supportive of Chávez.

The coup of April 2002 and the general strike of 2002–3 were both promoted and supported by the opposition with the help of the commercial media. By that time, most commercial media outlets had not only become supporting agents of the opposition, but also in many ways quasi-autonomous agents of political power. However, as Luis Brito García, a leading media sociologist and a Chávez supporter says,

> the media in Venezuela has a great influence and is able to shape the perceptions of part of the population, however it is not omnipotent. Venezuela is fascinating in two ways: On the one hand, the media has adopted an extreme position as a political actor; on the other, there is now a relative autonomy of one part of the public opinion in regards to that media.
>
> (interviewed by Carvajal 2003)

The political discourse of president Chávez and his followers has been characterized by the redefinition of the historical subject, changing its symbolic gravitational centre from the idea of class alliances to one of class struggle (Molero 2001: 221; Romero 2001, 2002b). The new discourse did not rely on the traditional argument of *policlassismo* (multi-class party politics), adopted by the traditional parties, which translated into an idealization of the so-called middle class and class alliances, but instead centred on the poor as its main discursive construction – the common citizen in public space. It is precisely this characteristic of the *Chavismo* that has created the most antagonism among the middle classes, since they had believed that they would be able to rescue some of their privileges under Chávez, an aspiration that had become manifest in the past three elections. Contrary to this, the middle and professional sectors saw that, in the name of the Bolivarian revolution, many of their former privileges disappeared. This was particularly simplified and exaggerated by the commercial media, which became regarded by the so-called middle class as the valid and legitimate vehicle to express their dissenting views against the Bolivarian project. Media owners and traditional elites were quick to see this as the perfect mechanism to create and mobilize discontent against Chávez. Once the pact of consensus between the media and the state was completely broken, the tense and confrontational relations between Chávez and the media knew no boundaries or contraints.

The increasingly subversive nature of the media clashed with the need of the new regime to consolidate itself. If some media owners were seduced at some point by the idea of expanding their sphere of influence beyond the traditional elites and could take advantage of the new institutional framework set up by Chávez, the reality was very different. As Romero (2002a) points out, it soon became clear that there was no space for them in the new process of the hegemonic construction of power implemented by the *Chavismo*, and that the new elites were not willing to negotiate. There is no evidence to suggest that it is either possible or desirable under the current conditions for the president to renew former pacts, such as *Punto Fijo*. It also seems that relations between the new political elites and the media have undergone significant transformations. Once symbiotic, they are now characterized by confrontation and submission. The Chávez administration has understood that it is no longer possible to galvanize support from the media by means of a symmetrical relationship, as in the past. It knows that its inability to liberate itself from the monopolistic control of the information imposed by the commercial and private media does not derive from a lack of media infrastructure and instead relates to its own inability to develop a coherent and effective information and communication policy. Because of this, the government has empowered itself and accepts that the realistic objective of its information policy is not to gain support from the media but to neutralize or reduce its influence. This new approach can be seen in the very recent 'social responsibility' law aimed at broadcast media outlets, which allocates new discretional powers to the government. Government power has increased with the re-nationalization of the main telecommunications company, CANTV, which controls over 65 per cent of the telecommunications market and 90 per cent of the infrastructure. However, this approach is no more evident than in the recent decision not to renew the RCTV licence for open terrestrial broadcasting and, later, the attempt to suspend its signal from cable and satellite.

The administration has been very adamant in insisting that it respects, and will continue to respect, media freedom. However, in effect, it is making use of sophisticated control mechanisms. The implementation of a new legal framework includes not only the new broadcasting law mentioned above, but also new laws that limit access to sources – the government in fact has banned many media from covering official acts, draconian and judicial measures that have led to the trial, house arrest and even imprisonment of some 32 journalists and civil rights activists. It is also directly and indirectly increasing the dependence of media outlets on the government while trying to promote a new and community-based supportive media. President Chávez did not renew RCTV's signal in the free terrestrial spectrum. This allowed him to neutralize the most influential broadcaster in terms of reach to poorest areas and substitute it with a government channel, *TeVes*. His government also struck a deal with Diego Cisneros, the owner of Venevisión. This agreement meant the support of this last channel during the last elections, resulting in more positive coverage towards the government; to the point that it broadcast a four hour interview with the president in prime time. A similar deal was made with Televén and other local broadcasters in exchange for renewing their licence for five years and additional advertising investment.

The other main strategy has consisted of promoting and supporting new media outlets. Some have completely failed, such as the newspaper *El Correo del Presidente* (*The President's Gazette*). Others, such as the promotion of community and local broadcasters such as TV Catia and the modernization of the government channel VTV, have produced mixed results. On top of this, there is another important strategy, namely the acquisition of some print and broadcast media by political and economic groups related to the government. The proposal for a new constitution is that not only will it allow the president to be re-elected indefinitely, but it redefines the terms of private property, allowing the government to expropriate any company that is considered of 'social interest'. This of course will include print and broadcast media. The precedent for this was set with the case of RCTV, when the government took, with military personnel, all the transmission facilities, equipment and antennae without compensating the owners or stating when they will return this property.

It is important to clarify, however, that direct censorship by political and legal means and the exercise of self-censorship using the government's resources were a reality in Venezuela long before Chávez came to power. Reporters Without Borders (RSF) (2001), for example, has acknowledged that veiled and open censorship has occurred in Venezuela on a regular basis for many years and that pressure on editors has been common practice for equally long. Self-censorship has been routinely achieved through threats, bribes or indirect pressures via editors. It is also necessary to underline the idea that the private commercial media was key in orchestrating the coup of 2002 and most of the later attempts to overthrow the regime (Ansidey and Díaz 2007: 56). The reaction of the regime has been an expected consequence and an attempt to guarantee its own political survival.

However, the most interesting developments in terms of Venezuela's media are with regard to the geopolitical positioning of the Chávez administration. The setting up of an international news channel, TeleSur, and the acquisition of a Chinese-built satellite are part of this project. Indeed, the tense relations with the USA have made intervention in global geopolitics and public diplomacy a fundamental element of the Chávez administration. Venezuela's authorities have justified and promoted TeleSur and the new Simon Bolívar satellite project – formerly known as Project Condor – as much needed infrastructures to counterbalance US and European dominance and secure Venezuela's communicative independence. According to Venezuelan officials, the aim of TeleSur is to associate itself with projects such as Al-Jazeera and the recently launched French International News Network (BBC 2005). This is in order to provide a voice for the region that can not only offer alternative views and perspectives imposed from the north, but also facilitate the integration of Latin America. In so doing, these two projects aim to take advantage of existing integrationist elements such as politics, culture and trade blocks (MERCOSUR, Andean Pact, CARICOM etc.). Nonetheless, poor ratings of state-owned media, delays in the execution of the main projects and a national and international backlash as a consequence of not renewing RCTV's broadcasting licence are proving, for the Chávez administration, that sometimes 'doing' media projects is far more difficult than 'doing' politics.

Notes

1   Interview with Pablo Bassim 12 September 2000.
2   This process had multiple causes, and in each case was related to the administration making a move against particular interests of media groups, therefore breaking the consensus, as explained previously. Three reasons are given to explain this rupture. In the case of *El Nacional* the sacking of Carmen Ramia, wife of one of its co-owners, from the Ministery of Information (OCI). In the case of Venevisión it is often said that it was the crystallization of support for the Cuban regime, and in the case of Televén government authorization – through the National Stock Commission – to sell Electricidad de Caracas.

14 BEYOND NATIONAL MEDIA SYSTEMS: A MEDIUM FOR LATIN AMERICA AND THE STRUGGLE FOR INTEGRATION

Andrés Cañizález and Jairo Lugo-Ocando

Amidst the response of national media systems to the development needs of its still-incipient democracies, Latin America has yet to face a long-standing aspiration: to create a federal political and economic community similar to the European Union or the USA. Not only would this allow the free circulation of goods and people, but it would provide an imaginary space to accommodate the vast and hybrid array of national and transnational identities and cultural diversities that characterize the sub-region. For now at least, the existence of what some have termed 'media space' and 'media politics' (Castells 1997: 329), makes this long-held aspiration seem possible. However, despite advanced state and market convergence, political integration in Europe has proved to be complex and difficult. One might suggest that Europe's distinctive languages and cultures have somehow limited its ability to create a common broadcasting space; something that has been highlighted in recent works (e.g. Fossum and Schlesinger 2007). Even in the USA, where, officially at least, there is a single language, media spaces tend to be shaped by distinctive geo-cultural realities that define their identities in very different ways (Husting 1999: 161).

This final chapter therefore discusses Latin American integration and its associated geopolitical agendas. The project of TeleSur is used as a case study since it represents the most ambitious attempt in recent years to provide such a space. The chapter argues that, while it remains still too early to provide a comprehensive assessment of the channel's viability, it is nevertheless possible to predict the series of likely challenges faced by TeleSur in the near future; these challenges will reshape its nature and its audiences. It is our contention that, because the channel aims to be both an instrument of asymmetrical confrontation with the USA and a means of facilitating geopolitical integration in the region, it must be analysed on two levels. TeleSur needs to be understood as a project that presupposes the existence of a common public sphere in Latin America in which the identities of its citizens are defined by means of the confrontation with, and struggle against, US/neo-liberalism, but that at the same time operates in a region where these common spaces do not actually exist in practice. By analysing its operation in this manner, we explore TeleSur's antecedents, organization and structure within the context of Latin America's media systems. The chapter also discusses the validity of comparisons (by the project's friends and foes alike) between TeleSur and other broadcasters such as Al-Jazeera and EuroNews in the context of geostrategic initiatives. We will argue, according to our criteria, that such comparisons require closer critical scrutiny.

Some background

Throughout this book, the contributors have explained that the political landscape in Latin America has dramatically shifted to the left in the past few years. After decades of dictatorship and a traumatic post-democratic period, several countries have recently elected left-wing leaders. Furthermore, for the fist time in their history, these leaders have not only come to power by democratic means, but they have not subsequently been overthrown or assassinated. Perhaps none is so influential and controversial as Venezuela's president, Hugo Chávez, a lieutenant colonel who, following the attempted coup in 1992 that brought him a three-year jail sentence, stormed to power in a landslide victory in the 1998 elections. Since then, President Chávez has led a process of institutional reform, including a new constitution and several referendums. He has also embarked on left-wing policies, including new land reforms – the first ones took place in the 1960s – substantially increasing health and education budgets, restructuring Venezuela's oil industry and realigning the country's foreign alliances away from the USA and closer to Cuba, China, Iran and Russia. The Chávez administration has placed particular emphasis on regional integration. It formally requested adherence to Mercosur,[1] after dropping its membership from the Andean Pact[2] as a result of Colombia's announcement that it would sign a free trade agreement with the USA in 2006. The Venezuelan government has also pushed for the creation of a political and trade area with Bolivia, Cuba and Nicaragua (ALBA)[3] and has expanded trade agreements and energy assistance agreements with many Caribbean countries. Venezuela is currently the architect of some ambitious integration projects such as the Banco del Sur, which aims to become a sort of South American central bank, and TeleSur, which aims to be the voice of Latin America. All these integration projects need to be analysed alongside two main situations: a) the confrontation between President Chávez's administration and the USA as geopolitical framework and b) the administration's aim to push for regional integration. Indeed, Venezuela's authorities have justified and promoted TeleSur as an alternative to the US/UK news networks (arguably CNN and the BBC), which have dominated the scene since the 1990s (White 1997: 131). According to Venezuelan officials the aim of TeleSur is to associate itself with projects such as Al-Jazeera and the French International News Network (BBC 2005). This is in order to provide a voice for the region that will counterbalance views and perspectives being imposed from the north, but also facilitate integration in the region. In so doing, the channel will take advantage of existing integrationist elements such as politics, culture and trade blocks.

Coming from those setting up TeleSur, this perspective conforms to existing conceptualizations of Latin America. Indeed, some authors have already pointed out that Latin America is commonly essentialized by politicians, academics and the general public alike as a single region with a common culture (Roncagliolo 2003). Such reductionism emanates from the belief that language, religion and history alone are culture's main determinants. It has therefore not been surprising to observe the prevalent discourse of a common Latin American space. The ideal of Latin American integration is commonly presented as a series of projects that aim to rescue the post-colonial romantic ideal of the nineteenth century. Among these voices can be discerned a wide range of integrationist projects ranging from common market initiatives (SELA, Andean Pact, Mercosur etc.) to joint ventures in cultural, scientific and, more recently, media spaces. It is a romantic view that tends to pursue the ideal of a common Latin American public sphere, and by so doing, it imaginatively collapses historical layers and patterns of diversity in order to provide a shared historical space and homogenous identity. By means of this interpretation of integration, Argentineans, Bolivians, Brazilians, Cubans, Uruguayans and Venezuelans alike are supposed to share the same cultural values and inhabit a common sphere.

While there is a widespread belief that Latin Americans share a sense of common identity rarely present in other regions, it is nevertheless a notion founded on superficial observations about a common indigenous symbolism, language and historical background. As such, this perspective obviates the fact that most of Latin America's 550 million people live now in urban and semi-urban areas. The emergence of these vast urban spaces across the region during the twentieth century challenges the notion of a rural-indigenous reality and trans-Latin American historical common space. Even the indigenous component of its population, which is often referred to as a key component of cultural-historical integration, cannot be seen as a referent for a common space beyond the realm of the symbolic. Instead, existing and historical networks among these segments of the population are not as widespread as commonly thought and are far more permeated by amalgamated urban realities than by their historical and sociocultural background. Therefore, to persist in pursuing this particular ideal of integration is to sideline, in the analysis, the rich diversity and heterogeneity that characterizes Latin America today.

The other aspect of our work departs from the fact that media systems in Latin America face a certain paradox. In a sense they are still framed and defined by nation-state prerogatives, while at the same time they are also influenced and defined by powerful global trends. Therefore, as some authors have pointed out, only a combined focus on local politics and global media can provide a comprehensive picture of Latin American media (Fox and Waisbord 2002: xxii). The project of TeleSur as a Latin

American broadcast network falls into this category in its aim to be an expression of a common space with the capacity to promote cultural and political integration. This last aspect resembles other networks such as the BBC, CNN and Al-Jazeera in the sense that, while not having explicitly claimed to do so, the capacity has nevertheless been acquired to project geopolitical interests at home and abroad.[4] For the main governments involved in TeleSur (Argentina, Cuba, Uruguay, Venezuela and, more recently, Bolivia), this was an important facet of the project, since it situated it among other initiatives that facilitated resistance movements and regional integration. To elaborate further, it is important to look at the origins of the TeleSur project. By so doing, we expect to encounter discursive elements that assist in clarifying and exploring the specificities of this project and its relation to geopolitics, regional integration and the public sphere. The analysis therefore includes the revision of secondary sources and semi-structured interviews in Caracas as well as the revision of secondary sources in both Venezuela and the UK.

Initial steps

From the outset, TeleSur was a political project of President Chávez's administration aimed at achieving an international presence. Its first chairman was Andrés Izarra, the Minister of Information in Venezuela. His presence in TeleSur undermined any pretence at government independence from the outset. This had important repercussions for subsequent debates over TeleSur as an alternative news paradigm.

One of the first official statements that flagged up the possibility of a Latin American broadcast network was made on 5 July 2005 by Andrés Izarra during the programme *Aló, Presidente* (*Panorama* 2005). Izarra announced that TV Sur – as it was originally called – would be launched in March that year. He also announced that the national news agency Venepres would be rebranded as the Agencia Bolivariana de Noticias (Bolivarian News Agency) (Weffer 2005). From that moment and throughout 2005 there were several official announcements in which the project of TeleSur was mentioned as part of the government's communication strategy. In January 2005, President Chávez appointed Blanca Eekhout as general director of Venezolana de Television (VTV), Venezuela's main government broadcaster. Eekhout was also appointed head of the new Televisora del Sur C.A., which would later adopt the commercial name of TeleSur (Santos 2005a). In his announcement, Chávez confirmed that the new network would incorporate content from public broadcasters of Argentina, Brazil and Venezuela and that the objective was to present the social realities of Latin America and the Caribbean. This has not been entirely achieved.

Most of the programmes, such as documentaries, are made by independent producers or bought from archives in these countries, and as Table 14.1 shows, the overall content tends to be overwhelmingly about news and current affairs.

Table 14.1 TeleSur programmes

Area	Programmes (%)
Current affairs and opinion	26.66
News	22.91
Documentaries/factual	18.75
Sports	12.50
Music and fine arts	8.33
Miscellaneous and entertainment	10.89

Source: Programación de TeleSur January-March, 2007

President Chávez also announced that the signal would reach Bogota, Mexico City, Lima, Brasilia and Los Angeles (*Diario de Caracas 2005*). Days later, Andrés Izarra provided details of the project. According to this new announcement, TeleSur would broadcast from a building annexed to that of (VTV), using three studios and a main control room in Caracas. It would also have a network of correspondents in Los Angeles, Mexico, Bogota, Lima, Buenos Aires and probably Brasilia or Rio de Janeiro. The initial investment was announced to be US$3 million, all set by the Venezuelan government. The idea, according to Izarra, was to establish a state company that would, in time, be able to sell shares to other nations (Santos 2005b). However, by the end of March 2005 when the channel still lacked a broadcast signal, Izarra announced that it would begin its transmissions in May and that, by June or July, it would be able to broadcast 24 hours by satellite (*Notitarde 2005*). He also announced that 40 per cent of the initial provision would be based on news and public affairs programmes (*El Nuevo País* 2005). Izarra established a 'communicational cabinet' with the purpose of designing strategies and policies to confront what he called 'the aggressions of the private media against the government'. Later that month he confirmed that the headquarters of TeleSur would be in Caracas but, even more importantly, that the channel's composite share would see Venezuela with 70 per cent, Argentina with 20 per cent and Uruguay with 10 per cent, and that Brazil and Cuba would also be contemplated as shareholders (*Diario 2001*; *Diario de Caracas* 2005). By then, the initial amount of the investment had risen to US$10 million, all paid by the Venezuelan government through the state-owned Venezuelan Petroleum Corporation (CVP), to cover the first years of the channel's operations (*Últimas Noticias* 2005).

The initial signal of TeleSur was broadcast on 24 May 2005. The director general of the channel, Aram Aharonian, pointed out that this was a significant time for the region since through this initiative 'it was possible to undermine the control of media conglomerates'. Aharonian said that the channel aimed to offer 'a competitive alternative to CNN and TVE, with an alternative agenda that was completely different from these multinational companies'. He admitted that there 'would be some bias towards Latin American political and economic integration, diversity and plurality', stressing that the intention was to 'challenge the hegemonic discourse' of the main international networks (Santos 2005c). Aharonian also emphasized that this initiative was only possible thanks to the new political environment in the region, characterized by left-wing governments, although on that occasion he rejected the charge that the channel would be used as a vehicle for Cuban and Venezuelan propaganda (*Tal Cual* 2005). From the beginning, therefore, TeleSur had a dual purpose. The first was to counteract what was perceived to be the hegemonic domination of international networks such as the BBC and CNN. The second was to promote cultural and political integration by means of strengthening the region's supposed common public sphere.

Adjusting to controversy

It is, therefore, possible to argue that while the creation of TeleSur was part of Venezuela's public diplomacy strategy aiming to serve national geopolitical interests, it was also conceived as a tool for enhancing regional integration. The advisory council of TeleSur is comprised of many international and regional left-wing intellectuals, including Nobel peace prize winner Adolfo Pérez Esquivel, Nicaraguan poet Ernesto Cardenal, writers Eduardo Galeano, Tariq Ali and Saul Landau, editor-in-chief of *Le Monde Diplomatique* and historian Ignacio Ramonet, free software pioneer Richard Stallman, Peruvian film director Javier Corcuera and US actor Danny Glover. The board's composition clearly has important implications in terms of linking the network to major resistance movements across the globe and achieving public diplomacy. The way in which the structure of the channel was established (shareholders, executives, bureaus and correspondents) confirms its aspiration to be a platform of regional integration.

However, even if this initiative has been laid open to other countries, Venezuela nevertheless remains the sole financial contributor to the project. Argentina, Cuba, Brazil and Uruguay were initially invited to participate in this initiative as partners, but Brazil dropped it almost from the start, instead announcing the establishment of its own initiative (TV Brazil), while Argentina, Bolivia, Cuba and Uruguay have yet to meet their financial commitments for 2005, 2006 and 2007. The final composition of shareholders is as follows: Venezuela has 46 per cent of the shares, Argentina 20 per cent, Cuba 19 per cent and Uruguay 10 per cent. Following the election of Evo Morales and Rafael Correa, Bolivia and Ecuador have become the most recent shareholders of TeleSur with 5 per cent each (MINCI 2006).[5] Other countries such as Colombia and Peru, which were originally willing to allow cable and satellite operators to transmit TeleSur's signal in their countries, backtracked after the initial broadcasting included in its opening an hour-long interview with the commander-in-chief of the largest guerrilla group in Colombia (FARC),

Manuel Marulanda while, in the case of Peru, there was growing tension between Presidents Alejandro Toledo (and later Alan García) and Hugo Chávez.[6]

Another aspect to analyse is the fact that, although Venezuela is the main sponsor of the channel, Cuban officials play an important role in defining strategic aims and orientation for the network, which gives the channel a very clear ideological orientation.[7] In addition to this, it is important to note that Argentinean and Uruguayan producers supply a significant number of the programmes commissioned by TeleSur. They are among the main recipients of the channel's production budgets.

Some initial comparisons

From the start, some Venezuelan officials have compared TeleSur with the Qatari news channel Al-Jazeera (Hernández Navarro 2004). By making this comparison, the people involved in the channel's set up have asserted that the new channel is there to provide an alternative view to that offered by traditional commercial broadcasters. Javier Corcuera, a member of the advisory group of TeleSur, has stressed that the network wanted to become 'a Latin American version of Al-Jazeera':

> We want to create a sort of Latin American Al-Jazeera, with a news agenda that currently does not exist in the region and present that other side of the news that we have not seen yet. The idea is to offer a new type of television, with a pluralist and independent approach, that can also support documentary makers from Latin America.
>
> (EFE 2005)

This comparison is often made in the context of the debate about a new international communication and information order that took place mainly between the 1970s and 1980s and was synthesized in the McBride Report (UNESCO 1980). According to the comparison with Al-Jazeera, both networks have the potential to offer an alternative news paradigm. For Venezuelan media expert Antonio Pascuali, who participated in the research and writing of the McBride Report, TeleSur was a good idea that went wrong:

> Telesur is conceptually a beautiful and important project, analogous to the initiatives one has fought for over decades. It is obviously a project that requires pluralism, tolerance and independence from the government. In its current version it is an ideological caricature, one-dimensional and linked to government. Financing and programming are both Chavista. Its main programming resounds with Stalinist, leftist rhetoric that went out of style a half a century ago. After the withdrawal of Brazil its only supporters are Cuba, Argentina and Uruguay and these last two countries have veto power over programs.
>
> (Coronel 2005)

Indeed, comparing both networks is far from straightforward. One commonly cited point of similarity is the initial funding and set up of Al-Jazeera and TeleSur as state-sponsored alternatives. This state-sponsored paradigm – often inspired by European public service broadcasters – aims to offer an alternative to that of commercial broadcasters such as CNN. This comparison is nevertheless problematic since these types of state-controlled media outlets are historically associated with repression and censorship in both regions. Furthermore, historical realities in these cases are far more complex than the common assumptions portrayed by some activists supporting TeleSur. While, in the case of Arab countries, the media has been historically state-owned, Latin America's media system has mostly been characterized by private ownership and commercial operations. Therefore, control and censorship within Latin America's media system was carried out with the overwhelming support – sometimes tacit and sometimes explicit – of media owners. Contrary to the narratives of organizations such as the Inter-American Press Association, resistance, defiance and challenges to the dictatorships in Latin America during the 1960s, 70s and 80s by media owners was the exception and not the rule in the region. Some observers have already pointed out that a comparison between both networks in these terms would be highly inaccurate, despite the efforts of some officials to emphasize the similarities as a self-promotion exercise. As US journalist Alan Simpson has pointed out, 'the audience models are completely different and the breakthrough in news reporting created by Al-Jazeera occurred twenty years ago in South America' (Simpson 2005). In most of these countries, commercial broadcasters copied the US model and applied it to their own news structures. This type of news model is not however what TeleSur is theoretically pursuing and therefore the comparison made with Al-Jazeera seems even more problematic.

In terms of funding and ownership, the comparison seems much more pertinent while still presenting some difficulties. Al-Jazeera and TeleSur initiated operations using large government grants, which are heavily dependent on oil exports for their revenues. Al-Jazeera received an original grant from Sheikh Hamad ibn Khalifa Al Thani, the Emir of Qatar. This was given to allow Al-Jazeera to become self-sufficient through advertising by 2001. Since then it has operated as a commercial broadcaster of 24/7 news (El-Nawawy and Iskandar 2002) although it has not yet broken even. TeleSur also received a government grant but has technically operated since its inception as a public service broadcaster. Contrary to Al-Jazeera, TeleSur has yet to find any major private sponsor and most advertising revenue comes from Venezuelan government agencies. However, this complies with initial expectations since from the start it was not assumed that TeleSur would become a strictly commercial operation. Therefore, the pressures on TeleSur to become commercially viable are far less demanding than those of its Arab counterpart. The size of the grants is also strikingly different. While the Qatari government gave US$150 million, TeleSur got less than a tenth of that to start transmissions. Furthermore, after the Arab station failed to achieve its self-financing goal in 2001, the Emir of Qatar agreed to provide a US$30 million subsidy per annum. Meanwhile, no official provisions have been made in the case of Venezuela for the government budget of 2007 (when this chapter went to print, the channel's resources were being funnelled directly from the state-owned oil company).

There are other important distinctions to be made between both channels. Unlike Al-Jazeera, TeleSur is not strictly a 24/7 news channel. Instead, it offers a schedule in which news only accounts for part of its programming. Most of the schedule of TeleSur relates to topics such as politics, history, community matters and interviews. Only between 20 and 30 per cent – it varies according to news events taking place – of the network's programmes can be considered factual news. Although both networks are broadcast mainly by means of cable, satellite and the internet, the audiences differ in their numbers and their nature. According to Moraima Martinez from AGB Panamericana, the country's leading ratings firm, the total audiences for TeleSur in Venezuela are limited by the fact that less than 30 per cent of the population have cable television.[8] In both cases the audiences for both satellite and cable are very fragmented and, according to most ratings, terrestrial television has retained its hold over most audiences. Another indication of the type of challenge that TeleSur faces in terms of audiences is exposed by the fact that the main government network, VTV, which has operated since the 1960s and broadcasts via a terrestrial open signal, attracts – according to most surveys – less than 6 per cent of the total audience share in the country. Other similar rating reports on Argentina, Uruguay and Bolivia carried out by the Brazilian Institute of Public Opinion and Statistics (IBOPE) and its affiliates suggest that the ratings for TeleSur (as for most cable and satellite channels) are not much better. In other words, while Al-Jazeera has an estimated 50 million viewers, TeleSur faces the prospect of being seen, at peak times, by less than half a million people across the whole of Latin America.[9] According to Antonio Marcano, a political and media consultant, this would not be so much of a problem 'if this was the right elite watching TeleSur, but I am afraid that the people with the economic resources to have access to satellite and cable are not necessarily the strongest supporters of the regime in Venezuela'.[10]

Some might argue that this is a very unfair comparison, since the contexts from which both channels emerged are very different. From the experience of Al-Jazeera we now know that certain events such as the US invasions of Afghanistan (2001) and Iraq (2003) can change viewing patterns in the same way that the Gulf War of 1991 made the consolidation of CNN as a global broadcaster possible (White 1997). Indeed, early lessons from the role played by the government-owned VTV during the attempted coup of 2002 show that major events often determine the impact of networks in the long run and galvanize new audiences. During these types of event, a news network or a website can become a crucial geopolitical referent in the struggle for power in media space. TeleSur has yet to face such a situation, which would probably be a major political crisis either in Venezuela, Cuba or Bolivia in the near future.

Integration and analysis paradigm

At this point we need to clarify that TeleSur is not the first government-sponsored initiative in Venezuela to propose a new geopolitical alternative to the prevalent news paradigm. In fact, during the first presidency of Carlos Andrés Pérez (1973–8), the Venezuelan ambassador to the UN, Diego Arria, proposed buying the US news agency United Press International (UPI) in order to have a tool for influencing foreign policy (Lugo-Ocando 1998: 18). Later on, during the second presidency of Pérez (1989–93), there was a similar strategy led by his Minister of Information Pastor Heydra, who oversaw the internationalization of the state-owned news agency Venpres. Heydra set up news desks and correspondents around the world in order to allow Venezuela to play a more active geopolitical role. Some of the people involved in that project are now part of the TeleSur initiative, for example, Aram Aharonian, then in charge of the internationalization of Venpres and now TeleSur's director general. According to him, the main objective of the internationalization at that time was 'to provide Venezuela with the ability to project itself geopolitically onto the world stage and exercise public diplomacy' (Lugo-Ocando 1998: 61). The project contemplated the association of all government news agencies in the region in order to create an alternative news network from Mexico to Argentina. The project was short lived and did not survive the impeachment of Carlos Andrés Pérez in 1993, after which all funding for the project was halted and all the correspondents had to return to the country.

However, what is innovative about TeleSur as a continental broadcasting initiative is its association with a renewed emphasis on Latin American integration. This is somehow reflected in its daily schedule, which includes programmes from the entire continent. On a weekly basis, the channel will broadcast programmes made or referring to each one of the countries who are shareholders. In addition to this, the news magazines and current affairs programmes are diverse in trying to incorporate elements from all over Latin America. Indeed, the idea of using TeleSur to foster political and economic integration is mostly based on the 'common sphere' philosophy, with all its attendant assumptions, together with the belief that this sphere can be further enhanced by electronic media. Not only is this approach consciously manufactured to gain political leverage, but it also has its basis in prior conceptualizations of a pan-Latin American community. This is why the idea of Al-Jazeera, as a pan-Arab referent, seems so appealing to those setting up the Latin American counterpart. According to this logic, TeleSur will allow the articulation of a common political and public space and its extension to every corner of Latin America.

Promoting the development of such a phenomenon in Latin America is, however, about as practicable and justifiable as that of a pan-European or Middle-Eastern sphere. More a romantic aspiration than a viable project, it has nevertheless been a persistent objective in political discourse, revitalized as a project for development since the re-democratization of

Latin America in the second half of the twentieth century (Avritzer and Costa 2004: 704). The notion that, somehow, Latin Americans share a common space is indeed profoundly rooted in the assumption that independence from Spain and Portugal and the emergence of national borders in the nineteenth century led to similar models of societies across the region; a notion that is fuelled by the idea that identities in that part of the world have all been constructed alike. This notion has been carefully deconstructed by many authors who have not only pointed out profound historical differences among emerging nation states in Latin America (López-Alves 2003) but also considerable variation in national identity formation (Anderson 1991). Despite this, the notion retains its currency in academic literature and political discourse (Avritzer 2002; Dagnino 2002).

This said, this notion of a common space for political debate in which social exchanges are possible has indeed become, in the past few years, a proposition of development within the Washington and post-Washington Consensus (Fine *et al.* 2003). The erruption of information and communication technologies into daily life – especially electronic media – as an opportunity for 'catching up' with the developed world (Drucker 1993) in both economic and institutional terms is a main component of the argument made by both left (articulation of resistance) and right (generation of social capital). This is particularly relevant in the case of Latin America where the ideal of the information society is linked to generalizations such as civil society (Delarbre 1994).

Those who embrace this notion see electronic media as a transformational element that can allow the creation of political common spaces, contributing to democratization, development and institutional convergence ('integration' in the case of Latin America). For those arguing this position, the introduction of electronic media is helping to reshape the political landscape in some regions in the world. They suggest that it has helped to democratize and modernize the Middle East (Lynch 2005) and Latin America (McNair 2006). Despite being predominantly a positivist paradigm, it is nevertheless shared by scholars from different ideological spectrums. It is a paradigm that suggests many parallels between Latin America and the Arab World. In it Al-Jazeera is often represented as a pan-Arab satellite channel that legitimately presents 'Arab views, opinions and beliefs' (El-Nawawy and Iskandar 2002: 44) and that somehow integrates the Arab world. Those defining TeleSur as a project are either suggesting the existence of a Latin American common public sphere or assuming that telecommunications have the potential to create one. In so doing, they refer to the existence of 'hybrid identities' (García-Canclini 1990), but from a pre-Hispanic perspective – that is, as a nostalgic pre-colonial construction. It is an appealing paradigm to political leaders in the region who, for a long time, have incorporated the integrationist narrative into their own discourses. Regional integration has been by far the most resonant element of the political discourse in Latin America. Both left and right have appealed to this ideal, which is often associated with pre-Hispanic utopias and cultural traditions (Hopenhayn 2002) but that at the same time draws inspiration from the European Union model.

The post-colonial and decolonization traditions, that often take the form of dependency theory in Latin America's political discourses, have also been very influential in the conceptualization of this paradigm. In the same way that the 'Baathification' of Arab politics following decolonization was hugely influenced by this pan-Arabic dream (Farah 1978), predominant development strategies in public policy in Latin America during the 1960s and 70s were based on integrationist aspirations. Although both ideals of pan-Arabism and pan-Latin Americanism have been thoroughly questioned (Said 1979, 1997; Martín-Barbero 2001) these ideals have nevertheless re-emerged in both political narrative, mostly due to the election of left-wing leaders in Latin America, and as a result of the intensification of the conflicts in the Middle East.

In this context Al-Jazeera and TeleSur have tried to exploit the perception of pan-Arabism and pan-Latin Americanism as a means of promoting themselves among potential audiences. The slogans in both cases suggest that they see themselves as catalysts for configuring broader identities that are able to transcend the artificial states created or derived from colonial powers. With the slogans 'When Al-Jazeera speaks, the world listens' or 'TeleSur makes the South become the North' the networks suggest that they give voice to their own regions as a whole on the world stage. In so doing, these media outlets also appear to rescue the failed notion of collective histories.[11] This paves the way for a wider and alternative collective derived from a notion of pre-Hispanic integration. If – as some authors point out – the convergence of capitalism and print technology created the possibility of a new form of imagined community (Anderson 1991: 46), the electronic media invites then the imaginative possibility of alternatives beyond capitalism and institutional convergence. These types of media are fundamental in establishing a postcolonial (or pre-Hispanic in the case of Latin America) notion of regional communities that are able to defy globalization (Americanization) on its own terms. Nevertheless, unlike to the Middle East, Latin America's political leadership – without a recent post-colonial past – looks towards Europe as a referent. After all, the European Union, as a successful economic, military and immigration and integration project in the post-World War II era has inspired several multilateral institutions in the region. The Andean Parliament, the Latin American Parliament, Mercosur, SELA and the Andean Pact are all inspired by – if not modelled on – European institutions.

One might suggest, therefore, that a comparison between TeleSur and Euronews as parallel media institutions is more appropriate. After all, they both aim to provide 'the views of Latin Americans' and 'the news of Europe' respectively. Indeed, Euronews devotes a significant amount of attention to European Union-related subjects due to its pan-European origins and nature. Similarly to TeleSur's original aims in Latin America, the European channel uses content from the main public service broadcasters in the region and was initially owned by member states of the

European Union. Indeed, Euronews was created in 1992 in Lyon as a European Broadcasting Union initiative by a group of 11 European public broadcasters that included CYBC (Cyprus), ERT (Greece), France Télévisions (France: the France 2, France 3 and France 5 channels), RAI (Italy), RTBF (Belgium), RTP (Portugal), RTVE (Spain), TMC (Monaco) and YLE (Finland). Its content is supplied by the shareholders and by Britain's ITN, which is owned by the main private broadcaster in the UK (ITV). Although the BBC, the main European public services broadcaster, is not a partner in this project, the rest of the associates are public service broadcasters.[12] EuroNews started as a pan-European television news channel that aimed to reach most European Union countries. It was selected from a total of seven candidates by the European Union itself to produce and broadcast, simultaneously in several languages, news programmes on issues about the Union and given the mission of becoming a European public service broadcaster. Like Al-Jazeera and TeleSur, it started with a government grant and nowadays receives €5 million each year to support its operations. EuroNews has set aside 10 per cent or more of its production for information, discussion and debates about European Union issues. This emphasizes the integrationist character of the channel despite the fact that EuroNews is now in the hands of the French government and can only be seen in places such as Britain through commercial satellite and cable operators.

However, there are important differences between TeleSur and EuroNews. These are not limited by the fact that one channel is a news channel and the other not, nor to the nature of the audiences, but fundamentally by the ability to draw resources from existing traditions of public service broadcasting outlets. The creation of a pan-Latin American public service broadcaster is problematic given the absence of national public service systems in each of the countries concerned. Contrary to Europe, the construction of media spaces in Latin America did not result from struggles for participation and debate but was conceived from the start as a series of commercial spaces to be exploited by the private sector. Most of the media in Latin America emerged and consolidated as private enterprises that did not answer to the citizens but instead supported existing elites, including military regimes. Hence it is difficult to create a regional public broadcasting service when there are few successful antecedents, sustainable experiences and viable proposals at a national level to provide a glimpse of quality and independence.

Another important aspect to be considered in this analysis is that, contrary to the European Union, most pan-Latin American experiments such as common markets and political institutions have had very limited success if they have been viable at all. The Central America–Dominican Republic Free Trade Agreement (DR-CAFTA), Mercosur (Argentina, Brazil, Paraguay, Uruguay and more recently Venezuela) and the Andean Community of Nations (Colombia, Ecuador, Peru and more recently Chile) are trade blocs that are still in a development stage and do not yet have any firm plans for the free movement of people across borders. Despite a wide range of agreements, institutions such as the Andean

Parliament or the G3 (the free trade agreement between Colombia, Mexico and Venezuela) rarely contemplate political frameworks bonding for the signatories or deliver on cultural issues. Because of this, Latin American integration is, for most citizens in the region, a chimerical utopia that seems to have little or no impact on their daily lives. We disagree nevertheless with those authors who suggest that the blurring of boundaries of the nation state confuses the definition of citizenship (Castells 1997: 309). On the contrary, if anything, integration projects such as the European Union have enhanced individual and collective citizens' rights, even though they have not necessarily translated into a common space (Schlesinger 2007: 68). A project such as TeleSur could therefore have the potential to widen, strengthen and demark the notion of citizenship in a region where human rights violations are still very much in evidence.

Challenges and the future

The problem is not to establish a universal set of aspirations, but to define in specific terms what it is to be a citizen in Latin America; not only in a way that can equal guarantee rights despite class divisions (something that not even the European Union has been able to offer), but also with regard to geographical, cultural and ethnic diversity. Furthermore, not all groups and countries have necessarily had the same degree of commitment or interest in the integrationist project. It is therefore not possible to talk about 'an integrationist project' in Latin America, but about different projects that coexist and that have parallel ideological and political aspirations. Many of these are driven by political and economic elites in the region that have not only different but in many cases competing agendas. Therefore, the creation of a common media space to strengthen integrationist projects cannot only be seen as an ideational aspiration, but also needs to be assessed – we would argue – as a project that is intrinsically linked to regional hegemonies. This is a troubling prospect, since these hegemonies perceive other integrationist projects as possible threats to their own interests.

It is no coincidence then that TeleSur is viewed differently across the region, even among the shareholders. In places such as Colombia, for example, many elites believe that the channel could become another ideological instrument of the Venezuela/Cuba alliance against the USA (*El Tiempo* 2005); in other countries, such as Brazil, some political elites – from the left and the right – perceive it to be a possible threat to their own regional hegemony and leadership (a threat made manifest in the nationalization of the gas industry in Bolivia, which mainly affected Brazilian interests). Even Cuba, the closest political ally of President Chávez, only allows a two-hour transmission of a censored and edited version of what TeleSur broadcast the previous day for the rest of the world (Cino 2005).

Equally challenging for TeleSur is the degree of independence from government intervention that can be attained. An advisory group to TeleSur recommended that it should be set up as a public trust, independent from government officials or state-controlled broadcasters (Villarroel 2005). However, independence of TeleSur's news agenda represents a dilemma in more ways than one. This is because the project aims to depart from the traditional Anglo-Saxon model, which has at its centre the notion of impartiality, often associated with the value of objectivity (McNair 1995), and that in turn is supposedly guaranteed by commercial values (questionable as they are). However, in comparing itself with Al-Jazeera, which had an infrastructure and ethos that were originally established by the BBC and which are based on similar news values, TeleSur is setting up a standard that contradicts its own aim of being an alternative to the predominant news agenda paradigm, thereby placing itself in a no-win situation.

Potential and limits

Overall, we suggest that TeleSur will have a very difficult time becoming a regional public broadcaster. In simple terms, this is because Latin America cannot be viably constructed as a single region with shared cultural values nor is there a tradition of public service broadcasting among the individual countries. Instead, the complexity and diversity of Latin America's cultural and political constructed hegemonies and realities provides an unavoidable challenge for the multiculturalism and cultural hybridity that TeleSur seems to want to incarnate.

However, if the channel intends to justify its existence as a geopolitical project in the context of increasingly polarized relations with the USA, then that is another story. TeleSur will not be alone in this strategic game of establishing networks to influence public diplomacy, competing directly with the USA. The French government gave initial funding of €30 million for 2006 to its partially owned French International News Network (CFII) and allocated another €65 million for 2007. CFII is owned by the French commercial network TF1 and the state-funded company France Télévision that started broadcasting in 2007. President Jacques Chirac floated the idea of a French global television channel back in 2002, this to raise the profile of his country's diplomacy, as France led international opposition to US plans to invade Iraq (Feuilherade 2005). Using similar geopolitical arguments, the BBC has cut the cost of some home-based services in order to fund an Arabic television channel (Sheppard 2006: 28).

For TeleSur, which has far less resources and internal conflicting interests, it will not be an easy game to play. In July 2005, the US House of Representatives approved a measure that authorizes the Bush administration to initiate radio and television broadcasts 'that will provide a consistently accurate, objective, and comprehensive source of news to Venezuela', while President Chávez responded that he would jam any signal coming into Venezuela in the same way that Cuba does with Radio Marti (Goodenough 2005). It is also possible to predict that some of the shareholders of TeleSur, who have much better relations with the USA than Cuba and Venezuela, would be reluctant to support a more open confrontation. If TeleSur is able to expand to all its intended markets (which include some parts of the USA) then we will probably see a radicalization towards the left, increasingly antagonizing the USA. Some member states will subsequently wriggle out of the project as Brazil did virtually at its inception. That is the real dilemma for TeleSur: in order to reach its peak audience and consolidate its position as an alternative communicational project it will probably have to sacrifice some of its partners together with its original aim of being Latin America's voice; so much for regional integration and a common media space.

Notes

1   Mercosur is South America's leading trading bloc. Known as the Common Market of the South, it aims to bring about the free movement of goods, capital, services and people among its member states.

2   The Andean Community of Nations (Spanish: Comunidad Andina de Naciones, CAN) is a trade bloc comprising the South American countries of Bolivia, Colombia, Ecuador and Peru. The trade bloc was called the Andean Pact until 1996 and came into existence with the signing of the Cartagena Agreement in 1969. Its headquarters are located in Lima, Peru.

3   The ALBA (Alternativa Bolivariana para las Américas), as its Spanish initials indicate, is a proposed alternative to the US-sponsored Free Trade Area of the Americas (FTAA, ALCA in its Spanish initials), differing from the latter in that it advocates a socially-oriented trade bloc rather than one strictly based on the logic of deregulated profit maximization.

4   In the case of the BBC this is more evident since the BBC World Service is not funded by the television licence but directly by the Foreign and Commonwealth Office, which justifies such funding, arguing that it is in aid of public diplomacy.

5   This raised important questions since at that time there was no official rise in the channel's overall capital and none of the shareholders gave away shares. Neither Bolivia nor Ecuador have been requested to pay cash for their shares.

6   The tensions rose when President Chávez made a series of public comments regarding Peru's electoral candidates that were considered by President Alejandro Toledo as an intrusion in the country's internal affairs. The tensions increased until both countries recalled their respective ambassadors.

7   Interview with media analyst Antonio J. Marcano, 12 February 2006.

8 In the interview on 27 August 2006, Martinez pointed out that her company has just started to include satellite in its surveys, but still mostly concentrated on the capital and other important cities.

9 In February 1994, AGB Nielsen Media Research (AGB Venezuela) first delivered people meter data for the Caracas region. As a result of successive panel expansions, the panel had 810 households and represented the nine most important urban areas of the country. From 1 April 2003, due to negative business conditions, the panel has been downsized to approximately 590 households in the four main cities: Caracas, Barquisimeto, Maracaibo and Valencia.

10 Interview with media analyst and journalist Antonio J. Marcano, 12 February 2006.

11 Moreover, it is perceived that integration as a political project has been suppressed by powerful interests in the West, according to which Simón Bolívar's and Gamal Abdel Nasser's integrationist aspirations failed to materialize due to western intervention.

12 The British approach to pan-European projects during the conservative period (1979–7) meant that private consortiums and companies, rather than the state, would take part in these types of project as in the case of the Eurostar, Concorde and Airbus.

REFERENCES

AAAP (2007) *Informe Oficial de Inversión Publicitaria Argentina 2006*, Buenos Aires, www.aaap.org.ar/inversion%2Dpublicitaria/interna.html (accessed 12 March 2007).

Acevedo Rojas, J. (2000) Perú: Derechos Humanos y Prensa, in *Chasqui, Revista Latinoamericana de Comunicación*, no. 72, www.chasqui.comunica.org.

Acevedo Rojas, J. (2002) *Prensa y violencia Política (1980–1995) Aproximación a las visiones de los Derechos Humanos en el Perú*. Lima: Calandria.

Acevedo Rojas, J. (2005) La Política, los políticos y los medios. Apuntes sobre el debate de la Ley de Radio y Televisión, in R.M. Alfaro (ed.) *Comunicación y Política en una democracia ética por construir*. Lima: Calandria, pp. 41–5.

AGB Panamericana de Venezuela Medición (2001) *Libro de Hábitos y Tendencias 2000–2001*. Caracas: AGB Panamericana.

Aldana, C. (1992) Síntesis de las palabras de Carlos Aldana en el acto por el Centenario de Patria e instauración del Día de la Prensa Cubana. In *Granma*, 17 March: 4.

Aldana, C. (1997) Racism and the conceptions of beauty: the relationship between media consumption and the definition of identity, MA dissertation, University of Sussex.

Alfaro, R.M. (2006) Hundidos en la Incertidumbre: Cultura Política y Proceso Electoral, in Rosa Maria Alfaro (ed.) *Indignación e Incertidumbre Política, Responsabilidades del Periodismo en el Proceso Electoral*. Lima: Calandria, pp. 54–82.

ANDA-FEVAP (2001) *Comité Certificador de Medios ANDA-FEVAP*. Caracas: Asociacion Nacional de Anunciantes.

Anderson, B.R. (1991) *Imagined Communities: Reflections on the Origin and Spread of Nationalism*. London: Verso.

Ansidey, G. and Díaz, M. (2007) *Libro blanco sobre RCTV*. Caracas: Ministerio del Poder Popular para la Comunicación y la Información.

Arbitron (2006) *RADAR 95 December 2006 Radio Listening Estimates.* New York: Arbitron Inc.

Ardito Vega, W. (1999) Racismo en el Perú y Estándares Internacionales. *En Revista Ideéle* 117: 15–17.

Ardito Vega, W. (2004) Racismo en el Perú Republicano. In *Revista Aportes Andinos* no. 9, Discriminación, Exclusión y Racismo. Programa Andino de Derechos Humanos – Universidad Andina Simón Bolívar.

Avila, A. (2006) Campaña, mentiras y videos, *La Revista de El Universal,* 26 June.

Avritzer, L. (2002) *Democracy and Public Space in Latin America.* Princenton, NJ: Princenton University Press.

Avritzer, L. and Costa, S. (2004) Teoria Crítica, Democracia e esfera Pública: Concepções Usis na América Latina. *Revista de Ciências Sociais,* 47(4): 703–28.

Barrera, E. (1999) *Mexico.* Encyclopedia of Broadcast Communications. Museum of Broadcast Communications.

Barriga, A. (2004): *Guía Boliviana de Medios de comunicación.* La Paz: Imagen y Color.

Bartelsman, E., Haltiwanger, J. and Scarpetta, S. (2004) Microeconomic evidence of creative destruction in industrial and developing countries. *Policy Research Working Papers.* Washington, DC: World Bank.

BBC (2005) Latin CNN' broadcasts first news, BBC World Service, 1 November.

Belinche, M., Vialey, P., Castro, J. and Tovar, C. (2004) *Medios, Política y Poder. La conformación de los multimedios de la Argentina de los 90.* Argentina: Editions of Periodismo y Comunicación.

Bernstein, C. (1977) The CIA and the Media, *Rolling Stone,* 20 October: 65–7.

Bisbal, M. and Pasquale Nicodemo (2002) *Impacto e imparcialidad en las primeras planas.* Caracas: UCV-Mimeo.

Blanco, D. and Germano, C. (2005) *20 años de medios & democracia en la Argentina.* Buenos Aires: La Cujía Ediciones.

Bohmann, K. (1989) *Medios de comunicación y sistemas informativos en México* México, DF: Alianza Editorial.

Bonilla, E. and González, J. (2004) *Regulación y concesiones en la televisión colombiana: destellos y sombras.* Bogotá: Comisión Nacional de Televisión, CID.

Borrat, H. (1989) *El periódico como actor político*. Barcelona: Gustavo Gili Editores S.A.

Bourdieu, P. ([1979] 1999) *La Distinción*. Madrid: Taurus.

Bourdieu, P. (1998) *On Television and Journalism*. London: Pluto Press.

Brito, B. (2005) *Books and Publishing Sector Profile – Argentina*. Buenos Aires: The Canadian Trade Commissioner Service.

Budde Communication PTY Ltd (2006) *Telecommunications Research Reports*. http://www.budde.com.au/reports/Category/main-Search-Categories-1.html (accessed 9 February 2007).

Cacho, L. (2006) *Los Demonios del Eden*. Mexico, DF: Grijalbo.

Calderón, F. (2004) Cultura Política y Desarrollo, www.cultureandpublicaction.org.

Cancio, W. (1998) El periodismo en Cuba, http://www.saladeprensa.org (accessed May 2006).

Cancio, W. (2005) Castro lanza una ofensiva contra el acceso ilegal a la televisión por satélite, http://www.miami.com/mld/elnuevo/news/world/cuba/13296485.htm (accessed December 2005).

Cañizales, A. (1990) Los Medios de Comunicación Social, *Cuadernos de Formación Socio-Política*, 26. Caracas: Centro Gumilla.

Caparelli, S. (1982) *Televisdo e Capitalismo no Brasil*. Sao Paulo: L & PM.

Cappellini, M. (2004) La prensa Chicha en Perú. In Chasqui, *Revista Latinoamericana de Comunicación*, no. 84.

Carvajal, Y. (2003) Entrevista con Luis Brito García, *Panorama*. 23 February.

Castellanos, N. (2001) La civilización del iletrado. El proyecto ilustrado de radiodifusión en Colombia, 1929–1940, in Bonilla, Jorge y Patiño, Gustavo (eds) *Comunicación y política. Viejos conflictos, nuevos desafíos*. Bogotá: Pontificia Universidad Javeriana.

Castells, M. (1997) *The Information Age: Economy, Society and Culture, Volume II: The Power of Identity*. London: Blackwell.

Castro, Fidel (1961a) Homenaje al periódico Revolución. In *Obra Revolucionaria*, 11: 6.

Castro, Fidel (1961b) *Palabras a los intelectuales*. Havana: Ediciones del Consejo Nacional de Cultura.

Castro, F. (1966) Respuesta a Frei. In *Documentos Políticos*. Havana: Editora Política, 1: 260.

Castro, F. (1975) Informe Central al I Congreso del Partido Comunista de Cuba. Havana: Departamento de Orientación Revolucionaria del Partido Comunista de Cuba.

Catalán, C. and Sunkel, G. (1992) *Algunas tendencias en el consumo de bienes culturales en America Latina.* Santiago: FLASCO.

Chamorro, C. (2001) *El turno de los medios en la agenda de la democratización.* Envio, 232, July 2001, www.envio.org.ni/articulo/1092 (accessed 17 September 2006).

Chamorro, C. (2002) *El Poder de la Prensa: entre el Mercado y el Estado.* Managua: CINCO.

Cino, L. (2005) Las desventuras de Telesur. Cubanet http://www.cubanet.org/CNews/y05/sep05/26a9.htm (accessed 10 May 2006).

Clarín (2006a) CableVisión y Multicanal forman un sistema regional de cable e Internet, www.clarin.com/diario/2006/09/29/elpais/p-02201.htm (accessed 12 March 2007).

Clarín (2006b) *El capital nacional regresa a uno de los líderes de la TV paga,* http://www.clarin.com/diario/2006/09/29/elpais/p-02301.htm (accessed 12 March 2007).

Colomina, M. (1968) *El huésped alienante.* Maracaibo: Prensaluz.

Comisión de la Verdad y Reconciliación (2003) *Informe Final,* www.cverdad.org.pe.

CONATEL (2007) *Estadísticas del Sector Telecomunicaciones,* www.conatel.gob.ve/indicadores/Indicadores2007/Presentacion_Estadisticas_del_Sector_ano_2006.pdf (accessed 12 March 2007).

Consejo de Investigación de Medios (2006) *Conexión. Media data 2006.* Distrito Federal, México: Consejo d e Investigación de Medios.

Convenio Andrés Bello (CAB) (2003) *El impacto económico de las industrias culturales en Colombia.* Bogotá: CAB, CERLALC, Ministerio de Cultura.

Cordova-Claure, T. (2002) Chávez: Golpe mediático o burocrático? *Revista Chasqui,* 78: 22–6.

Corrales, O. and Sandoval, J. (2005) Concentration of the media market, pluralism and freedom of speech. Santiago: Fundación Chile, 21 *Ideas Coleccion,* 5(53).

Coronel, G. (2005) A conversation with Antonio Pasquali about Telesur, www.venezuelatoday.net/gustavo-coronel/antonio-pasquali+telesur.html (accessed 12 January 2006).

Corte Nacional Electoral (2005) *Democracia en Bolivia. Cinco análisis temáticos del Segundo Estudio Nacional sobre Democracia y Valores Democráticos.* La Paz: Edit. G&S Producciones.

Costa, J. *et al.* (2003) *Investigación Diagnóstica sobre los Partidos Políticos con Representación Parlamentaria en Bolivia.* La Paz: Fundación Boliviana para la Democracia Multipartidaria. Informe final.

Crabtree, R. (1996) Community radio in Sandinista Nicaragua, 1979–1992: participatory communication and the revolutionary process, *Historical Journal of Film, Radio and Television*, www.findarticles.com/p/articles/mi_m2584/is_n2_v16/ai_18897249 (accessed 17 September 2006).

CRIS (2007) Crisinfo. Communication rights in the information society, http://comunica.org/mailman/listinfo/crisinfo_comunica.org (accessed 21 August 2007).

Cuneo, C. (2002) *Globalized and localized digital divides along the information highway: a fragile synthesis across bridges.* Paper presented at 'Ramps, Cloverleaves, and Ladders', the 33rd Annual Sorokin Lecture. University of Saskatchewan.

Curran, J. (1981) Capitalismo y control de la prensa, 1800–1975, in J. Curran *et al. Sociedad y comunicación de masas.* México: Fondo de Cultura Económica, pp. 222–61.

Dagnino, E. (2002) *Sociedad Civil, Esfera Pública y Democratización en América Latina.* México, D.F.: Fondo de Cultura Económica.

Delarbre, R.T. (1994) Videopolítica vs. Mediocracia? Los Medios y la Cultura Democrática, *Revista Mexicana de Sociologia*, 3(94).

DGEEC (2002) *Censo de la Pubalcion y por Hogar.* La Asunción: Dirección General de Estadísticas, Encuestas y Censos.

DGEEC (2004) *Encuesta Permanente por Hogar.* La Asunción: Dirección General de Estadísticas, Encuestas y Censos.

Diario 2001 (April 15, 2005) Combatirá campañas de agresión mediática. Izarra anunció creación de gabinete comunicacional, *Diario 2001*: 15.

Diario de Caracas (2005) Nombran nueva presidenta de VTV, *Diario de Caracas,* 10 January: 5.

Díaz Castañón, M. (2004) *Perfiles de la nación.* Havana: Editorial de Ciencias Sociales.

Díaz Rangel, E. (1976) *Pueblos subinformados.* Caracas: Monte Avila Editores.

Díaz Rangel, E. (2004) ¿Dónde está la sociedad civil? *Ultimas Noticias,* 9 March: 4.

Díaz Rangel (1976) Eleazar. Dónde esta la sociedad civil? *Ultimas Noticias*, 9 March.

Doyle, K. (2002) *Mexico's New Freedom of Expression Law.* Washington, DC: The National Security Archive.

Drucker, P. (1993) *Post-Capitalist Society.* Oxford: Butterworth-Heinemann.

Edelman, M. (2005) *Campesinos contra la globalización. Movimientos sociales rurales en Costa Rica.* San José: Editorial Universidad de Costa Rica.

EFE (2005) *Consejero dice que Telesur quiere ser Al Yazira latinoamericano,* http://www.efe.es (accessed 8 August 2005).

Egypto, L. and Osorio P. (2002) *Quem são os donos da mídia no Brasil?* Brasil: Observatório da Imprensa.

El Comercio (2006) La profundidad y el servicio, 30 July.

El Nuevo País (2005) Anuncian estructura de TeleSur, *El Nuevo País,* 3 March: 10.

El Tiempo (2005) Emisiones de prueba de Telesur incluyen imagenes de Tirofijo y una mujer que canta 'Eta, Eta, Eta', *El Tiempo,* 14 July: 6.

El-Nawawy, M. and Iskandar, A. (2002) *Al-Jazeera. How the Free Arab News Network Scooped the World and Changed the Middle East.* Cambridge, MA: Westview.

Eliades, A. (2005) *Red-Com magazine.* Redefiniciones, 1.

Encuestas and Estudios (2004) *Segundo Estudio Nacional sobre Democracia y Valores Democráticos en Bolivia.* Servicio de Información Pública. La Paz: Corte Nacional Electoral.

Eltzer, B.A. (1986) *El periodismo político argentino durante la época militar, 1976–1983.* Buenos Aires: Ediciones S.J.L.

Estrada, I. (1996) *Retóricas, astucias, convenciones. Ideologías profesionales de los periodistas cubanos.* Havana: Editorial de Ciencias Sociales.

ETIC (2005) *Estrategia Nacional de TIC para el desarrollo,* http://www.etic.bo (accessed 9 September 2007).

Farah, E. (1978) *Partido Ba'th Arabe y Socialista. El Pensamiento Árabe Revolucionario frente al desafío actual.* Madrid: Fareso.

Fárber, G. (2003) *Bomba de Tiempo.* La Palabra.com. http://esp.mexico.com/lapalabra/una/13622/bomba-de-tiempo.

Febres, C.E. *et al.* (1991) 27 de Febrero. Dos años después, o para no olvidar. Apuntes. *Cuadernos de la Escuela de Comunicación Social.* (UCV) Apuntes Especial 1.

Federico, M.E.B. (1982) *História da Comunicação, Rádio e TV no Brasil.* São Paulo: Vozes.

Fernández, C.F.F. (1985) *Los medios de comunicación masivos en México.* México, D.F: Juan Pablos Editor.

Festa, R. and Santoro, L.F. (1991) A Terceira Idade da TV: o Local e o Internacional, in Adauto Novaes (ed.) *Rêde Imaginária: Televisão e Democracia.* São Paulo, Brazil: Companhia das Letras, pp. 179–95.

Feuilherade, P. (2005) French channel set for 2006 start. BBC Monitoring, http://news.bbc.co.uk/1/hi/world/europe/4485256.stm (accessed 12 May 2006).

Fine, B., Lapavitsas, C. and Pincus, J. (2003) *Development Policy in the Twenty-First Century.* London: Routledge.

Flores, M.I. and Gardela, I. (1983) Origen, desarrrollo y actualidad de la radiodifusión, *Revista de Ciencias Sociales*, 26: 17–26.

Fossum, J.E. and Schlesinger, P. (2007) *The European Union and the Public Sphere: A Communicative Space in the Making?* London: Routledge.

Fox, E. (1997) *Latin American Broadcasting: From Tango to Telenovela.* Luton: John Libbey Media, University of Luton.

Fox, E. and Waisbod, S. (eds) (2002) *Global Media, Local Politics: Broadcasting Policies in Latin America.* Austin, TX: University of Texas.

Fox, P.D. (2006) *Being and Blackness in Latin America: Uprootedness and Improvisation.* Gainesville, FL: University Press of Florida.

France Press (2002) La prensa cubana escamotea críticas de Carter, www.cubanet.org/CNews/y02/may02/16o1.htm (accessed March 2006).

Galperín, H. (2002) Transforming television in Argentina: market development and policy reform in the 1990s, in E. Fox and S. Waisbrod (eds) *Latin Politics, Global Media: Broadcasting Policies in Latin America.* Austin, TX: University of Texas.

García-Canclini, N. (1990) *Culturas Híbridas.* Mexico, D.F.: Grijalbo.

Gargurevich Regal, J. (1987) *Prensa, Radio y Televisión: Historia Crítica.* Lima: Editorial Horizonte.

Gargurevich Regal, J. (2005) Peru, Medios del Estado y Gobiernos, Un Breve Recorrido Historico, in Rosa Maria Alfaro (ed.) *Comunicación y Politica en una Democracia Ética por Construir.* Lima: Calandria, pp. 175–85.

Gerbner, G. *et al.* (1996) Crecer con la televisión: perspectiva de aculturación, in B. Jennings and D. Zillman (eds) *Los efectos de los medios de comunicación. Investigación y teorías.* Barcelona: Editorial Paidós, pp. 35–66.

Gervasi, S. (1979) CIA Covert propaganda capability, *Covert Action Information Bulletin,* 7: 18–20.

Giglio, J. (2006) Crean la mayor red de cable de la región, La Nación, 29 September, http://buscador.lanacion.com.ar/Nota.asp?nota_id=844701 &high=cable (accessed 29 September 2006).

Gil, E. and Ricardo Luis, R. (2000) *La Verdad Útil.* Universidad de La Habana: Facultad de Comunicación.

Gill, J. and Hughes, S. (2005) Bureaucratic compliance with Mexico's new access to information law, *Critical Studies in Media Communication,* 22: 121–37.

Glassner, B. (1999) *The Culture of Fear: Why Americans are Afraid of the Wrong Things.* New York: Basic Books.

Goodenough, P. (2005) Chavez promises airwave warfare over US broadcast plans, http://www.cnsnews.com//ViewForeignBureaus.asp?Page=%5C %5CForeignBureaus%5C%5Carchive%5C%5C200507%5C%5CFOR2 0050722c.html (accessed 21 May 2006).

Grupo Radio Centro, S.A. de C.V. (2006) *Reporte Anual.* Distrito Federal, México: Comision Nacional Bancaria y de Valores.

Guest, I. (2000) Behind the Disappearances: Argentina's Dirty War Against Human Rights and the United Nations. Pennsylvania: University of Pennsylvania Press.

Guevara, A. (1998) Indice de una polémica con Blas Roca (dossier incompleto), in *Revolución es lucidez, La Habana,* Ediciones ICAIC, pp. 201–18.

Habermas, J. (1994) *Historia y crítica de la opinión pública.* México: G. Gili.

Hallin, D.C. and Papathanassopoulos, S. (2002) Political clientelism and the media: southern Europe and Latin America in comparative perspective, *Media, Culture & Society,* 24(2).

Hernández Navarro, L. (2004) Latinoamérica: ¿hacia un Al Jazeera hemisférico? *La Jornada*, 7 December, www.jornada.unam.mx/ 2004/12/ 07/027a2pol.php (accessed 14 February 2006).

Herrán, M.T. (1991) *La industria de los medios de comunicación en Colombia*. Bogotá: Fescol.

Hopenhayn, M. (2002) *No Apocalypse, No Integration: Modernism and Postmodernism in Latin America*. Durham, NC: Duke University Press.

Hughes, S. and Lawson, C. (2005a) Propaganda and crony capitalism. Partisan bias in Mexican Television News, *Latin American Research Review*, 39: 81–105.

Human Development Report (2005b) *Human Development Report 2005*, http://hdr.undp.org/reports/global/2005/pdf/HDR05_complete.pdf (accessed May 2006).

Human Rights Watch (1998) *The Limits of Tolerance: Freedom of Speech and Public Debate in Chile*. Santiago: Lom Editions.

Husting, G. (1999) When a war is not a war: Abortion, Desert Storm, and representations of protest in American TV news, *Sociological Quarterly*, 40(1): 159–76.

IBOPE AGB (2005) *Share TV Abierta, 28 Ciudades*. México: Distrito Federal.

IBOPE AGB México (2007). *Reportes de rating*, http://www.ibope.com.mx/ hgxpp001.aspx (accessed 20 July2007).

INEC (2002) *Informe General Encuesta Nacional Sobre Medición De Nivel De Vida, 2001*. Managua: Instituto Nicaraguense de Estadísticas y Censos.

Instituto Nacional de Estadística – INEI (2006) Códigos de Lenguas Nativas, http://www.inei.gob.pe/siscodes/LenguasMarco.htm.

Instituto Venezolano de Publicidad (IVP) (2001) *Histórico Inversión Publicitaria Período 1981–2000*. Caracas: IVP.

International Federation of Journalists (2002) *Missing Link in Venezuela's Political Crisis. Report of IFJ to Caracas*. Brussels: International Federation of Journalists.

IPSO-BIMSA (2004) *Estudio General de Medios*. México: D.F.

IPSO-BIMSA (2005) *Estudio General de Medios*. México: D.F.

IVC (2006) Boletín: Diarios de Circulación Pagada. Instituto Verificador de Circulaciones (IVC), http://www.ivc.com.ar/consulta (accessed 12 March 2006).

IWS (2007) *Bolivia: Internet Usage and Market Report*, Internet World Statistics, www.internetworldstats.com/sa/bo.htm (accessed 1 September 2007).

Jiménez, S. (2007) YVKE Mundial dependerá del MINCI, *El Universal*, http://buscador.eluniversal.com/2007/08/13/til_art_yvke-mundial-depende_403005.shtml (accessed 8 August 2007).

Klich, I. and Rapoport, M. (1997) *Discriminacion y racismo en America Latina*. Buenos Aires: Grupo Editor Latinoamericano.

Kodrich, K. (2002) *Tradition and Change in the Nicaraguan Press*. Lanham, MD: University Press of America.

Kunzle, D. (1984) Nicaragua's *La Prensa* – capitalist thorn in socialist flesh, *Media, Culture and Society*, 6: 151–76.

La Prensa (2005) Pocos dignos de confianza, *La Prensa* 21 September, http://www-ni.laprensa.com.ni/archivo/2005/septiembre/21/nacionales/nacionales-20050921–14.html (accessed 17 September 2006).

La Prensa (2006) FSLN censura entrevista, 27 August, http://www-ni.laprensa.com.ni/archivo/2006/agosto/27/noticias/nacionales/139875.shtml (accessed 17 September 2006).

Landi, Oscar (1993) *Devórame Otra Vez. ¿Qué hizo la televisión con la gente? ¿Qué hace la gente con la televisión?* Buenos Aires: Editorial Planeta.

Lara Klahr, M. (2005) *Diarismo: Cultura e industria del periodismo impreso en México y el mundo*. México: D.F.

Latinbarómetro (2005) *Informe Latinbarómetro 2005*, www.latinobarometro.org/uploads/media/2005.pdf (accessed 17 September 2006).

Leiken, R.S. (2003) *Why Nicaragua Vanished: A Story of Reporters and Revolutionaries*. New York: Rowman & Littlefield.

Lenin, V.I. (1979) *Acerca de la prensa*. Moscow: Progress.

León Enrique, R. (1975) *Ultima Edición*. Havana: Arte y Literatura.

Lerner, S. (2003) *Discurso de Presentación del Informe Final de la Comision de la Verdad y Reconciliación*, www.cverdad.org.pe.

Linz, J. (1996) *La quiebra de las democracias*. Madrid: Alianza Universidad.

López-Alves, F. (2003) *La Formación del Estado y la democracia en América Latina*. Bogota: Groupo Editorial Norma.

Lugo-Ocando, J. (1998) *Información de Estado*. Maracaibo: Vennet Editores.

Lugo-Ocando, J. (1990) Interview with Ramon J. Velásquez: A La democracia se le están agotando los recursos, *La Columna*, 29 February: 3.

Lugo-Ocando, J. and Romero, J. (2002) From friends to foes: Venezuela's media goes from consensual space to confrontational actor, *Sincronía*, 7(1).

Lynch, M. (2005) *Voices of the New Arab Public: Iraq, al-Jazeera, and Middle East Politics Today.* New York: Columbia University Press.

Macassi, S. (2006) Entre la Cultura Política y la Oferta Informativa: Reflexiones Sobre el Debate Electoral en Noticieros, in Rosa Maria Alfaro (ed.) *Indignación e Incertidumbre Política, Responsabilidades del Periodismo en el Proceso Electoral.* Lima: A.C.S. Calandria, pp. 44–53.

Manrique Galvez, N. (2006) Democracia y Nación. La Promesa Pendiente, in *La Democracia en el Perú: Proceso Histórico y Agenda Pendiente.* Lima: PNUD.

Márquez, H. (2007) *Venezuela: Petrodollars for Local Film Industry,* http://ipsnews.net/news.asp?idnews=36151 (accessed 12 March 2007).

Marrero, J. (1999) *Dos siglos de periodismo en Cuba.* Havana: Editorial Pablo de la Torriente.

Martín-Barbero, J. (1993) *Communication, Culture and Hegemony: From the Media to Mediations.* London: Sage.

Martín-Barbero, J. and Rey, G. (1997) El periodismo en Colombia: de los oficios y los medios, *Signo y Pensamiento*, XVI(30): 13–30.

Mato, D. (1999) Telenovelas: transnacionalización de la industria y transformaciones del género, in N. García Canclini (ed.) *Industrias culturales e integración latinoamericana.* México: Grijalbo.

Mattelart, A. (1998) *La mundialización de la comunicación.* Barcelona: Paidós.

Mattelart, A. (1986) *Communicating in Popular Nicaragua.* New York: International General.

Mattelart, A. (1972) *Agresión desde el espacio. Cultura y napalm en la era de los satélites.* Santiago: Ediciones Tercer Mundo.

Matus, A. (1999) *The Black Book of Chilean Justice.* Santiago: Planeta.

May, C. (2002) *The Information Society: A Sceptical View.* London: Polity.

McAnany, E.C. (1984) The logic of cultural industries in Latin America: the television industry in Brazil, in V. Mosco and J. Wasko (eds) *The*

Critical Communications Review, Vol. II: Changing Patterns of Communications Control. New Jersey: Ablex, pp. 185–208.

McNair, B. (1995) *An Introduction to Political Communication.* London: Routledge.

McNair, B. (2003) *News and Journalism in the UK.* London: Routledge.

McNair, B. (2006) *Cultural Chaos: Journalism, News and Power in a Globalised World.* London: Routledge.

Medios para la Paz (2004) *La guerra: una amenaza para la prensa.* Bogotá: MPP.

Méndez, A.I. and Morales, E. (2001) La democracia Venezolana desde el discurso de los líderes tradicionales, *Utopía y Praxis Latinoamericana,* 6(14): 9–39.

Merklen, D. (2001) *Politiques de lutte contre la pauvreté urbaine: Un cadre général pour l'action.* Paris: Organisation des Nations Unies.

Mesa-Lago, C. (1994) *Breve historia económica de la Cuba socialista. Políticas, resultados y perspectivas.* Madrid: Alianza Editorial.

MINCI (2006) *Bolivia se suma a TeleSUR.* MINCI, Boletín de Prensa.

Ministerio de Comunicaciones (2004) *Serie Cuadernos de Política Sectorial,* 3. Bogotá: Imprenta Nacional.

Ministerio de Transportes y Comunicaciones (2006) *Estaciones de Radiodifusión por Televisión a Nivel Nacional.* Ministerio de Transportes y Comunicaciones del Perú, www.mtc.gob.pe/portal/comunicacion/concesion/radiodifusion/tv.pdf (accessed 21 January 2007).

MIT/Reforma Survey (2005) *First Installment. Panel Survey,* http://web.mit.edu/polisci/research/mexico06/MReport.pdf (accessed 12 February 2007).

Molero, L. (2001) Recursos lingüísticos y estrategias discursivas en la construcción de la imagen del pueblo en el discurso político Venezolano, *Oralia: Análisis del discurso oral,* 6: 215–35.

Molina, J.I. (1997) Explorando las bases de la cultura impresa en Costa Rica: la alfabetización popular (1821–1950), in J. Patricia Vega (ed.) *Comunicación y construcción de lo cotidiano.* San José: DEI.

Molina, J.I. (2002) *Costarricense por dicha.* San José: Editorial de la Universidad de Costa Rica.

Molina, J.I. (2003) *Identidad nacional y cambio cultural en Costa Rica durante la segunda mitad del siglo XX.* San José: Serie Cuadernos de Historia de las Instituciones de Costa Rica, Editorial de la Universidad de Costa Rica, no. 11.

Molina, J.I. and Fumero, P. (1997) *La Sonora Libertad del Viento. Sociedad y Cultura en Costa Rica y Nicaragua (1821–1914)*. México: Instituto Panamericano de Geografía e Historia.

Moncayo Jiménez, E. (2004) Nuevos Enfoques del Desarrollo Territorial: Colombia en una Perspectiva Latinoamericana. Bogotá: Naciones Unidos.

Montes, R. (2006) Rebajas de temporada para Creel. La Revista de El Universal.

Moreno, A. (1999) Campaign awareness and voting in the 1997 Mexican Congressional elections, in J.D.A.A. Poire (ed.) *Toward Mexico's Democratization: Parties, Campaigns, Elections and Pubic Opinion*. New York: Routledge.

Moreno, A. (2002) *Negative campaigns and voting in the 2000 Mexican presidential election*. Working papers in political science. Distrito Federal, México.

Morley, D. (2000) *Home Territories: Media, Mobility and Identity*. London: Routledge.

Morris, N. and Waisbord, S. (eds) (2001) *Media and Gloablization: Why the State Matters*. Lanham, MD: Rowan & Littlefield.

Murdock, G. (1999) Rights and representations: public discourse and cultural citizenship, in J. Gripsrud (ed.) *Television and Common Knowledge*. London: Routledge, pp. 7–17.

Norris, P. (2001) *Digital Divide: Civic Engagement, Information Poverty, and the Internet Worldwide*. Cambridge: Cambridge University Press.

Notitarde (2005) TeleSur transmitirá por satélite, *Notitarde*, 27 March: 15.

Núñcz Machín, A. (1983) *Pensamiento revolucionario y medios de difusión masiva*. Havana: Editora Política.

O'Donnell, P. (1995) *Dar la palabra al pueblo*. Mexico: Universidad Iberoamericana.

O'Neill, O. (2002) *A Question of Trust*. Cambridge: Cambridge University Press.

OECD (Organization for Economic Cooperation and Development) (2007) OECD statistics, http://stats.oecd.org/WBOS/default.aspx?Dataset Code=CSP2007 (accessed 21 May 2007).

OEI (2005) *Industrias Culturales y Desarrollo Sustentable*. Mexico, D.F.: Organización de Estados Iberoamericanos para la Educación, la Ciencia y la Cultura.

Orozco Gómez, G. (1997) *La Investigación de la Comunicación dentro y fuera de América Latina*. Argentina: Ediciones de Periodismo y Comunicación.

Palomino, F. (2001) Marketing Político y Vladivideos. In Chasqui, Revista Latinoamericana de Comunicación, no. 75, www.comunica.org/chasqui.

Panorama (2005) Gobierno relanza Política Comunicacional, *Panorama*, 1 June.

Pascuali, A. (1991) *Comunicación Cercenada. El Caso Venezuela*. Caracas: Monte Avila Editores.

Pedelty, M. (1995) *War Stories: The Culture of Foreign Correspondents*. London: Routledge.

Pedraglio, S. (2006) Balance del Comportamiento Informativo de los Medios en Procesos Electorales. Elecciones en Perú: 1990, 1995, 2001 y 2005, in R.M. Alfaro (ed.) *Indignación e Incertidumbre Política, Responsabilidades del Periodismo en el Proceso Electoral*. Lima: A.C.S. Calandria, pp. 11–43.

Pellegrino, F. (1999) *Los Medios de Comunicación Social*. Caracas: Centro Gumilla.

Pérez González, J.O. (2005) *The Son of the Scribe: The Professional Ideologies of the Young Cuban Journalists*. London: University of Westminster.

Pérez Roque, F. (2003) *Conferencia de prensa del canciller Felipe Pérez Roque con relación a los mercenarios al servicio del imperio que fueron juzgados los días 3, 4, 4 y 7 de abril*, www.cuba.cu/gobierno/documentos/2003/esp/r090403e.html (accessed May 2006).

Petkoff, T. (2002) Chávez y los medios, in A. Francés and C. Machado (eds) *Venezuela: la crisis de abril*. Caracas: Ediciones IESA.

PNUD (2004) Interculturalismo y Globalización. La Bolivia posible. Informe Nacional de Desarrollo Humano 2004. La Paz: Plural Editorial.

PNUD (2005a) *Informe de Desarrollo Humano en Costa Rica*. San José: PNUD.

PNUD (2005b) Venciendo el Temor. (In)seguridad Ciudadana y Desarrollo Humano en Costa Rica. http://hdr.undp.org/en/reports/nationalreports/latinamericathecaribbean/costarica/name,3342,en.html (accessed 12 November 2006).

Portuondo, F. (1965) *Historia de Cuba 1492–1898*. Havana: Pueblo y Educación.

Preston, J. (1996) Mexico's elite caught in scandal's harsh glare, *The New York Times*, 12 July: 56.

Protzel, J. (2001) Televisión, la Legitimidad Perdida, *Quehacer Magazine*, 130.

RACSA (2006) *Disminuye Brecha digital en el país*. RACSA Noticias, www.racsa.co.cr/racsa_noticias/brecha_digital.htm (accessed 7 March 2007).

RACSA (2007) *Historia del servicio de Internet de RACSA en Costa Rica*, https://www.racsa.co.cr/info_general/historia_internet_cr.html (accessed 27 March 2007).

Radio Habana Cuba (2006) *Quiénes sómos los realizadores de Radio Habana Cuba,* www.radiohc.cu/espanol/quienes.htm (accessed May 2006).

Ramos, E. (2003) *Medios de comunicación por municipio*. El Alto: Directorio Nacional.

Raventós, C.C. *et al.* (2004) *Abstencionistas en Costa Rica ¿Quiénes son y por qué no votan?* San José: Editorial Universidad de Costa Rica.

Reporters Without Borders (2006) *Cuba: Annual Report,* www.rsf.org/article.php3?id_article=17421&Valider=OK (accessed May 2006).

Rey, G. (2002) La televisión en Colombia, in G. Orozco (ed.) *Historias de la televisión en América Latina*. Barcelona: Gedisa, pp. 117–62.

Rionda, G. (1997) TV Households in Latin America expected to increase from the present 90 mil to 110 mil by the year 2000, *Multichannel News International Supplement*, 3(10): 1–4.

Rivas Leone, J. (2002) Antipolítica y nuevos actores políticos en Venezuela, in A. Ramos Jiménez (ed.) *La transición venezolana: aproximación al fenómeno Chávez*. Mérida: Centro de Investigaciones de Política Comparada. Universidad de los Andes.

Robinson, W. (2003) *Transnational Conflicts: Central America – Social Change, and Globalization*. London: Verso.

Rockwell, R.J. and Janus, N. (2003) *Media Power in Central America*. Chicago: University of Illinois Press.

Rodríguez Neyra, J.R. (1983) *La Enseñanza del Periodismo en Cuba*. Habana: Universidad de La Habana, Facultad de Periodismo.

Rogers, E.M. and Antola, L. (1985) Telenovelas: a Latin American success story, *Journal of Communication*, 35(4): 24–35.

Romero, J. (2001) El discurso del poder en Hugo Chávez (1996–1999), in *Revista Espacio Abierto*, 2.

Romero, J. (2002a) Hugo Chávez: construcción hegemónica del poder y desplazamiento de los actores políticos tradicionales, *Revista Utopia y Praxis,* La Universidad del Zulia-Venezuela.

Romero, J. (2002b) Discurso y filosofía política en Hugo Chávez (1996–1999), *Revista Ecuador Debate,* 55.

Romero, J. (2002c) Transición política, democracia y espacio público en Venezuela (1998–2001), *Revista Cuestiones Políticas,* 28.

Romero, J. *et al.* (1999) Relaciones entre el poder civil y militar: el caso de Venezuela (1958–1998), in *Revista de Historia de América de La Universidad de Costa Rica,* 126.

Roncagliolo, R. and Macassi, S. (1989) Prensa y Poder, *Diálogos de la Comunicación,* 24. Lima: FELAFACS.

Roncagliolo, R. (2003) *Problemas de la integración cultural: América Latina.* Barcelona: Grupo Editorial Norma.

Rosabal, H. and Sanz, L. (2005) Insatisfacciones, logros y proyectos, *Punto cu.,* 1: 4–5.

Rothschuh, G. (1988) *La Onda Pervertida.* Managua: Tierra Arada.

Rothschuh, G. (1990) *Volver a Empezar.* Managua: Universidad Centroamericana.

Rothschuh, G. (1995) *¡Cogé la onda!* Managua: Ediciones Centro de Investigaciones de la Comunicación, CINCO – Fundación Friedrich Ebert.

Salas, B. (2003) Con espacios noticiosos y de opinión e interminables cadenas presidenciales, el canal del Estado apenas logra el 4,9% de rating, *El Universal.* 8 April: 7b.

Sampaio, M.F. (1984) *História do rádio e da televisão no Brasil e no mundo.* Rio de Janeiro: Achiamé.

Sandoval, G.C. (1991) *Costa Rica: Muchos canales y poca televisión. Contribuciones 21.* Costa Rica: Institute for Social Research, University of Costa Rica.

Sandoval, G.C. (1996) *Una aproximación al campo profesional de la publicidad en Costa Rica. Reflexiones,* no. 49. San José: University of Costa Rica.

Sandoval, G.C. (2004) *Threatening Others: Nicaraguans and the Formation of National Identities in Costa Rica.* Athens, OH: Ohio University Press.

Sandoval, G.C. (2006) *Fuera de juego. Fútbol, identidades nacionales y masculinidades en Costa Rica.* San José: Editorial de la Universidad de Costa Rica.

Sandoval, G.C. and Al-Ghassani, A. (1987) *Inventario de medios de comunicación en Costa Rica.* San José: Institute for Social Research, Universidad de Costa Rica.

Sandoval, G.C. and Karina Fonseca, V. (2006) *Medios de comunicación e inseguridad ciudadana.* UNDP-CostaRica: Cuadernos de Desarrollo Humano, N° 2.

Santos, B. (2005a) Presidente de la República también aprobó Proyecto TVSur. VTV estrena presidenta y alista cambio en programación, *El Universal,* 10 January: 2–9.

Santos, B. (2005b) El proyecto abordará lo social e informativo. Telesur busca la integración, *El Universal,* 13 January: 2–9.

Santos, B. (2005c) Una muestra de su programación se transmite en Vive TV y VTV. Telesur a prueba, *El Universal,* 5 May: C-14.

Santos, E. (1989) El periodismo en Colombia, 1886–1986, in A. Tirado Mejía (ed.) *Nueva Historia de Colombia.* Bogotá: Planeta, pp. 109–36.

Schlesinger, P. (2007) Nacion y espacio communicativo, in L. Luchessi and M.G. Rodriguez (eds) *Fronteras Globales: Culturas Politica y Medios de Communicacion.* Buenos Aires: La Crujia Ediciones.

Segura, R. *et al.* (1991) *La construcción de la noticia. Estudio del proceso de producción noticiosa en el Noticiero Nacional de Televisión.* Habana: Universidad de La Habana, Facultad de Comunicación.

Sen, A. (1999). *Development as Freedom.* New York: Anchor.

Sheppard, F. (2006) BBC's mission to take on Al-Jazeera with free Arabic TV channel, *The Scotsman,* 16 August: 28.

Siebert, F.S. *et al.* (1963) *Four Theories of the Press.* Chicago: University of Illinois Press.

SIL International (2006) Languages of Peru, /www.cthnologue.com/show_country.asp?name=PE (accessed 21 February 2007).

Silva Colmenares, J. (2003) *El gran capital en Colombia. Proyección al siglo XXI.* Bogotá: Planeta.

Simpson, A. (2005) Telesur: television of the South, Intel Briefing, www.comlinks.com/polintel/pi050602.htm (accessed 12 February 2006).

Sinclair, J. (1986) Dependent development and broadcasting: 'The Mexican Formula', *Media, Culture & Society,* 6(2).

SIP (2006) *Mapa de riesgos para periodistas: Brasil, Colombia, Mexico* [Risk map for journalists: Brazil, Colombia, Mexico]. Miami: Sociedad Interamericana de Prensa.

SITTEL (1999) *Regulación de las telecomunicaciones en Bolivia*. La Paz: SITTEL.

SITTEL (2000) *Regulación de las telecomunicaciones en Bolivia 2000*. La Paz: SITTEL.

Sklair (2001) *The Transnational Capitalist Class*. Oxford: Blackwell.

Sociedad Interamericana de Prensa (Inter-American Press Association) (2006) *Mapa de riesgos para periodistas: Brasil, Colombia, Mexico* (*Risk Map for Journalists: Brazil, Colombia, Mexico*). Miami, FL: Sociedad Interamericana de Prensa.

Solís, M. (2002) Entre el cambio y la tradición: el fracaso de la privatización de la energia y las telecomunicaciones en Costa Rica, *Revista de Ciencias*.

Straubhaar, J.D. (1989a) Mass communication and the elites, in M.L. Conniff and F.D. McCann (eds) *Modern Brazil — Élites and Masses in Historical Perspective*. Lincoln, NE: University of Nebraska Press, pp. 225–45.

Sunkel, G. and Geoffry, E. (2001) *Economic Concentration of the Media*. Santiago: Lom Editions.

Tal Cual (2005) Contra el 'latifundio mediático', *Tal Cual*, 24 April: 2.

Terra (2003) *Hace dos años, Cavallo imponía el corralito*, www.terra.com.ar/ctematicos/crisis_economica/81/81556.html (accessed 2 November 2006).

Torres, A.F.J. (1997) *El periodismo mexicano. Ardua lucha por su integridad*. México, D.F.: Ediciones Coyoacán.

Trotti, R. and Williamson, B. (1996) Should journalists be required to belong to *colegios* and have university degrees? in R.R. Cole (ed.) *Communication in Latin America: Journalism, Mass Media and Society*, pp. 105–12.

UCA (2003) *Encuesta General de Preferencia de Medios*. Managua: Universidad Centroamericana.

Últimas Noticias (2005) CVP y Minci se bajaron de la mula con TVSur, *Últimas Noticias*, 23 April: 18.

UNDP (2005a) *Informe sobre Desarrollo Humano Perú 2005: Hagamos de la Competitividad una Oportunidad para Todos*. Lima: UNDP.

UNDP (1999) *Auditoría ciudadana sobre la calidad de la democracia*. San José: PNUD.

UNDP (2004) *La democracia en América Latina: hacia una democracia de ciudadanas y ciudadanos,* 2nd edn. Buenos Aires: Aguilar, Altea, Taurus, Alfaguara.

UNDP (2005) *Human Development Report Country Sheet.* United Nations Development Fund, http://hdr.undp.org/statistics/data/countries.cfm? c=NIC (accessed 17 September 2006).

UNESCO (1980) *Many Voices, One World.* Paris: UNESCO.

UNESCO (2006) *Statistical Yearbook.* UNESCO Institute for Statistics, http://www.uis.unesco.org/en/stats/stats0.htm.

UNICEF (2006) At a glance: Nicaragua. *United Nations Children Fund.* http://www.unicef.org/infobycountry/nicaragua.html (accessed 17 September 2006).

Unión de Periodistas de Cuba (2006) *Incrementa EE.UU. financiamiento para las transmisiones de propaganda anticubana,* www.cubaperiodistas.cu/ 000_INFO/786.htm (accessed May 2006).

Uribe, M.T. and Álvarez, J. (1985) *Cien años de prensa en Colombia, 1840–1940.* Medellín: Universidad de Antioquia.

Vallejo, M. (2006) A plomo herido. Una crónica del periodismo en Colombia (1880_1980). Bogotá: Planeta.

Vega, P. (1987) Historia de la televisión en Costa Rica. Unpublished manuscript.

Vega, P. (1995) El mundo impreso se consolida: Análisis de los periódicos costarricenses (1851–1870), in *Revista de Ciencias Sociales.* San José (Costa Rica), No. 70.

Vega, P. (forthcoming) Prensa, escritores y lectores. Desarrollo de la comunicación social en Costa Rica 1850–1900.

Villarroel, D. (2005) ¡Aló Telesur! *El Mundo,* 25 July: 2.

Villasmil, X. (1980) *Difusión masiva y hegemonía ideológica.* Valencia: Badell Hermanos.

Vivas, F. (2001) *En Vivo y En Directo, Una Historia de la televisión de la Peruana.* Lima: Editorial de la Universidad de Lima.

Vizcaíno, M. (1999) La televisión educativa en Colombia. Balances y perspectivas, in M. Vizcaino (ed.) *Historia de una travesía.* Bogotá: Inravisión.

Waisbord, S. (2000) *Watchdog Journalism in South America: News, Accountability, and Democracy.* New York: Columbia University Press.

Wallace, A. (2007) *Sangre en la pantalla y otras tendencias del periodismo nicaragüense*. Managua: Amerrisque.

Web Reports (2007a) *Argentina – Convergence, Broadband and Internet Market,* www.budde.com.au/Reports/Contents/Argentina-Convergence-Broadband-and-Internet-Market-3014.html (accessed 21 March 2007).

Web Reports (2007b) *Argentina – Mobile Communications and Mobile Data Market,* www.budde.com.au/Reports/Contents/Argentina-Mobile-Communications-and-Mobile-Data-Market-1788.html (accessed 28 March 2007).

Weffer, L. (2005) Aló, Presidente volverá al aire el próximo, *El Nacional*, 6 January : A-3.

White, P. (1997) *Le Village CNN*. Montreal: Les Presses de l'Université de Montréal.

Wilson, P.A. (1992) *Exports and Local Development: Mexico's New Maquiladoras*. Austin, TX: University of Texas Press.

Wisdom, J.T. (2001) The media and democratisation in Africa: contributions, constraints and concerns of the private press, *Media, Culture & Society*, 23(1): 5–32.

Zapata, M. A. (2004) *Un año de buenas notas*. Caracas: Merca2.0.

Zúñiga Fajuri, A. (2006) La formación del pensamiento libre el caso de La Ultima Tentación de Cristo, in F. González (ed.) *Libertad de Prensa en Chile*. Santiago de Chile: Prensa Universidad Diego Portales.

INDEX

THE MEDIA IN ITALY

Matthew Hibberd

The Italian media – the press, cinema, radio and television – is one of the largest and most controversial media industries in mainland Europe. In this introductory text Matthew Hibberd explores the key historical processes and events in the growth and development of Italy's main media and considers it in the context of the economic, political, socio-cultural and technological movements that have affected Italy.

Featuring a timeline of key Italian events, the book begins with the Unification – or Risorgimento – of Italy in 1861, and charts the rise of Italy from a fragmented and rural-based society through to a leading industrialised and urbanised world power. It details Fascism's reliance on the exploitation of the mass media, analyses Italy's remarkable post-war recovery, the development of democratic institutions and the contribution that a pluralistic media has made to this. Finally, it examines Silvio Berlusconi's rise to high political office and questions whether the involvement of Italy's leading media mogul in politics has harmed Italy's international reputation.

The Media in Italy addresses key themes that show how the Italian state and Italian media operate, such as:

- How governing parties and individuals have been able to assert influence over media intuitions
- Why there is a close relationship between political elites and media professionals
- The lack of consensus over key media reforms
- The importance of the Catholic Church in the development of the Italian media
- How a unique Italian media system has been shaped by issues of citizenship, democracy and nation-state

The Media in Italy is key reading for students on media, journalism, politics, and modern language courses.

Contents: The media and the Unification of Italy – The liberal years, 1861–1922 – The media in Fascist Italy – The First Italian Republic: cinema and the press in the postwar years – The First Italian Republic and 'Mamma RAI' – Broadcasting and the Wild West years – The Second Italian Republic: cinema and the press since 1992 – Silvio Berlusconi – Moving towards digital: Italian media in the new millennium – Conclusion

2007 192pp

978-0-335-22285-8 (Paperback)

KEY THEMES IN MEDIA THEORY

Dan Laughey

'Key Themes in Media Theory is wonderfully wide-ranging and deservedly destined to become a key text for students of Media Studies.'

Professor John Storey, University of Sunderland, UK

- What is media theory?
- How do media affect our actions, opinions and beliefs?
- In what ways do media serve powerful political and economic interests?
- Is media consumerism unhealthy or is it empowering?

Key Themes in Media Theory provides a thorough and critical introduction to the key theories of media studies. It is unique in bringing together different schools of media theory into a single, comprehensive text, examining in depth the ideas of key media theorists such as Lasswell, McLuhan, Hall, Williams, Barthes, Adorno, Baudrillard and Bourdieu.

Using up-to-date case studies the book embraces media in their everyday cultural forms – music, internet, film, television, radio, newspapers and magazines – to enable a clearer view of the 'big picture' of media theory.

In ten succinct chapters Dan Laughey discusses a broad range of themes, issues and perspectives that inform our contemporary understanding of media production and consumption. These include:

- Behaviourism and media effects
- Feminist media theory
- Postmodernity and information society
- Political economy
- Media consumerism

With images and diagrams to illustrate chapter themes, examples that apply media theory to media practice, recommended reading at the end of every chapter, and a useful glossary of key terms, this book is the definitive guide to understanding media theory.

Contents: What is media theory? – Behaviourism and media effects – Modernity and medium theory – Structuralism and semiotics – Interactionism and structuration Feminisms and gender – Political economy and postcolonial theory – Postmodernity and information society – Consumerism and everyday life – Debating media theory

2007 248pp

MEDIA TECHNOLOGY

Joost van Loon

- What are media?
- Why are more and more objects being turned into media?
- How do people interconnect with the media in structuring their everyday lives?

In *Media Technology: Critical Perspectives*, Joost van Loon illustrates how throughout the course of society, different forms of media have helped to shape our perceptions, expectations and interpretations of reality.

Drawing on the work of media scholars such as Marshall McLuhan, Walter Benjamin, Roland Barthes and Raymond Williams, the author provides a theoretical analysis of the complexity of media processes. He urges the reader to challenge mainstream assumptions of media merely as instruments of communication, and shows how the matter, form, use and purpose of media technologies can affect content.

The book uses practical examples from both old and new media to help readers think through complex issues about the place of media. This helps to create a more innovative toolkit for understanding what media actually are and the basis for trying to make sense of what media actually do. It uses case studies and examples from television, radio, print, computer games and domestic appliances.

Media Technology is essential reading for undergraduate and postgraduate students on media, social theory and critical theory-related courses.

Contents: Introduction – A critical history of media technology – Alternative trajectories: Technology as culture – 'Media as extensions of wo/man': Feminist perspectives on mediation and technological embodiment – New media and networked (dis)embodiment – Conclusion: Theorizing media technology

2007 192pp

2008 978-0-335-21446-4 (Paperback)

2008 978-0-335-21813-4 (Paperback)